FOUR THOUSAND
LIVES LOST

FOUR THOUSAND LIVES LOST

THE INQUIRIES OF
LORD MERSEY
INTO THE SINKING OF

the *TITANIC*,
the *EMPRESS*
OF IRELAND,
the *FALABA*
and the
LUSITANIA

ALASTAIR WALKER

The History Press

Dr Alastair Walker has had a lifelong interest in maritime history and was a committee member of the Ulster Titanic Society. He is a retired educationalist and is the author of several books and many articles in that field. He is a trustee of National Museums NI and lives in Bangor, Northern Ireland.

Back cover image: 'Remember the little lost children of the *Lusitania*', published in the *New York Herald*, 7 May 1918, artist W. A. Rogers (1854–1931). LOC

First published 2012

The History Press
The Mill, Brimscombe Port
Stroud, Gloucestershire, GL5 2QG
www.thehistorypress.co.uk

British Library Cataloguing in Publication Data.
A catalogue record for this book is available from the British Library.

ISBN 978 0 7524 6571 5
Typesetting and origination by The History Press
Printed in Great Britain

CONTENTS

	Acknowledgements	6
	Introduction	7
1	A Maritime World in Transition	11
2	The Peacetime Risks	19
3	The Wartime Risks	30
4	The Nature of Inquiries	38
5	The Commissioner of Wrecks	47
6	The Eight Captains	55
7	Improbable Things Do Happen	69
8	Men of Steel	76
9	Issues	88
10	E.J. Smith	96
11	Stanley Lord	116
12	Henry Kendall and Thomas Andersen	126
13	Frederick Davies and Will Turner	144
14	Gunther von Forstner and Walther Schwieger	166
15	Eight Captains and a Judge: The Links	177
	Postscript	185
	Bibliography	186
	Index	188

ACKNOWLEDGEMENTS

My interest in maritime matters began at the age of seven with the entry for Horatio Nelson in my parents' 1923 edition of the *Harmsworth Encyclopedia*, was nurtured by Arthur Ransome's wonderful Swallows and Amazons stories and came of age in yacht races in Belfast Lough. The fascination for the nautical never waned. An interest in *Titanic* was natural as my mother had seen the ship as a child of nine and a near neighbour of the family in the Woodvale area of Belfast had been lost. An uncle was a survivor of the torpedoing of the *Athenia* on the first day of the Second World War, so the topics covered here have a personal resonance.

I would particularly like to thank the Canadian National Archives for making me aware that the proceedings of the inquiry into the loss of the *Empress of Ireland* were available on the internet. I also express my appreciation for the work of the Titanic Inquiry Project in making the proceedings of both the *Titanic* and *Luisitania* inquires likewise accessible, and the Law Library of Yale University for the digitisation of the proceedings of the *Falaba* inquiry.

I am deeply indebted to two friends who agreed to read the draft of this book. Una Reilly and Stephen Cameron both provided very helpful and constructive comments. Thanks to Shaun Barrington and the staff at The History Press with whom it has been a pleasure to work.

Finally, go thanks go to my wife Barbara for the patience, understanding and forbearance without which a writing project such as this would never be started, let alone finished.

INTRODUCTION

The *Titanic* slowly disappeared into the chasm of the deep Atlantic, the *Empress of Ireland* rolled over in the shallows of the St Lawrence, the *Falaba* was dispatched into the waters off the south west of England and the *Lusitania* crashed bow first into the seabed off the south coast of Ireland. The man who links these four terrible tragedies, that cost close to 4000 lives, is Lord Mersey, who, as Commissioner of Wrecks, presided over a series of inquiries into the sinkings between 1912 and 1915. In the process of the inquiries he came to many significant conclusions, some of which, in retrospect, have turned out to be common sense, some have become controversial and some have been shown to be quite simply wrong. Many of those conclusions were judgements about the behaviour of eight men who were in charge of ships involved directly (or indirectly in one case) in the incidents. The purpose of this book is to look at those judgements, at the man who made them, the methods used to arrive at them and the captains whose lives or reputations were affected by them. Our concern will not principally be with the aspects of the tragedies linked to the actions of those in boardrooms, ministries and shipbuilders but rather with those who were held accountable for their actions at sea as the events took place.

Only four of the eight captains appeared before Mersey and, of these, two captained ships that had been lost. Two of the eight died with their ships and two were German submariners. The intention is to give a brief picture of their lives as well as an indication of their personalities and then to look at the way in which they were dealt with during the inquiries and to consider whether the outcomes affected their careers, in the cases of those who survived, or their reputations, in the cases of the two who did not. They are disparate in background and character. Three were quite well known to the public before the disasters took place. Of two we still know comparatively little. Most were reluctant actors in public events (the submariners of course not taking part in the inquiries) but there were also a couple of self-publicists.

It is important to place the incidents themselves and the people concerned firmly into historical context. It is all too easy to level criticisms based upon knowledge and understanding that has accrued over the century since then. We should therefore consider the maritime context of the early twentieth century, including commercial and technical factors, political and military developments and the activities of the press. To help in doing so we will consider some of the other accidents and tragedies that took place at sea during the same period so that we can better pick up patterns.

A great deal of research has already been undertaken into the sinkings of *Titanic* and *Lusitania* and there are many publications. Regarding the former, some might use the term 'overkill'. I have therefore approached that tragedy with some trepidation, but it would make little sense to look at the quartet of Mersey's inquiries without spending some time on the first and the longest. Less has been written about the *Empress of Ireland*, but the main events have been documented.

The story of the *Falaba*, however, has been entirely overshadowed by that of the *Lusitania*, which followed so closely after it and which resulted in the deaths of many more people. Nonetheless, the sinking of the *Falaba* raised significant issues and it contrasts with that of the *Lusitania* in interesting ways. Given the number of sources already in the public domain, a selection of which is listed in the Bibliography, this book is not intended to provide a full narrative of the incidents into which Mersey inquired and only sufficient background has been included to elucidate the issues being discussed.

In some of the material produced about these sinkings, particularly amongst the proliferation of books and films on *Titanic*, a mythology has developed that bears little relation to the actual events. Indeed, Mersey may have contributed, wittingly or otherwise, to the generation of some of the myths. What follows may help to puncture one or two of these; but the intention is to take an overview, to look for links and patterns and, perhaps by so doing, to gain some insight into the nature of disaster-related inquiries and their impact on the decision makers involved.

There are two themes that recur throughout. One, as just indicated, concerns the nature of the inquiry process and how it was influenced by the backgrounds and personalities of those who took part in it. The second is the extent to which events and reactions to them were influenced by the rapid technological change that was taking place at the time. There may be echoes of those themes that resonate down to the present day. Some of the major government-sponsored inquiries of recent times have demonstrated more than a few of the characteristics of those discussed here. We too live in a period of technological change, one even more rapid than that of the early twentieth century. To what extent do some of today's disasters arise from a mis-match between the pace of technological change and the speed with which people adapt their thinking and their practices to new circumstances?

In reviewing the judgements that were made about the eight captains, it will prove helpful to set them against two 'courts of opinion'. Firstly, how were those judgements received by other seafarers? Peer judgements by those who had to face the possibility themselves of being involved in this type of event are particularly valuable. There is also the court of public opinion. It may not be as well informed as the seafaring group and it may be considerably more variable, but it is important, particularly so far as reputation is concerned. The difficulty now, of course, is ascertaining, at this remove, what were the opinions of contemporary seafarers or of the general public on the conclusions reached by Lord Mersey. There are, however, some indications from the actions taken by shipping companies and others after the inquiries as to what those opinions were. The views which Mersey expressed, particularly in relation to *Titanic,* continue to influence writers today. Even in recent publications it is possible to see those opinions repeated uncritically, including some that have since been shown to be entirely in error. Perhaps one of the lessons we shall learn is the ease with which anything produced under judicial imprimatur acquires for some people the supposed infallibility of pronouncements 'ex cathedra'.

Altogether the loss of the four ships cost almost 4000 lives. Few people have chaired more than one inquiry into a maritime disaster. Mersey was unique in chairing four encompassing such a tragic number of deaths in a period of just three years and three months. Yet, to some he remains little more than a laughing stock, to others a symbol of judicial mediocrity, while a third group see him as a pawn of shipping bosses and government. Over the years he has received little appreciation for undertaking what must have been a series of daunting tasks and, while he is unlikely ever to be showered with accolades, we may just be able to qualify his infamy with a little more understanding.

1

A MARITIME WORLD IN TRANSITION

Shortly before he left England for the last time, in the late summer of 1805, Nelson attended a meeting at the Admiralty to discuss some new technological developments being promoted by Robert Fulton, an American inventor. Fulton had lived in England for some time, before moving to France and trying to persuade the French government that his ideas for a submersible boat were practicable. Having failed to do so, he was now back in Britain and trying to interest the British government in the same idea as well as his suggestions for an early form of 'torpedo', the term then being used to describe a transportable mine. Being a man of broad interests he was also raising the possibility of the navy making use of steam propulsion. There is no record as to how Nelson responded to such technological advances, although being conservative by nature he was probably not impressed. However, while Fulton made little progress with his submersible boat, in October 1805, the same month as Trafalgar, he demonstrated the potential of his torpedo when the resulting explosion sank a 200-ton brig. Just two years later, back in America, Fulton provided the first real evidence, with the *Clermont,* that steam propulsion was commercially viable.

Over the period of the next century one thinks of developments in maritime technology proceeding in a steady manner, decade by decade, culminating in the great liners, Dreadnoughts and submarines of the early years of the twentieth century. In fact, 50 years after his death Nelson would not have found the ships of the navy or of commerce so very different from those that he had known. Given the continued dominance of wood and sail, there would have been little to amaze him. Most of the really rapid changes took place in the period right at the end of that century and the beginning of the next.

Isambard Kingdom Brunel decided in 1852 to build a ship that was several times larger than any that had gone before. It was an idea ahead of its time, because, although it was then technically possible to create a hull of the requisite size, other elements of the technology necessary effectively to power and to control such a large ship were not in place. Some consider The *Great Eastern* to have been the biggest white elephant of all time, although it did achieve considerable success, not as the passenger ship it had been designed to be, but as a very effective cable layer. The iron monster, mixing paddle wheels, propeller and sails, laid much of the infrastructure required for the embryonic communications revolution. It was not until 1899 that the White Star *Oceanic* exceeded it in length and two years later the *Celtic,* also White Star and also built by *Titanic's* builder, Harland and Wolff in Belfast, exceeded it in tonnage. Within a decade, however, there were ships that were twice as large.

The speed that steamships were built to travel at depended on the purpose for which they were intended. The liners hoping to carry mails were normally the fastest of their day. Speeds did not increase dramatically with improvements to steam engines in the 1870s to 1890s. Rather, the quantity of coal needed to produce those speeds dropped significantly. Fuel costs were reduced and a greater proportion of ships' internal space was given over to revenue-generating passengers or cargoes. That changed suddenly on a single day, 26 June 1897. At the great Naval Review held at Spithead to celebrate the 60th anniversary of Queen Victoria coming to the throne, a small steamboat called *Turbinia* streaked through the lines of ships, clearly visible to the Prince of Wales watching from the Royal Yacht (his mother was indisposed) and from every ship in the fleet. In modern times it would have caused a tremendous security alert, possibly with dire consequences. In 1897 it certainly created a stir, but for a very different reason. *Turbinia* was travelling at over 30 knots, a speed that not one of the other ships present could have approached. She was the product of a Dr Charles Parsons, who was aboard her at the time, and she had been built to show off his newly developed steam turbine engine. Instead of cylinders with pistons, cranks and shafts, all in a blur of reciprocating movement, *Turbinia* was driven by steam jets hitting blades in a casing on the shaft that led directly to the propeller. It was much smoother, involved much less wasteful thrashing of machinery, was more compact and it was much, much faster.

It is an immense tribute to the ability of late Victorian and Edwardian society to take hold of a new idea and apply it rapidly that, just ten years after the Jubilee Naval Review, a battleship, the *Dreadnought,* the biggest ever built to that time, was powered by the new engines. In the same year, the first of a new class of turbine-driven liner, *Lusitania,* emerged to take the Blue Riband speed record for crossing the Atlantic. The twentieth century has sometimes been called the century of the internal combustion engine because it is considered to be the most influential technical development of the period and also, perhaps, the most visible. The century could, with equal validity, be called 'the turbine century'. Not only did the turbine revolutionise propulsion at sea, it became the basis for all electricity generation, whether from coal, from nuclear power, from gas or from wind and water. Add to that the turbo-jet, turbo-prop and turbo-fan and we have the turbine to thank for modern flight as well.

For many ships not requiring high speeds the new propulsion system was not particularly advantageous and normal reciprocating engines continued to be built for several decades. A very few ships, of which *Titanic* was one, had a hybrid system of large, advanced reciprocating engines and a turbine as well. One effect was that the difference in speed between the fastest liners and the slowest cargo ships increased greatly. Plodding tramps continued to move at around 8 to 10 knots while some passenger ships raced past at 25 knots.

The first application of electricity in ships came in 1882. Cunard's *Servia* used it for lighting in passenger spaces. Over the next few years, however, applications relating to the operation of the ship gradually took effect. At around the same time, hydraulic control systems became available and the combination of electrical and hydraulic power made it feasible to manage the complexity of larger, faster ships in ways that had not been possible previously.

By the end of the century, all ships of any size were built of riveted steel plates. In a process of gradual development, rather than through any spectacular leap forward, the design of hulls gradually evolved to include watertight divisions both across the ship from side to side and also along the length of the ship. These divisions, or bulkheads, required doors through which crew members or passengers could pass. When, for any reason, it was necessary for the bulkheads to be watertight the doors needed to be quickly closed. At first this was done manually, then electro-mechanical methods were developed that allowed the doors to be closed by operating a single control on the bridge.

So, within a decade the means of propulsion, the size, speed and complexity of ships had all taken an enormous leap forward. However, there were two further inventions that were also to have a fundamental influence on the whole maritime world of the early twentieth century and were of major importance in the incidents with which we are concerned. These were the fruition of Robert Fulton's belief in the feasibility of submersible boats and the invention of wireless telegraphy.

The submarine was not the product of a single inventor. Going back to Fulton and beyond, many ideas for submersible boats had been produced and a few had made it off the drawing board. The American Civil War saw the first successful use of the submarine as a weapon of war, if an operation can be called successful that results in the loss of the submarine and its crew. Those early attempts at submarines were, like the contemporaneous *Great Eastern,* ahead of their time – navigating submerged was an aspiration that required further technical development before it could become established practice. Submarines could only become effective with a propulsion system, other than manpower, that could be made to work under water. They also needed much more sophisticated control systems to maintain the delicate balance of neutral buoyancy and trim which they required to operate submerged.

It was the electric motor and battery storage that provided the underwater motive power and it was electro-mechanical and hydraulic systems that facilitated sustainable trim with neutral buoyancy. Strictly speaking, the internal combustion engine was not necessary for submarine development. Britain built the K-Class steam turbine-powered submarines during the First World War, although they proved to be a failure that was costly in both material and human terms. Large-scale use of steam turbine propulsion in submarines had to wait for the emergence of nuclear reactors. The internal combustion engine, with its ability to stop and start readily and its absence of bulky boilers, made design of the early submarines so much easier; the coming of the marine diesel engine around 1910 made them safer, albeit never safe.

Marconi was not the only person who contributed to the early beginnings of wireless, but he was by far the dominant one and it is his name above all others that has come to be associated with it. His experiments, particularly the trans-Atlantic transmission in 1904, demonstrated the possibilities of radio as a communication tool and not just as a scientific curiosity. There had been earlier experiments at sea. In 1891, Captain Henry Jackson RN (later First Sea Lord) sent wireless Morse signals over a distance of a few hundred yards. In 1899 wireless technology was first used in naval manoeuvres. As with the turbine, the rapidity with which the new invention was applied was startling. The first occasion when radio enabled major loss of life to be averted in a maritime disaster was as early as 1909 during the sinking of the White Star *Republic.* Despite that success, the initial employment of radio at sea in the merchant service was primarily as a convenience for rich passengers and only marginally as a contribution to the operation of the ship. The terms of employment of the radio operators by The Marconi Company (not the ship owners) and their job descriptions left no doubt as to their commercial priorities. As with the submarine, it was how the invention was used that became controversial rather than the invention itself.

In the next two chapters we will be examining in some detail the nature of the risks that seafarers faced in the early 1900s, in peacetime and in wartime and both wireless and the submarine will feature strongly. Obviously the submarine only appears in the wartime scenarios, but wireless had major roles in both contexts. In one case it should have mitigated risk, but in the other it may well have exacerbated it.

One aspect of ship technology did not change over the two decades before the outbreak of the First World War, although it did so shortly thereafter. Coal continued to provide the energy source for steamships. That meant large bunkers had to be included in the ship's structure in such a way as to allow the coal to be loaded easily. The stability of the ship had to be managed during a voyage while bunkers were gradually depleted. There had to be arrangements for the movement of the coal to the stokeholds even under severe weather conditions and, finally, there needed to be large numbers of stokers to maintain the fires. For large, fast steamships of the period, the logistics of these processes were daunting and there were considerable dangers from bunker coal catching fire, or from explosion of the air and coal dust mixture remaining once the bunker was nearly empty.

The 'black gang' on an Atlantic liner moved hundreds of tons of coal every single day into the boilers. Smaller amounts, but still in the hundreds of tons, of ashes also had to be removed and dumped overboard. Although steam power was used in a large number of different contexts – on trains, in factories and mines and many others – there was something unique about the coal-fired stokeholds in ships, largely because they were subject to the vagaries of the sea and to changing temperature and weather patterns as ships moved through different climate zones. While the heat of the boiler fires might be quite welcome in the North Atlantic in winter, it was utterly intolerable in the Red Sea in summer. Keeping fires lit and steam pressure up in a severe gale required prodigious efforts by stokers and engineers. As can be imagined, the accident rate was appalling. It is a world which, apart from a few preserved ships, has now disappeared. Little remains by way of a record of the life of the men involved because few were communicators or even thought that their story might be of interest in the future.

Perhaps the most striking feature about the maritime scene of the early twentieth century was its variety. As well as the spread of steamers from large, fast passenger ships to small, slow cargo ones, there were still large numbers of sailing ships, both sea-going square riggers and coastal schooners and ketches. Add to them vast fleets of fishing vessels, both sail and steam and one is left with a vision of crowded seas in many parts of the world. The number of sailing ships, particularly ocean-going square riggers, was in steep decline although they continued to be built in small numbers right up to the outbreak of the First World War. The *Passat,* now preserved in Travemunde in Germany, was one of two sister ships launched in 1911. By the end of the First World War numbers of active ocean going sailing ships had dropped dramatically. Indeed, it has recently been calculated that with the building of replicas and of new sail training ships, there are more square riggers on the ocean now than at any time since 1919.

There were particular niches of the maritime world in which sail continued to flourish long after it had disappeared from the major trading routes. For example, the Grand Banks schooners from Canada and from Portugal continued to fish for cod on the Grand Banks almost as long as the cod held out. Sealers continued to hunt on the ice from small purpose-designed schooners well beyond the Second World War. Indeed, the last example of working sail in UK waters, the Falmouth Oyster fishery, continues to this day because the use of engines over the oyster beds is forbidden in order to reduce the risk of pollution.

We have seen that the early decades of the twentieth century were a period of intense change. It is interesting to reflect on the equally rapid changes in the latter part of that same century. When we look back to the events of 1912–1915 we do so from the perspective of a very different maritime world. Since 1980, there has been an enormous increase in the size of the largest ships, in propulsion systems and in the complexity of the electronics used for navigation and safety. Passenger liners have now largely disappeared except for ferries on short sea routes, but they have been replaced by large numbers of cruise ships. The biggest of those cruise ships are now the equivalent, in gross tonnage terms, of more than four *Titanics*. Taking into account the increase in the global population, there are probably now more passengers at sea around the world at any given time than was ever previously the case.

Perhaps the biggest change in recent decades has been in cargo handling methods. We still require bulk cargoes to be carried and the specialist ships that do this job are now much larger and more versatile but, in operating principle, they are much the same as they have been since oil stopped being transported in barrels. The real change has been in containerisation and the rapidly increasing numbers of containers being carried on a single ship. Where, early in the twentieth century, most non-bulk cargoes were carried loose in the holds of cargo ships, packed as well as possible to prevent them from being damaged, they are now almost all carried in standard containers on ships designed for that purpose alone. Very large container ships travel on ocean routes between massive container ports. Much smaller short-sea container ships then move goods between the container ports and ports around the coasts.

How does the maritime world of today contrast with that of a century ago? There is no longer such an enormous variety of ships. Standardisation of container ships, of the design of engines-aft bulk carriers and of smaller, but similarly standardised coasters means that there is a rather boring similarity to most modern ships. Cruise ships look like (and are like) floating hotels. They may be designed with some thought to an attractive appearance; but everyone seems to be using the same computer program to do so. The fleets of small fishing craft have disappeared in favour of large, super-efficient trawlers, each of which is capable of hoovering up complete shoals of fish.

On a flight across the Irish Sea it is now quite possible to go from one side to the other on a clear day and see hardly any ships at all. Had it been possible to fly across a hundred years ago, there would have been dozens. There are, of course, seas that remain as busy as ever because they contain main routes. The English Channel is the best known area where congestion, with its greatly increased risk of collision, is a continual concern. Out in the oceans, however, the great container ships, tankers and other bulk carriers travel along narrow sea corridors like juggernauts along motorways. Although the total amount of cargo carried has multiplied greatly over the last hundred years, the jump in the quantity carried by each ship and the speed with which they can be turned around, means that the total number of ships at sea has greatly decreased. The oceans are much emptier places.

Cruise ships, unlike the former passenger liners, frequent areas well away from those narrow corridors. They travel amongst the Caribbean islands, along the coast of Alaska, into Norwegian fjords and around the continent of Antarctica. For extremely large, deep ships they spend a lot of time in narrow, shallow waters, some of which are not as reliably charted as the main shipping routes. Many cruise in remote areas where there are few other ships. Some recent accidents, happily without large numbers of casualties, have demonstrated the element of risk that this type of cruising can sometimes involve.

The purpose of examining the changing maritime world from 1880 to 1910 is to help us to judge the events of the subsequent five years properly within their historical context. It helps us to understand better the minds of the principal actors, either those at sea or those in the inquiry rooms. The men who, in 1910, were at the apex of their profession, captaining large passenger or cargo liners, had spent their formative years in quite a different world. The ships in which they learned their craft were smaller, slower, usually wind- rather than steam-powered and relied only on lights and flags for communication. If they thought about wars at all (and they had little reason to do so) it was of fleets of battleships or of gun-firing surface raiders. It was probably even more difficult for those involved in the inquiries who were not seamen. The world of the big liners provided many stories for the newspapers and a lot of publicity centred on their size and speed. Some of the lawyers and others may have had first-hand experience of crossing the Atlantic on one of the modern leviathans, but even that would have provided them with little understanding of what was involved in guiding one at speed across a crowded ocean. None would have been aboard a submarine; indeed most would never have seen one. Even amongst the seamen, understanding of the dynamics of submarine operation and of their capabilities in terms of offensive action would have been quite limited.

Wireless did not become part of the daily experience of the population until broadcasting began in the 1920s. Until then it was rather a mysterious, almost slightly miraculous, technology confined to a relatively small range of applications. The size, power requirements and fragility of wireless equipment limited its use even in most military contexts. It was never a major factor in the great battles of the Western Front and did not appear in aircraft at all until much later. Most long-range communication continued to use telegraph technology based on the cables of the type that the *Great Eastern* pioneered, as is still the case to a certain extent today. Neither the seamen nor the lawyers at the inquiries would have had much understanding about how the new invention worked or what its capabilities and limitations were. As we shall see, however, one of the captains had become famous prior to the disaster in which he was involved by exploiting wireless in a new way.

A few years ago the author asked a group of educational technologists how they considered education had changed as a result of the immense increase in the availability of computers. Their answer was a unanimous one; the pace of change of technology was much faster than changes in the practice of the teachers using it. This is an issue that will interest us as we consider the events of 1912-15. To what extent were the disasters themselves the consequence of men not sufficiently adapting their habits at sea to the dramatic technological changes? To what extent also were the outcomes of the inquiries influenced by a failure to understand the new conditions under which seamen were operating? Finally, how much of our thinking about all of those events is a product of our own quite different perspective?

2

PEACETIME RISKS

Fear of flying is a well-known phenomenon and there are consultant psychiatrists who specialise in dealing with it. This is despite the fact that, statistically, travel by modern jet passenger aircraft is amongst the safest means of moving about the planet. In the 1950s, when jets were first being used for long distance flight, that was not the case. It seemed that rarely a month went by without a news announcer solemnly intoning the fate of yet another flight that had come down as a result of bad weather or mechanical problems. A lot of people died before the issue of metal fatigue on the early Comets was diagnosed. However, even the hazards of flying in early jet aircraft were small compared to ocean travel in the first days of steamships.

Our interest is in passenger ships in the North Atlantic in particular and, in order to arrive at an informed view about the actions of the captains and the pronouncements on them by the judge, we need to have some sense of the types of risk they faced at sea. In this chapter we will consider risks faced in peacetime before August 1914 and in the next the additional ones that war amongst the major powers rather obviously brought. Risk management is now a powerful tool that assists in the running of businesses and other organisations. Audit Committees review and update registers which detail the risks that an organisation faces, estimate the severity of those risks and set out measures which, it is hoped, will mitigate them. In a sense what we are now about to do is create retrospectively a sort of risk register for a liner at sea in the second decade of the twentieth century, such as the captain might have produced on the basis of his own knowledge and experience had he been asked.

Identifying risks is not the difficult part of the exercise, nor is listing the mitigating measures that either were or were not then in force. The contentious element in the process is measuring the relative severity of the risks. In modern management practice there is now a fairly standard approach to this.

Severity is quantified as the product of two estimations, the first of which is the likelihood of the risk materialising. The second is the level of damage created if it does. The risks that are easy to categorise in this way and to plan for are those at either extreme. An event that is highly likely to happen and is potentially very damaging requires urgent and extensive mitigating measures. It is probable that such risks are well understood and good preventative precautions are already in place. One which is unlikely and of little potential impact can largely be ignored. Even risks which are quite likely to materialise but which are of minimal potential impact do not cause too much concern so long as there are reliable procedures in place to deal with them.

The risks that most often give rise to sleepless nights are the ones that, although highly unlikely to happen, could have disastrous consequences. Their very improbability adds to the difficulty of establishing appropriate means of preventing them. If they are improbable, relatively few people in the past are likely to have experienced them. The underlying causes that give rise to such events may, for the same reason, be less well understood, so the effectiveness of any mitigating measures may be difficult to judge. The failure of some of the world's most prestigious financial institutions to prevent their own collapse in 2008 as a consequence of the effects of new types of highly complex but poorly secured loans is a classic example.

Audit Committees regularly update risk registers because the severity of risks changes over time and new ones are always emerging. That brings us back to the issue that we identified in the last chapter. How good were our captains at updating their personal estimates of the risks they were facing in the light of changing circumstances principally resulting from rapid developments in technology? For that matter, how well did the judge understand the relevant patterns of risk, even with the help of the nautical assessors who were provided to sit with him and assist him to do so? In the court of public opinion, guided by newspaper reports, it could only be expected that appreciation of what was involved in directing a voyage of a large, fast passenger liner was extremely limited.

In the era of wooden sailing ships casualty rates were extremely high. Indeed, it is surprising how many people were prepared to jeopardise their lives on long and perilous ocean voyages. Even well crewed and well found ships frequently came to grief. In 1707 Sir Cloudesley Shovell and his entire crew on HMS *Association*, as well as the crews of *Eagle, Romney* and *Firebrand* were lost when the squadron of which he was admiral ran foul of the Scillies in bad weather. Almost 2000 men died as the result of an inability to calculate longitude correctly. In 1811 an escorted convoy of merchantmen left the Baltic very late in the season and was caught in atrocious weather in the North Sea. Many ships were overwhelmed and, again, at least 2000 men and women perished.

The early liners were really wooden sailing vessels to which engines had been added. The engines were of limited power and did little to increase the ships' capacity to withstand hazards. Replacing the wooden hulls with iron allowed for larger ships to be built but had little impact on safety. The catalogue of disasters in the 1850s illustrates just how vulnerable these ships were; 1854 was an awful year. In March the Inman Line *City of Glasgow* left Liverpool for Philadephia with 480 on board but did not arrive. The sailing ship *Baldaur* reported sighting a ship of similar appearance to the *City of Glasgow* which seemed to be in some difficulty but was unable to get to her to help. In the days before wireless, hope lasted longer. For weeks people clung to the possibility that the ship had become disabled but had remained afloat. Eventually hope faded and nothing more was ever discovered as to her fate. She is likely to have foundered in heavy weather, but at that time of year there could have been icebergs in the area through which she was travelling and collision with one of them cannot be ruled out.

In September of that year the same line's *City of Philadelphia* grounded on Cape Race. All 600 on board were ferried ashore safely in the ship's boats, but the ship was lost. That same month the Collins Line *Arctic*, a large, fairly new and prestigious wooden paddle steamer, collided in fog in the area of the Grand Banks with the smaller iron-hulled French steam schooner *Vesta*. The badly mangled schooner managed to stay afloat but the damage to the *Arctic* proved fatal. So did the lack of discipline amongst some members of the crew who commandeered the boats and left the passengers, including many women and children, to fend for themselves. Only 21 of the 281 passengers survived, all of them male, while around 40 per cent of the crew were saved. Altogether around 350 perished and this remains the worst disaster to happen to an American flagged liner. The appalling stories brought back by the survivors created a wave of dramatic headlines in the press. Unlike the *City of Glasgow*, which simply faded out of public consciousness with little notice, the *Arctic* became notorious.

One aspect of that disaster which resonates with a later one was the fact that the number of lifeboats carried by the *Arctic* was nowhere near sufficient for the number of passengers that she carried, despite having the number that was required by law. Just as in the case of *Titanic* nearly 70 years later, the law had failed to keep up with an increase in the size of ships and the number of passengers carried. Also significant in terms of the level of media attention was the social standing of the passengers. Like the *Titanic*, the *Arctic* carried a number of wealthy citizens from both sides of the Atlantic while the *City of Glasgow* was transporting mostly poor immigrants.

The Collins Line suffered a further tragedy less than two years later. In January 1856 the *Arctic's* sister ship, *Pacific*, departed from Liverpool with 186 on board and was never seen or heard from again, at least not for almost a century and a half. When she failed to arrive the process of waiting and speculation began. There had previously been incidents when ships had gone missing for long periods but had eventually emerged having been damaged or in some way incapacitated. Although her normal passage time was ten or eleven days, it was three months before all hope was officially given up. Reports from other ships in the Atlantic at that time talked about a severe winter, with ice coming farther south than usual and there was speculation that this might have been the cause of her loss. It is difficult to know the extent to which that media speculation was shared by the community of seafarers who were better able to judge the risk. Only in 1991 was the question answered as to where the *Pacific* sank when her wreck was positively identified in the Irish Sea about 60 miles from Liverpool. It seems that some catastrophe occurred shortly after she left port that must have caused her to sink very quickly. Not only did no one on board survive, nothing identifiable from the ship reached the shore a mere twelve miles away. The riddle remains; we are none the wiser as to the cause of her loss except, of course, that we can remove ice from the list of possibilities. It is a tribute to the power of myth that still, in 2011, on the Ice Data website (http://www.icedata.ca/Pages/ShipCollisions/ShipCol_OnlineSearch. php), the ship is listed as having sunk following collision with an iceberg, the evidence quoted being a message in a bottle supposedly washed up in the Hebrides. The same website states that the *City of Boston*, which disappeared in January 1870 between Halifax and Liverpool, 'is assumed to have hit a berg.' There is, in fact, no evidence to that effect and many at the time considered it more likely that she was overwhelmed in an exceptionally severe storm reported by a number of other ships.

By the 1870s liners were steel-built with more efficient compound engines driving propellers rather than paddle wheels. They were therefore less dependent on their auxiliary sails, although they still carried them. Better control and reduced dependence on the wind helped to improve safety somewhat. A lee shore, with the wind forcing a sailing ship ever closer, does not present the same danger to a well powered steamship. Nonetheless, the changes in the structure and propulsion of ships also created some additional risk. As ships became bigger they carried more people so that a single accident put more lives in jeopardy. Greater speeds, without compensating improvements in navigation aids, meant some types of accidents were more likely to happen and not less. Two awful losses in just over a year illustrate the point.

In April 1873 the White Star Liner *Atlantic* crashed into rocks close to Halifax in atrocious weather. At least 550 died including all of the women. Only one child was saved. The ship had been turned towards Halifax because of fears aboard that she had insufficient coal left after days of fighting into heavy gales to reach New York. Her captain had left the bridge for a rest but was not awakened at the time he instructed. Either the speed of the ship was greater than estimated as a result of an easing in the weather, or the course plotted was incorrect, or both. Like *Arctic* before her and *Titanic* after, the agonies of the passengers were protracted and the stories of survivors heart-rending. An inquiry in Canada found that the captain had been negligent in not ensuring that greater care was taken in approaching a dangerous coast in bad weather. His certificate was suspended for two years, effectively ending his career. The owners, however, were also censured and were found negligent in sending the ship to sea with insufficient fuel. They raised such a clamour that a further inquiry was held in London and only after a very protracted process did they get the result that they wanted. Certainly on paper it seemed as if there ought to have been sufficient coal, so perhaps their exoneration was justified, but the fact that they were able to pursue the matter at such great length and to such good effect illustrated the extent to which, at that time, the Board of Trade, which was responsible for such matters, was open to lobbying by business interests. It is much more unlikely that the ship's captain, had he disputed the outcome of the first inquiry in Canada, could have achieved any such resolution.

As we have noted, the largest ship afloat in the 1870s was the *Great Eastern*. For a short time the second largest – although only one fifth of her tonnage – was the French Line *Ville du Havre*. Initially designed as a paddle wheeler she had been re-engined with screw propulsion as well as being lengthened and was fast, luxurious and well received on her return to service in 1873. Her nemesis was the sailing ship *Loch Earn* with which she collided in mid-Atlantic in the absence of fog in the early hours of 21 November 1874. Neither ship seems to have been aware of the other until the very last minute. There were heavy seas and it was overcast so, although visibility was good, the darkness meant that only the lights each ship was burning could have acted as warning. Either those lights or the look-outs on both ships were ineffective. *Ville du Havre* received a massive hole in her side allowing the sea access to the wide open spaces of her engine room; she sank in minutes. The loss of life amounted to 226 passengers and crew. It was over a week before news reached shore that the *Ville du Havre* had sunk and, despite all of the anguished analysis of survivors' reports, little emerged by way of explanation as to the reason for the collision. The disaster did illustrate the vulnerability of steel ships to collisions of this nature. As the number of bulkheads and watertight compartments gradually increased in the years following, the level of risk declined. Even so, ten years later, the Cunarder *Oregon,* then the fastest ship on the

Atlantic, was rammed off New York by a sailing ship and likewise sank as a consequence. In her case there was ample time to get the passengers off and assistance on hand to get them to shore, so no lives were lost. However, as the *Empress of Ireland* was to show in 1914, the potential consequences of such a collision remained extremely severe.

To the people involved in the peacetime accidents of 1912–1914, the losses that we have been considering would have seemed a long time ago, although well within the living memory of a significant number of them. Events of the 1890s and 1900s would have had a more significant impact on their understanding of the nature of the risks that they faced at sea. Unfortunately, there was no shortage of examples for them to consider. Some of those examples would not have provided help in determining the severity of risks because they were so unusual that their repetition was highly unlikely. They were extreme examples of the 'improbable but drastic' type of risk that we noted previously. On 17 March 1891, in Gibraltar harbour, the steamer *Utopia* was caught by wind and current as she came into the anchorage and was driven onto the ram of the anchored British battleship HMS *Anson*. The ram proved its effectiveness as a weapon by piercing the side of the *Utopia*, causing her to take on water so rapidly that she sank almost immediately with the loss of 571 lives. An even more bizarre accident, but fortunately one without loss of life, occurred on 22 September 1907 at Spezia in the Gulf of Genoa at the launch of what was then the largest liner built in Italy, the *Principessa Jolanda*. Some of the launching cradle remained stuck on the side of the ship as she went down the ways, causing her to take a list to port. As the openings in the side of the ship had not yet had their doors fitted at this stage, water flooded in and the list gradually became greater and greater until she capsized and sank in the harbour, a total loss witnessed by thousands of spectators.

Of much more relevance to the understanding of more general dangers at sea were the losses of the *Islander, Norge, Republic* and *Waratah*. The *Islander* accident was not in the Atlantic and did not involve a large liner, but it did involve ice. She foundered off Alaska after collision with an iceberg with the loss of 90 lives. Most collisions between ships and icebergs naturally involved ships that customarily went into ice prevalent areas because of the nature of the work that they did. Whalers, sealers, Grand Banks fishermen were all at significant risk from ice, although the great majority of collisions only involved damage rather than loss of the ship. Nonetheless, significant numbers of ships were lost and crew members killed. *Islander* was unusual in that passengers were lost, but the ship was engaged in travelling on a coastal route that took it through waters well known to have large numbers of bergs.

The risk from ice in the North Atlantic has already been noted. There was media speculation that the *City of Glasgow* and the *Pacific* had been lost through collision with ice and the latter possibility had not been discounted in 1912. The *Lady of the Lake,* a brig sailing from Belfast to Quebec in 1833, was caught in an icefield that eventually pierced her hull and caused to her sink. Reports of the numbers lost vary from 70 to 215. However, when it comes to collisions between Atlantic passenger liners and icebergs, there were, in fact, only two confirmed instances prior to the *Titanic* and neither resulted in any deaths. In January 1856 the Cunard liner *Persia* set out on her maiden voyage. She was at the time the largest and most luxurious ship afloat, although mechanically a little behind the times. Five days out she collided with an iceberg at 11 knots. Although quite badly damaged the ship survived and all aboard arrived safely, although very late, in New York. It may be that the knowledge of what had happened to the *Persia* encouraged speculation about ice being involved in the disappearance of the *Pacific* which set out on her fatal voyage on the 23rd of the same month. It was only weeks after the *Persia* arrived bruised and battered in New York that an explanation was being sought for the non-arrival of the *Pacific.*

The second liner to collide with an iceberg was the *Arizona* in 1879. The collision took place in the dark on a calm, clear night with good visibility. Again, the *Arizona* ran into the berg head on at almost full speed, again about 11 knots. The result was similar to the case of the *Persia,* a badly crumpled bow with the ship kept afloat by her watertight compartments. She limped to the closest port, St John's Newfoundland, and had to go back to the Clyde for repairs from there. There were some injuries amongst the crew but no fatalities. The excuse from the lookouts was that they thought the berg was low-lying cloud right up until the moment the bow crunched into it.

The danger of ice was, therefore, acknowledged by all, especially in combination with fog, but the overall risk assessment placed it much lower than many other hazards. In clear visibility, whether in daylight or at night, icebergs are easily seen. At night the phosphorescence from waves breaking on the base makes them readily visible from a considerable distance away as does the glint of moonlight or even starlight on the crystals formed on the surface. What probably was not recognised until after the *Titanic* disaster was that there was a particular set of circumstances where these conditions were not in force and an iceberg might not be seen until it was much closer. After some time drifting south into warmer water, the part of an iceberg under the water begins to melt. Eventually the berg becomes top heavy and rolls over. At that stage the part now out of the water is smooth, dark and free of crystals. On the very rare occasions in the North Atlantic when the sea is so calm as to be free of swell there is no phosphorescence at the base. Those were the circumstances that may have conspired together on the night of 14 April 1912 to create the most studied disaster in history.

It was early in the morning of the 28 June 1904 when the Danish immigrant ship *Norge* steamed at full speed into Hasselwood Rock just beside Rockall. Most passengers were in their bunks. The ship sank in only 20 minutes and, of the 800 or so on board, only 168 got away in the lifeboats, some of whom were not picked up for 8 days. It was the worst loss of life on the Atlantic up to that time and remains the worst sea disaster that Denmark has experienced. It resulted from a navigational error; clearly those on the bridge thought that they were many miles away from what is a well marked hazard on every chart. Although the sinking of the *Norge* has now largely been forgotten, it would have been very much in the minds of those responsible for navigating ships across the Atlantic for many years afterwards.

Navigational error leading to stranding was clearly therefore a major risk, but not one that featured in the peacetime accidents with which we are concerned, except that one of them took place in confined waters in fog and the risk of stranding may have influenced decisions about movements. The possibility of stranding did, however, feature in one of the wartime incidents, the sinking of the *Lusitania,* but we will have to consider that in the context of the additional risks that war created. Navigational error can lead to dangers other than possible collision with land and these include a risk that only emerged with the advent of wireless. If a ship is in distress and wishes to summon assistance with wireless, it is necessary to let others know accurately where the ship is. Prior to wireless a ship could only communicate with other ships that could see it. Sending out a wrong position by wireless could well jeopardise any rescue. That was a risk that materialised in the case of *Titanic.* It could have been significant in the case of the *Republic,* the first ever ship to summon assistance by wireless, as we shall see.

The area off the coast of America east of New York is notorious for persistent and dense fogs. During the night of 22/23 January 1909 the White Star liner *Republic* was slowly feeling her way through one of those fogs close to the Nantucket Light Vessel when she was struck amidships by the smaller Italian emigrant liner *Florida*. Although *Florida* was travelling slowly as well, this was another of those accidents, of which we have already noted several, where the smaller ramming vessel suffers serious bow damage but survives while the larger vessel struck in the side is fatally incapacitated. The difference in this case was that one of the two ships, *Republic*, was fitted with the new wireless technology manned by a single operator employed by the Marconi Company. Jack Binns took the brave decision to send out the world's first wireless distress call when he saw the damage to the ship without even wait-ing for instructions from the bridge. He followed that up with accurate details of the ship's position which were re-broadcast by much more powerful shore-based wireless stations. Nonetheless, it was over twelve hours before the first major rescue ship found *Republic* in the fog, also a White Star ship, the much larger *Baltic*. Had the position sent out by the *Republic* not been correct, it is extremely unlikely that the *Baltic* would have found her before she sank. By the time the *Baltic* did arrive the passengers had been transferred from the *Republic* to the *Florida,* who stood by despite the damage she had received, a process that required many hours. Eventually the passengers from both ships were rowed across to the *Baltic* and members of the *Republic's* crew were also rescued, the last two, Captain Sealby and Second Officer Williams, as the ship sank beneath them.

The stories of the protracted and dramatic rescue of almost all of those on the two ships became major world wide news. The collision itself killed three passengers on *Republic* and three crewmen on *Florida* but other than that everyone survived. One effect was to make a hero of Binns and raise the profile of wireless as a means of effecting rescue when a ship is in distress. Thereafter it became accepted without question that all ocean-going ships should be fitted with wireless capability. Nonetheless it is worth noting that, had the watertight bulkheads of the *Republic* not held out long enough to permit transfer of passengers and crew and had the ship been totally depend-ent on rescue by ships summoned through the distress calls, the story might have been quite different. At least the ship carried sufficient lifeboats for all on board and, in the absence of a rescue ship standing by, everyone might still have been evacuated. One of the notable features of the accident and the sub-sequent rescue was the quality of the leadership provided by Captain Sealby whose calm and powerful voice directed and reassured effectively throughout.

While the *Republic* was sinking off New York a brand new medium-sized liner was completing her maiden voyage from the UK to Australia. The *Waratah* was one of the last ships of her type to leave her builders without any wireless equipment. By the time she left on her return voyage to the UK in April 1909, possibly as a result of the publicity surrounding the loss of the *Republic*, the decision had already been taken to have it fitted on arrival back in the UK. That never happened because, having called at Durban and departed for Capetown on 27 July 1909, the *Waratah* disappeared. The loss of the ship has never been fully explained, partly because, despite extensive searches, the wreck has never been found. The most likely cause is an extremely large wave in the atrocious weather conditions that she headed into on leaving Durban. While stories emerged after her loss doubting her stability, these were never substantiated. It is the case that the area she passed through does experience combinations of wind and currents that, from time to time, give rise to freakishly large waves. However, the seabed along the course she would have taken has been meticulously searched for her wreck and it has not been located. A number of wrecks provisionally thought to be hers have been shown to be similar sized ships sunk by submarines during the Second World War; the mystery may never be solved.

What is of interest to us is not, however, the cause of her sinking but the reaction to the loss, given the fact that the ship did not have wireless. We have already noted that when the *City of Glasgow* and *Pacific* failed to arrive at their destinations, hope lasted for some time that they were still afloat. The same was true of the *Waratah*. For example, had the bad weather she experienced caused the loss of her propeller, the ship would have drifted disabled, but otherwise intact, with electrical and hydraulic power to operate her other life support systems on board and with sufficient food and water to last for a considerable time. Her drift would have taken her down into the roaring forties and gradually south towards Antarctica. Hence, several Royal Navy ships and a pair of chartered merchant ships mounted searches for the *Waratah* for a period of more than six months but nothing was ever found. Eventually all hope disappeared. Had the ship been fitted with wireless, how would that have affected what happened?

It is quite possible, likely even, that the *Waratah* was indeed suddenly overwhelmed and capsized by a freak wave. In such circumstances it is unlikely that a distress call could have been transmitted. In September 1980, the large bulk carrier *Derbyshire* sank during Typhoon Orchid in the Sea of Japan as a result, we now know, of structural failure. Her sinking was also so sudden that there was no time for a distress call and a search ensued that lasted a week before she was declared lost.

In her case it was the absence of radio messages that raised concerns about her safety. Had *Waratah* had wireless then the likelihood of her drifting for a prolonged period without contact would have been greatly reduced and the search would probably have been called off sooner. If the sinking was actually for a different reason and took place over a longer period of time, then of course the possibility exists that distress calls might have alerted other shipping in time to rescue some or all of those on board. The ability to make contact over long distances well beyond the horizon was, only a few years after it came about, beginning to alter the way people thought about risks at sea and how they were dealt with.

Without attempting any formal arithmetic in order to calculate estimates of the severity of the different risks, we can see that, in addition to the hazards of damage to a ship from bad weather, liner captains on North Atlantic routes were probably most concerned with avoiding other ships and avoiding running aground, particularly in fog, but that collision with icebergs was not particularly high on their list of worries, other than when visibility was restricted in certain parts of the ocean at certain times of year. The rapid increase in the size and speed of liners had not been matched by any significant improvement in their ability to see hazards or to determine their exact position. The human eye at high points on the ship remained the sole means of spotting any dangers. While the latest binoculars provided greater magnification than was available early in the nineteenth century this was of little benefit at night or in fog. In both situations binoculars tended to reduce the effectiveness of lookouts and not improve it. Navigation relied, as it had for a hundred years and more, on a combination of dead reckoning checked against sun or star positions calculated with a sextant. On a steam ship travelling on a course not subject to the vagaries of the wind, dead reckoning was generally more accurate than on sailing ships, except that, at higher speeds, any error became rapidly magnified over time. Captains of large liners racing across the Atlantic in poor weather, when the opportunity to take sights was limited, could find themselves with more uncertainty about their actual position at a given time than a sailing ship captain in Nelson's era.

Greater speed also reduced the available time in which to take avoiding action. It is a modern cliché, often used by politicians as an excuse for not having achieved what they promised, that it takes an awfully long time to turn around a supertanker. While modern supertankers may be many times the size of the Atlantic steamships, the principle does apply. The new large, fast generation of ships that emerged in the 1900s required greater distances in which to turn and much more time to stop than the slower, smaller predecessors to which their officers had previously been accustomed. Yet, as we have seen, the ability to spot potentially serious hazards had not changed.

These then were the major risks that liner captains had to consider as they traversed the Atlantic up to August 1914. Then the world went to war and an entirely new risk register had to be created.

3

THE WARTIME RISKS

Prize money paid for captured merchant ships and their cargo was one of the great recruitment motivators for the Royal Navy in the Napoleonic Wars at the beginning of the nineteenth century. Warships and their semi-official privateering colleagues of all navies saw the pursuit and capture of enemy merchant ships as a major part of their role. With the dominance of the Royal Navy and the navies of other European powers that followed those wars the need for the privateering element diminished and, eventually, the award of prize money was discontinued. One of the purposes of the Declaration of Paris at the end of the Crimean War was to regularise the position by international agreement. The result was the emergence over a period of time of a set of rules governing the behaviour of belligerent navies towards merchant ships, known as the Cruiser Rules. These were far from new, going back in much the same form to the time of Henry VIII. The Hague Conventions of 1899 and 1907 provided the last refinement of international codes of behaviour by belligerents prior to the First World War but did not materially alter the Cruiser Rules.

The Rules envisaged a scenario in which a warship of one nation encountered at sea a merchant ship belonging to a nation with which it was formally at war. There were separate agreements around the treatment of neutral ships which, while they proved highly controversial, do not directly affect the incidents with which we are concerned. Like all legalistic determinations, much hangs upon understanding what the terms mean and before looking at the rules themselves it is important at least to be clear as to when, so far as the rules are concerned, a merchant ship is a merchant ship. Obviously a ship mounting its own armament cannot claim to be solely a merchant ship. If a ship has been built so as to be easily converted into an armed cruiser, (as some liners were) that cast some doubt on its merchant status. Also of significance is the nature of the cargo the ship is carrying. If the ship is carrying cargo that is directly aimed at furthering the war effort of the country to which it belongs, then it is no longer a merchant ship under the rules. Such cargo is referred to as 'contraband'. The difficulty with that proviso is that the 'cruiser' may have no means of knowing what cargo the ship is carrying until its crew can board the ship and search it.

Thus the procedure envisaged by the Cruiser Rules was that the cruiser would order the merchant ship to stop, an order which the Rules required it to obey, so that the cruiser could send across crew members to carry out a search; if contraband cargo were found then the ship could be impounded. Ideally, the ship should then be directed into a port of the nation to which the cruiser belongs, or an ally. Should that prove impossible the Rules allowed the cruiser to sink the merchant ship on condition that the safety of the crew was ensured. 'Safety' here implied that the cruiser would take the merchant ship's crew on board itself or would put them into lifeboats, provided that they were close to shore and the crew could land easily. If, on approach, the cruiser could see that the ship was armed it was entitled to open fire without warning and without giving the crew time to leave the ship.

The rules were fine as far as they went, except that the scenario upon which they were based proved to be the exception rather than the rule when war broke out. That is not to say that they were ignored entirely. R K Lockner entitled his book about Captain Karl von Muller and his ship, the German Light Cruiser *Emden,* 'The Last Gentleman of War'. During the *Emden*'s cruise in the Pacific in the autumn of 1914 a number of merchant ships were sunk, but always the Cruiser Rules were meticulously obeyed and the safety of the crews was assured.

Defining contraband cargo as anything intended to further the war effort was an immediate source of controversy. Both sides eventually attempted to impose total blockades on the basis that even foodstuffs which sustained the population enabled that population to keep the war going. On that defini-tion all merchant ships were deemed to be carrying contraband and therefore could be legitimately seized or sunk. Nonetheless, under the Rules the ship must first be stopped and the safety of the crew attended to. Unfortunately the Cruiser Rules were designed to deal with a surface warship as the cruiser and a merchant ship unable to send distress signals by wireless when approached. A submerged warship and a wireless-equipped merchant ship distorted the picture. It would be hard to blame the Tudor diplomats who penned the rules initially for a lack of foresight, but perhaps an opportunity was missed to update the rules in line with new technological developments when the refinements to the Hague Convention were agreed in 1907.

It is surprising, but also enlightening, to note how poorly the impact on
warfare of both submarines and wireless were foreseen before the event.
The occasional Jeremiah predicted the end of the battleship era as a result
of the threat of submarine attack but, in fact, no Dreadnought type battleship on either side was lost to submarine action throughout the war. It was
aircraft, not submarines, which eventually made battleships extinct. Likewise,
the potential of German submarines to create complete mayhem with the
seaborne trade of what was then the premier maritime nation was almost
entirely unforeseen. Furthermore, the capability of wireless to provide intelligence and orders to widely spread warships at sea was also underestimated.

Submarines posed a major challenge to the Cruiser Rules because they
combined enormous offensive potential with great defensive vulnerability,
especially on the surface. They were capable of targeting a very large high
explosive load, unseen and from great distances. But on the surface, damage
that, to a surface ship, would be regarded as minor, could prove fatal to a submarine. It was quite unrealistic to expect a submarine to stay for a prolonged
period on the surface in hostile waters while a party went across to a merchant ship to search the cargo and then facilitate the evacuation of the crew.
It was also unrealistic to expect the merchant ship to sit quietly and not to use
its wireless while this was going on.

What emerged as the war progressed was complete confusion characterised by partial adherence to the Rules by both sides, when to do so carried
little risk, but total disobedience when judged expedient – and that was most
of the time. What turned out to be almost as significant as actual behaviour
in the war at sea was the propaganda campaign that each side mounted to
exploit the supposed breaching of the rules by the other. Indeed, the two
aspects interacted in that some of the activity at sea was engaged in for the
purpose of generating a propagandist rather than a military success. The level
of hypocrisy was quite extraordinary. The two incidents that we are interested
in occurred quite early in the war at a time when both sides were still feeling
their way with the new technology, uncertain as to what it could achieve,
uncertain as to what they could legitimately use it for and, likewise, uncertain
as to what they could get away with that was not legitimate.

The confusion as to how the war at sea with submarines would be fought
was evident very quickly. A number of warships were sunk in August and
September 1914, but the first merchant ship to be attacked was the *Glitra* on
20 October. The captain of U-17, Feldkirchner, kept his ship on the surface,
requested the *Glitra* to stop, sent a party over to inspect the cargo, ordered the
crew off on the lifeboats and then sank the ship. Just six days later, in the Dover
Strait, the *Admiral Gentaume* was torpedoed without warning by Rudolph

Schneider in U-24, although she did not sink and was towed into port. By the end of 1914 just 10 merchant ships had been sunk by German submarines.

It must be remembered that the Allies were also making use of their submarines. Britain had declared a long range blockade of Germany and her submarines were involved in the North Sea and Baltic in enforcing it. In the North Sea the submarines were acting as scouts gathering intelligence as to the likely movements of the main German warships and they did not therefore pursue a very active role in stopping and sinking ships. In the Baltic they had a rapid impact on the carriage of iron ore from Sweden to Germany, sinking a large number of ore carriers in a short period. When the Gallipoli campaign began in April 1915, submarines were sent through the Dardanelles to the Sea of Marmara and the Bosphorus in order to disrupt Turkish supplies to their troops. It was a campaign that demanded much of the submarine crews in navigating very confined waters in a hostile environment and in operating completely isolated over long periods. Their bravery was recognised by the award of three Victoria Crosses. One of the commanders so honoured was Lieutenant Commander E.C. Boyle of E-14 for a patrol that lasted from 27 April to 18 May 1915. On 3 May, just four days prior to the sinking of the *Lusitania,* Boyle torpedoed the Turkish troop carrier *Gul Djemal.* This was a ship of 5000 tons which had begun life in Harland and Wolff's shipyard in Belfast as the White Star Line *Germanic* in 1875. There are several versions of what happened as a consequence of the torpedoing. In one, the ship sinks with the loss of almost all of the 6000 troops on board. In another, the ship is only slightly damaged and proceeds to port for repair with no human loss whatsoever. An 'intermediate' version has the *Guj Djemal* sinks in very shallow water so that her superstructure remains above water, but a large number of the 4000 troops on board drown. What is certain is that the ship was repaired and returned to service and performed various roles until scrapped in 1950. It is also the case that in 1922 surviving members of the crew of E14 shared £30 000 in 'bounty money' (at £5 per head of the supposed 6000 troops on the *Gul Djemal*) awarded by a British court, the largest such payment received by any group of individuals as a result of actions in the First World War. The court ruled that the rifles that the troops were carrying constituted 'ship's armament' and so the ship could be classified legally as a warship.

The commander of E14 knew that the *Gul Djemal* was in the service of the Turkish government as a troopship and, therefore, opened fire without warning as he was entitled to do. Towards the end of his patrol he also torpedoed a coal-carrying ship as it berthed in the harbour of Constantinople, also without warning, on the basis that coal was vital to the Turkish war effort. Altogether, during the Gallipoli campaign, British submarines sank 2 large warships, 1 destroyer, 5 gunboats, 11 transports, 44 steamships and 148 sailing boats. Although the actions of British submarines were never strategically as important as those of the U-boats and did not raise the same issues concerning the fate of neutral citizens or non-combatants, it would be wrong to suggest that the manner of their employment was radically different. That was not apparent from the statements of either government.

On 18 February 1915 the German government announced that, from that point on, in the area around the British Isles, its submarines would conduct 'unrestricted warfare'. That meant that the Cruiser Rules were being abandoned because all ships irrespective of cargo or of nationality were declared liable to be sunk without warning. Although the Germans withdrew the announcement in September that year as a result of pressure from neutral nations, particularly America, (only to re-instate it two years later) it was in effect during the period in which we are interested, through the spring of 1915. The U-boats immediately began to put the new policy into practice and numbers of ships sunk without warning increased. However, some U-boat commanders, where it was judged safe to do so, tried to follow the Cruiser Rules at least so far as giving the crew of the merchant ship a chance to get clear before the torpedo was fired. This most frequently occurred when small ships were attacked such as coastal steamers or sailing ships. Quite often the value of the target was judged to be so low as not to justify the expenditure of a torpedo. In such cases the submarine surfaced and used its gun to sink the merchant ship, often waiting long enough for the crew to get away in the boats before opening fire.

It is hard to pin down precisely why, in some cases, there was a genuine attempt to minimise losses amongst merchant ship crews and, in other cases, no attempt at all. It does seem to be the case that different U-boat captains exhibited different patterns of behaviour. Whether this was because they happened to operate in different patrol areas, some with high populations of British warships and others with fewer, or because some targets provided more opportunity for humanitarian gestures it is difficult to tell. A third possible explanation is that the different patterns of behaviour simply reflected the personalities of the captains involved and we will consider this further at a later stage.

The British Government attempted to hold the Germans to account in relation to the abandonment of the Cruiser Rules and some of the pressure from neutral nations demonstrated a measure of success in doing so. However, from the beginning of the war the British Admiralty had, in effect, abandoned the Rules as well, albeit in a different way. The advice given to the captains of merchant ships was that if they spotted a U-boat, they should ignore any instructions from it and either turn their stern towards it and run or else turn towards the submarine and attempt to ram it. They should also use their wireless to call for assistance, giving as much information about the submarine as possible. Turning stern on to the U-boat minimised the target size for the U-boat's gun or torpedo tubes and, obviously, going to full speed increased the chance of escape. Although we will later encounter one ship that did make an attempt to ram a submarine, the most common practice, certainly where passengers were involved, was to turn and run. However, the Cruiser Rules indicated that, if instructed to do so, the merchant ship should stop and permit a boarding party. The merchant ship was also not supposed to try to summon assistance.

The Admiralty encouraged captains to fly the flags of neutral nations instead of the Red Ensign so as to discourage U-boats. This was a legitimate 'ruse of war' sanctioned under the 1907 Hague Convention and was not itself a breach of the rules because, clearly, a search party could see through the ruse immediately. However, if a ship flying a neutral flag, which is told to stop by a U-boat, turns away at speed and calls for help on its wireless, it is difficult to see what option the captain of the submarine has other than to force the ship to stop by opening fire.

The advice given by the Admiralty was designed to try to reduce the success rate of U-boats and, if possible, to find them and attack them. Getting merchant ships to use their wirelesses increased the chance of warships being alerted in time to get to the scene before the U-boat had left. The priority of the Admiralty was to win the war. While they would not deliberately have put lives unnecessarily at risk, the saving of lives per se was not their first consideration.

The other advice that the Admiralty gave to captains was less contentious as it principally concerned the navigation of merchant ships in such a way as to avoid attack. Captains were advised to zig-zag irregularly in order to make it difficult for U-boats to target them with torpedoes. It was also suggested that merchant ships should not stay too close to coastlines and, in particular, they should avoid headlands. Headlands tended to be 'turning points' that also gave good opportunities for bearings to be taken that confirmed a ship's position. U-boat captains recognised this and tried to exploit the natural inclination of merchant ship captains to employ them in this way. Thus there was a tension between the advice offered by the Admiralty and what was regarded as normal, safe peacetime practice. Ships that perpetually zig-zagged had more difficulty in determining their dead reckoning position. If opportunities for taking sights with sextants had been limited for some time by weather conditions, then there was a greater need for sighting land in good time and good visibility. Running on towards land without knowing a ship's exact position of course raises the risk of stranding. As we have already observed, high speeds

tended to magnify errors in dead reckoning positions. One degree of inaccuracy in a course steered at 10 knots over 12 hours produces half of the error
that the same inaccuracy generates at 20 knots.

The British Admiralty also made adherence to the Cruiser Rules almost
impossible through its use of Q-ships. These were small merchant ships, trawlers or sailing ships which were secretly converted into warships with hidden
guns. They acted as decoys luring U-boats as close as possible before opening
fire. They did have some success, although probably not commensurate with
the effort and cost involved in terms of resources invested and manpower lost.
They are not relevant to the episodes with which we are concerned as the
first Q-ship success was not until 24 July 1915. It is worth noting, however, in
the context of some of the attitudes being struck by the British Government
in relation to the sinking of *Falaba* and *Lusitania,* that Q-ships had been conceived, had been taken up and converted and were operational by the time the
second of those sinkings had occurred and before either inquiry had opened.

One criticism frequently levelled against the Admiralty is that it failed to
put a convoy system in place at the very beginning of the war. After all, it
is sometimes argued, convoys were successfully employed throughout the
Napoleonic wars a century previously. Surely it was obvious that they were
needed in 1914. In fact it would have been wrong simply to have extrapolated
directly from actions fought by slow wooden sailing ships firing short range
cannons to attacks on steamships by submerged, torpedo-firing submarines.
Twentieth-century surface warships were also a world away from the sloops,
brigs and frigates that used to prey on merchant ships in the early 1800s, being
capable of accurate plunging fire from rifled guns fired at a distance of several
miles. In the end the Admiralty became convinced that convoys would be
beneficial and introduced them in 1917. Arguably they should have come
to that conclusion a little sooner, but given the nature of the threat in early
1915 and the poor understanding there was about how effective the new
technology would be and how best to counter it, the decision not to instigate
a convoy system at that stage is at least defensible.

Perhaps the single word that captures the situation in the first half of 1915,
therefore, is confusion. There was confusion amongst the politicians about
the rules of war, confusion amongst the admirals and shipping companies as
to how to interpret them and confusion amongst captains at sea, on either
side, as to how best to balance out the risks of the new warfare while at the
same time dealing with the peacetime risks that had not gone away when war
was declared. And confusion persisted for a long time after 1915. The Cruiser
Rules were included in the provisions of the 1930 Naval Treaty of London.
Germany was not a signatory but added the relevant parts into German law.

Nonetheless, on 3 September 1939, the day Britain declared war on Germany again, a torpedo sank the Donaldson Line steamship *Athenia* off the north coast of Ireland with the loss of 117 lives. Oberleutnant Fitz-Julius Lemp, whose U-30 fired the torpedo, claimed afterwards that he had mistaken the ship for a troopship or armed merchant cruiser. Towards the end of that year, however, in the South Atlantic, Captain Langsdorf of the pocket battleship *Graf Spee* did make some attempt to avoid loss of life amongst the crews of merchant ships that he sank by taking them on board and transferring them to supply ships. He was almost the last person to do so. After that, war at sea became completely no holds barred.

4

THE NATURE OF INQUIRIES

Although by the beginning of the twentieth century, the UK was no longer the largest manufacturing nation in the world, having already been overtaken by Germany and soon to be relegated to third place by the USA, she was still the largest trading nation, handling a much greater proportion of the world's trade than any other. It is not surprising, therefore, that the post of President of the Board of Trade was an extremely important one, deemed to be of cabinet rank. Indeed, that remained the case until well into the second half of the century. It was one of the responsibilities of the holder of that office to decide when a public inquiry into a matter affecting trade was required and to determine its terms of reference.

There was never any doubt that the loss of the *Titanic* would be the subject of an inquiry, but it was not automatic. The President of the Board of Trade, Sydney Buxton in this case, had the right to consider the nature of any accident involving a British flagged ship and decide whether or not an inquiry was warranted. The Merchant Shipping Acts, 1894-1906 provided the relevant legislation. The most important appointment in an inquiry into the loss of a ship was the man (and in those days it was of course always a man) who would act as the rather oddly named Commissioner of Wrecks. This person was required to chair the inquiry and to write the report. It was normal for the Commissioner to have a legal background because the proceedings of the inquiry were quasi-judicial and, in the case of a judge being appointed, that was a matter for the Lord Chancellor. That meant that evidence was given as in court and witnesses could be cross-examined. It is important, however, to stress that an inquiry was not a court case in that there was no accused, no plaintiff, no jury and no 'verdict'. In the Royal Navy when an event occurred that caused damage to or loss of a ship, the captain of that ship was automatically charged, at least, with hazarding the vessel, if not with gross negligence. The Court Martial that followed was a trial in the usual sense with an accused, prosecutor, defence, verdict and, if appropriate, sentence. Sentence could include not only ignominious dismissal from the service but also a prison term.

Board of Trade inquiries, because there was no verdict as such, could not impose sentences. However, they could find that the accident into which the inquiry was being held had been the result of negligence on the part of one or more people involved. Acting on that finding, the Board of Trade could, for example, suspend or remove a certificate of competence from a captain or other officer of a ship. Even if no such steps were taken, a finding of fault against a seaman could adversely affect that person's career for many years afterwards. Not only seamen, however, could be considered to have been the cause of accidents, or the loss of life that resulted. Ship owners and ship build- ers, for example, were very sensitive to the findings of inquiries as a negative comment about them in a report could harm their reputation and future business. It would also greatly increase the likelihood of them being found liable for damages. For these reasons an inquiry had much of the feel of a trial about it; after all the consequences of the report might well be seen in other courts subsequently and the proceedings of the inquiry had to be such as to stand up to scrutiny in those courts.

One protection in case of future scrutiny of the proceedings of an inquiry was permission given to persons who were at all likely to be the subject of criticism in a report to be represented by counsel. At the discretion of the Commissioner of Wrecks, the counsel was permitted to cross-examine those witnesses whose testimony had a bearing on the behaviour of their client. In one of the inquiries in which we are interested, the issue of permitting repre- sentation became controversial and has remained so since.

One of Mersey's four inquiries was not a British Board of Inquiry but was created on a similar model by the government of the new Dominion of Canada. In fact it required an amendment to the existing legislation in order to establish an inquiry because no provision for one had previously been made. There were some differences in its constitution and that of the British ones, particularly in that it took the form of a tribunal with Lord Mersey acting as President and two Canadians sitting as Commissioners. It differed further in that the Canadian Ministry of Justice had a role in deciding which witnesses would be called to give evidence, a degree of government influence regarded as controversial at the time.

There was very little variation in the terms of reference given to inquiries into the loss of ships whether in peace or war. The terms of reference normally consisted of a long series of questions that the inquiry was asked to answer. The questions were specific to the incident being investigated, but taken together their overall effect was to require the inquiry to establish the cause or causes and to decide what should be done to prevent a repetition. There was a great deal of difference, however, between how a peacetime loss could be investigated and a wartime one. All of those surviving a peacetime sinking who had any hand in the event could be asked to provide testimony and have that testimony challenged. In wartime the enemy could not be made subject to questioning. An inquiry into a peacetime accident could make recommendations about the construction or navigation of ships, or their manning that would reduce the likelihood of a similar accident happening again. A Board of Trade inquiry, however, was not the place for the formulation of wartime strategy. The Admiralty was under no obligation to pay any heed to the suggestions of a Commissioner of Wrecks appointed by the Board of Trade. The first priority of the Admiralty was victory; the safe passage of ships came second.

The value of holding inquiries into wartime losses might therefore be questioned. If the Commissioner was limited in how he was able to investigate the event and not considered to be of any weight in determining future actions, there would appear to be little point in the inquiry taking place. As the number of merchant ship losses mounted during the First World War, the holding of inquiries became less frequent. The principal criterion for justifying an inquiry was loss of civilian lives and the great majority of sinkings did not meet that criterion. For those with responsibility for conducting the propaganda war, inquiries were significant events, either for good or bad and there was clearly a desire on their part to have some say in whether or not an inquiry was held and, if one were held, to influence the outcome. The extent to which that desire was or was not translated into action in the cases of the *Falaba* and the *Lusitania* is a highly controversial question to which we shall return in some detail.

The Commissioner of Wrecks was required to look into the actions of professional seamen and to make judgements as to whether or not those actions were correct. Coming from a legal background he was unlikely to have sufficient nautical expertise. For that reason, sitting with him, were Assessors whose job was to provide expertise in matters to do with the construction, equipping, manning and navigation of ships. The Assessors were not appointed by the Board of Trade but by the Home Secretary. So, although the inquiry (referred to in recognition of its quasi-judicial status as a Court of Inquiry) was regarded as a Board of Trade animal (and it was to the Board that it addressed its report) its personnel were appointed by other authorities, albeit within the same government. The number of assessors and their backgrounds were dictated by the circumstances of the sinking. In both of the wartime inquiries naval personnel were heavily involved, not always the case in inquiries into peacetime accidents.

Undoubtedly the assessors involved in the inquiries were all competent people with a good understanding of the issues faced by seamen and the nature of the decisions that they were required to make. It was not always the case, however, that they were able to convey their understanding fully to the Commissioner of Wrecks. In any situation involving expertise garnered from years of practical experience, communicating that expertise to a non-expert who has not had the benefit of that experience is difficult and it is not a negative reflection on either the Commissioner or his assessors to suggest that this did not always happen successfully. The origins of nautical terminology are often abstruse and their usage does not always appear logical. The terms 'larboard' and 'starboard' have little obvious meaning and the replacement for the former, 'port', no more so. That lack of any clear connection between the term and its meaning was compounded at the time of the inquiries by the archaic usage of giving helm, or tiller orders to steer a ship rather than wheel orders. A tiller is pushed to starboard if it is desired to make the ship turn to port. A ship's wheel, however, is turned anti-clockwise (i.e. the top of the wheel goes to port) in order to achieve the same effect. Yet, even on large ships using wheels operating hydraulically powered steering engines, orders on the bridge were still given as if the helmsman were operating a tiller. That was a matter of some significance in the *Titanic* inquiry but was eventually resolved, although not, it seems, to the satisfaction of many subsequent commentators right up to the present day.

One example of terminologically induced confusion that was not successfully resolved was the difference between a 'heading' and a 'bearing'. A heading is the compass direction in which a ship is pointing. A bearing is the compass direction from that ship to some other object, for example a headland or another ship. If two ships in sight of each other are stationary, either may swing clockwise or anti-clockwise with the wind or current and so its heading will alter. However, as long as neither ship actually changes position, the bearing of the one from the other will not change.

That seems really quite simple and had all of the evidence and discussion at the inquiries been based on compass directions confusion might (just might) have been avoided. Consider our two stationary ships again. If a witness is asked, for example,

'Where did you see the other ship?'
Answer: 'On the starboard beam.'
'Was it still there an hour later?'

'No, it was on the port quarter.'

'So it had moved then?'

'No it had not.'

Result, confusion. If the ship the witness was observing from had merely swung and changed its heading then the witness would have to look over a different part of it in order to see the other ship. When the conversation referred to a night time situation in which ships were observed only by their lights then the confusion could deepen when red lights changed into green lights and white lights altered their relative positions. Having got caught in this minefield, when a witness then reported that the bearing of a ship he was observing had altered over time, implying that it had changed its position, the significance was not always appreciated. The situation became so bad on occasion that witnesses themselves became confused and used terminology incorrectly.

Once an inquiry had been properly constituted under the legislation, its Commissioner appointed by the Lord Chancellor and its Assessors by the Home Secretary (or, in Canada, their equivalents), it was required to complete its business as speedily as possible and independently of any vested interest. Speed was not a problem with our judge who was never accused of being dilatory, but the matter of independence was an issue at the time of the inquiries and remains so.

Whatever we may think about someone's behaviour in the past from our own perspective, it is also important to judge them against the behaviour that their peers would have expected of them. Conflict of interest for example is much more clearly defined, and disregarding it more explicitly proscribed, now than was the case in Edwardian times; but it was still recognised as a potential source of bias. There was a famous exchange in the House of Commons when the *Titanic* inquiry was announced. Sir Edward Carson challenged Prime Minister Asquith for an assurance that the Board of Trade itself would not seek to influence the inquiry such that it would avoid criticism of itself. The irony of that exchange will become apparent when we consider the role that Sir Edward himself played in the inquiry into the loss of the *Lusitania*. The Canadian Deputy Minister of Justice was also challenged by the then Leader of the Opposition as to how he could select from a long list a much shorter list of witnesses to be called in the inquiry into the loss of the *Empress of Ireland* without compromising the inquiry's independence.

The potential for the inquiries to be biased as a result of influence from one quarter or another was not just a matter of formal representation or procedures. Despite the nineteenth century Reform Acts, power in the UK remained concentrated in the hands of a relatively small number of people, the great majority of them living within an hour's travel of the centre of London.

Not only was political power concentrated in this way, so was the ownership and management of the large industries. Although commercial interests in shipping were sometimes located at other major ports, there was normally a London HQ. Even Lord Pirrie, an Ulsterman chairing the then biggest shipbuilder in the world, operating in Belfast and Glasgow, had a house in London in addition to his splendid residence on the outskirts of Belfast. It was at a dinner party in that house in 1907 that the first discussions took place with White Star's Ismay on the shape of the new *Olympic* class liners of which *Titanic* was the second.

The ease with which interested parties could communicate with each other in the course of social gatherings or casual meetings was such (especially since the invention of the telephone, by then ubiquitous amongst the political and commercial elites) that knowing who was subject to influence and from whom was very difficult. It might almost be said that the concentration of power and influence amongst relatively small numbers of people all in close proximity meant that maintaining even the appearance of independence was almost impossible. Those who wanted to could point to potential sources of bias through X knowing Y, or having been in the same meeting as Z, or being married to a sister of P, or being seen having lunch with Q (also a cousin, perhaps) or any one of a hundred other forms of interaction amongst the coterie of males who ran the country and its industries. That is why it has been so easy to assert that the independence of some or all the four inquiries we are dealing with was subverted either by political or commercial vested interest. There was never going to be any shortage of circumstantial evidence. That is also why it is difficult to prove the case either way, although in at least one instance there now remains little doubt.

Having discussed the generalities of potential bias there is one specific issue that needs to be highlighted at this point and that is the difference between the independence of an inquiry in peacetime and wartime. In theory, of course, there is no difference. Once appointed and asked its questions, it is up to an inquiry to answer those questions as completely and as objectively as the evidence permits whether it is inquiring into a peacetime accident or an act of war. Only the most idealistic, however, would expect practice to match theory. It is inevitable that, irrespective of any undue influence that may be brought to bear, the personnel involved in an inquiry will be biased towards their own country's interests to some degree. There will be a tendency to make the most of any faults determined to lie with the other side and to minimise any on their own side. However, and this is a major caveat, there is a line to be drawn, on the one hand, between exhibiting in wartime some degree of bias in apportioning blame and, on the other hand, deliberately reporting something known to be untrue as a means of supporting the propaganda war. We will be looking to see whether that line may have been crossed.

There are four inquiries within the scope of this book, but there were also two other inquiries concerning two of the same incidents. In the case of *Titanic* there was an American inquiry and, in the case of the *Empress of Ireland,* one conducted in Canada under the auspices of the Norwegian Government. Both were quite unlike their British and Canadian equivalents. Senator William Alden Smith chaired the American Inquiry into the loss of *Titanic* that opened in the Waldorf Hotel in New York only days after the disaster. Senator Smith was a member of the Senate Committee on Commerce and when the proposal was put to the Committee that it should investigate the disaster, he was nominated as the Chairman of a Sub-Committee charged with doing so. Senators, of course are quite entitled to inquire into any matter they choose. However, in order to do so effectively they need the power to compel witnesses to attend. The legal basis for the right to subpoena witnesses, including witnesses not of US nationality, in this case came from the US Attorney General. He based his opinion on the ship's destination being New York, the landing of the survivors at New York and the American nationality of many of those on board. So, like the British inquiry, the US inquiry operated within a legal framework, but it was overtly political in nature.

The executive and legislative branches of government in the United States are separated in a way that is not the case in the United Kingdom. None of the Senators involved in the inquiry had personal responsibility for any actions of the American government in relation to shipping. In that sense, therefore, it was at least as free from conflict of interest as the British inquiry. Not that the American government would have had any particular reason to feel itself in the firing line, despite the owners of the White Star Line being an American company and the ship itself having been built to meet American quality standards rather than those of Lloyds of London. Each ship was certified when built as having met certain building standards. The most famous is the Lloyd's 100A1 classification. *Titanic* was never certified as being 100A1 because she was not assessed using that system, but using an equivalent American one. Some people have implied that not being awarded the prestigious 100A1 label meant that somehow the *Titanic* was inferior in quality. In fact, there is no reason to believe that the quality standards applied to her and her sisters were any less rigorous than would have been the case had Lloyds been the assessing authority.

The benefit of holding an inquiry very rapidly after the event was that witnesses generally were on hand in New York and could be told to remain there. It also meant that memories were fresh and the minds of those inquiring were less contaminated by the tidal waves of speculation that were already beginning to sweep both sides of the Atlantic. The drawback of course was that the proceedings were rushed and those involved had little time to prepare background documentation. Furthermore, although the Senate inquiry was independent of the American government, it was less clear that it was free of commercial interests.

International Mercantile Marine (IMM) was the American parent company of the White Star Line and it was a company that was part of the vast interests of J P Morgan. Senator Smith was a known critic of J P Morgan and he had had interests himself in railroads and Great Lakes shipping that competed with parts of the Morgan empire. There was a suspicion that Smith's intense interest in the *Titanic* disaster was motivated by a hope that the outcome of an inquiry would leave IMM exposed to claims for damages by survivors and the relatives of those who had perished. In fact, the disaster did prove a contributory factor in the demise of IMM just three years later, although the Senate inquiry itself did not materially affect that process. The inquiry was something of a one-man show with Smith leading from the front and peppering every witness with a multitude of questions. However, there did seem a genuine attempt in his interrogations to get at the truth, rather than to accumulate evidence against any particular party. For our purpose it is perhaps most important to note that for all their differences in constitution, timing and manner of investigation, the two inquiries came to quite similar conclusions.

That is far from the case when the outcomes of the Canadian and Norwegian inquiries into the loss of the *Empress of Ireland* are compared. The two sets of conclusions were diametrically opposed. It has already been noted that Canada was a very young nation in 1912 and required some additional legislation before an inquiry could be instituted. Norway was also a young country having only attained independence from Sweden nine years prior to the disaster. Because the ship that struck the *Empress of Ireland* was the Norwegian collier *Storstad*, the Norwegian government decided to hold an inquiry. It was held two days after the Canadian inquiry completed its hearings but before the findings were known. A Norwegian diplomat from Washington, W Maithe Johannesen, was chairman with two Norwegian captains acting as assessors. The inquiry, held at the Norwegian Consulate in Montreal, lasted just one day and the only witnesses heard were from the *Storstad*. Not surprisingly it found that all fault lay with the officers of the *Empress of Ireland*. The flawed process of the Norwegian inquiry must largely destroy its credibility, irrespective of the findings. Given the appalling scale of the loss of life involved in the sinking of the *Empress of Ireland*, it is rather a pity that there was not a second inquiry with reputable methodology, the conclusions of which could have been compared with that chaired by Lord Mersey.

There was one feature that all of the inquiries into these sinkings had in common. Each in their own way illustrated how poor the human ability to observe events and to record those observations accurately can be. Many of those giving evidence were recalling incidents that happened when they were under enormous stress and such conditions are bound to affect how we see and remember the things going on around us. Nevertheless, there were many instances of witnesses reporting on matters that happened when they were not under stress and many of the same weaknesses are apparent. In passing judgement on Mersey himself and the assessors who sat with him, it is important to remember the amount of doubt that witnesses expressed about their own memories of what they had seen and heard and also the extent to which different witnesses gave mutually conflicting evidence; indeed, some witnesses gave evidence which was not internally consistent. Whatever conclusions the inquiries came to they were inevitably going to be at variance with a proportion of the evidence. One of Mersey's principal roles was to try to determine which of the witnesses provided the most reliable evidence. As a judge that should have been second nature to him. His direction to juries must frequently have involved drawing their attention to the apparent reliability or otherwise of the different witnesses in a case. But as well as being a reputable and successful man of the law, Mersey was also a man of his time, a time when people were frequently judged by their background and their position in life as much as by their actions. One of the issues that we will be exploring is the extent to which his judgement about witnesses was subject to that type of influence.

The opening page of each of the four inquiry reports records the formalities of the constitution of the court of inquiry and the manner in which it went about its business. Following that there is a statement of the overall finding of the inquiry as to the reason for the sinking of the ship. Underneath that statement is Mersey's signature, followed by the words: 'We concur in the above Report'. Then appear the signatures of each of the Assessors. The Assessors were there primarily to provide the expertise that the inquiry required to assess the issues brought before it. They were not, however, just advisers. In theory, at least, they had the right to express a dissenting view on any of those issues. That did not happen in any of the four inquiries. All of the Assessors involved were content to go along with the conclusions reached and to sign their names to that effect. Some of the more extreme critics of those conclusions treat them as if they were attributable entirely to the personality, susceptibility to influence, prejudice or, indeed, ignorance of one man. However much Mersey may have been the dominant figure as the Commissioner of Wrecks, we must not ignore the role of the expert Assessors, many of them leaders in their professions.

5

THE COMMISSIONER OF WRECKS

When John Charles Bigham, Viscount Mersey, celebrated his 89th birthday on 3 August 1929, he probably looked back over his life with some considerable satisfaction. He had been a very successful lawyer, had risen to an elevated position in the judiciary, had been made Baronet and then raised to a Viscount. His saddest memory would have been of the death of his wife some four years previously after a marriage lasting 54 years. His two sons were each successful in their own spheres, the younger being Assistant Commissioner of the Metropolitan Police in charge of the CID. The elder, shortly to succeed to his title, had given him four grandchildren, and had also acted as Secretary to the *Titanic* inquiry. His satisfaction might have been moderated a little had he been able to read the obituary that *The Times* had prepared and which was to appear just a month later. He would have been quite appalled had he had any inkling that, half a century after that, people referred to as '*Titanic* buffs' would come to regard him almost as a figure of fun, or even as an icon of everything that was wrong with early twentieth-century British society.

The fact that his obituary in *The Times* ran to 2500 words was in itself an indication that he had achieved some standing in society; only a few sentences referred to his role as Commissioner of Wrecks. Given the social rigidities that existed during his lifetime and the journey he had travelled that was a considerable achievement. He came from 'trade' as they said, father John Bigham being a Liverpool merchant. He was educated in Liverpool and at the University of London, the latter after a short period in his father's business. In 1870 he was called to the bar at the Middle Temple and joined the Northern circuit, rapidly gaining a considerable reputation as someone who could grasp the essentials of a case quickly and expound them with confidence. He was not a particularly attractive speaker, but a deliberate and measured delivery gave him a gravitas appropriate to his calling. He quickly built up a successful practice and, in 1883, became a Queen's Counsel. By then he was specialising in commercial cases, although by no means exclusively, and he was becoming well known in London as well as on the Northern circuit. For someone ambitious to move up the professional and social ladders, politics provided a way of gaining attention and it was probably for this reason, more than from any desire to make a significant political impact, that he sought election as a member of parliament.

It was almost inevitable coming from a 'trade' background that he would choose the Liberal Party. He made his first unsuccessful attempt to become Liberal MP for the East Toxteth Division of Liverpool in 1885, one year before the Liberal Party split. Gladstone's Home Rule Bill for Ireland was the cause of the split and the dissidents formed the Liberal Unionist Party to indicate their opposition to self-government for Ireland because they felt that it would threaten the union of the United Kingdom. They were a disparate group with a conservative wing quite content to be allied closely with the Tories and a much more radical wing strongly influenced and eventually led by Joseph Chamberlain. Mersey stood for his second election in the Exchange Division of Liverpool in 1892 as a Liberal Unionist and there is little in his character or record to suggest that he was aligned with the radical element of the party. It took a third attempt in 1895, also in the Exchange Division, before he succeeded. He made little political impact in his two brief years in the House of Commons or in the House of Lords after 1910, when he was created Baron Mersey.

It was his ability as a barrister rather than any visibility as a politician that brought him success in the legal field. He had an excellent reputation as an able and hard-working advocate and when he was appointed as a Judge in the Queen's Bench Division in 1897 (and received the knighthood that went with it) it was generally considered a well merited promotion. He continued to specialise in commercial cases, including many involving bankruptcy, but also tried criminal cases. His record as a judge was generally sound and, unlike some others, he did not experience regular overturning of his judgements on appeal. Indeed, in some of the more difficult points of law with which he had to deal, his opinions were eventually upheld by the Law Lords. Not that he was untouched by criticism. On one occasion he was heavily castigated for a lenient sentence on a mother who had mistreated her child. As the mother in question was socially very well connected, the suspicion was that Sir Charles was operating a more lenient standard for the well-to-do than he would for the poor. His defence was that the worst of the accusations against the defendant had not in fact been proved.

The Edwardian era was one in which there was great public fascination with the dramas being played out in courtrooms up and down the land.

Court reports in newspapers were very extensive and lawyers along with others involved in the criminal justice system competed with the names in lights on theatres for celebrity status. Bigham never would have been into that celebrity league but one of his cases became quite notorious and his behaviour during the case is of relvant to what came later. Whitaker Wright was a self-made financier whose financial empire collapsed in suspicious circumstances that resulted in his prosecution for fraud. It was a high-profile case as the demise of Wright's company had caused a minor panic on the stock market and there can be little doubt that there was indeed fraud at the root of it. One of those caught up (although never suspected of fraud) was the man Wright had persuaded to act as Chairman of his company, the Marquess of Dufferin and Ava, ex-Viceroy of India and perhaps the most prominent of all the British Imperial diplomats. When news of the bankruptcy reached him, shortly after he had learned of the death of his son in the Boer War, the Marquess retired to his estate in Co Down and died a short time later in 1902.

It seems that Bigham was chosen for the case because he was regarded as one of the most astute corporate law experts at that time. The person prosecuting was Rufus Isaacs KC who was later, as Attorney General, to represent the Board of Trade at the *Titanic* inquiry. Even Bigham's *Times* obituarist was to comment that the manner with which he dealt with Wright was strange in that he showed open hostility to the defendant from the start of the trial. Bigham had clearly decided on the man's guilt irrespective of anything that was to come out at the trial and the defence lawyer complained that at one stage Bigham had made fun of Wright causing the jury to laugh at him. Wright was, as expected, found guilty and sentenced to seven years penal servitude. He left the courtroom and, in the room he was taken into, swallowed a cyanide capsule and died immediately. One might wonder what would have been the outcome had there been an appeal against sentence on the grounds of the judge's hostile attitude to the defendant throughout the trial.

Such behaviour was rather typical of the man. He was credited with a quick mind, but one that was quick not just to assimilate facts but to come to conclusions; having arrived at a conclusion he was not one for easily changing his opinion. He had a brusque manner in court and did not suffer either fools or solicitors gladly. Witnesses frequently got the sharp end of his tongue, but for all the tetchiness he was not thought to be knowingly unkind. In old age he was well regarded as a patron of the arts, particularly drama and a good companion who liked a bit of gossip, a pastime that became more difficult as deafness encroached in his late seventies.

Promotion came in 1909 to the post of President of the Probate, Divorce and Admiralty Division. His commercial work having included a number of cases involving the shipping industry, he was quite content with the Admiralty part of it and financial affairs in Probate caused him no concern. The matrimonial disputes that came before him, however, he disliked intensely and he resigned after only one year. Immediately he was elevated to the peerage, to the lowest rank as Baron Mersey. In the Lords, as already mentioned, he was not politically significant, but he did remain very active in appeals and in the Judiciary Committee.

When the *Titanic* disaster occurred and a Commissioner was required to lead the investigation, Lord Mersey was an obvious choice. Although approaching 72, he was fit, keen to work and a continuing participant in the legal system, albeit not in a full-time capacity. His previous experience in the commercial context, including shipping, was regarded as an advantage and his well known ability to assimilate a lot of information quickly meant that he could be expected to get to grips with this new context. Many people, however, now believe that his was actually a poor appointment, given the output of his work as a Commissioner. Obviously, succeeding Lord Chancellors and the Canadian authorities thought otherwise as he was re-appointed on three occasions, including undertaking a role that was recognised as being of some significance in the political and diplomatic dimensions of the First World War.

It is not a hypothetical question to ask if there were available to the Lord Chancellor other judges who, on the basis of their experience and records, were better qualified to investigate the *Titanic* disaster and who were available to take the role. Perusal of the judicial lists of the time may well identify some likely candidates. It is hypothetical to ask if it is likely that another judge, as well or better qualified as Mersey, would have accepted the role and would have done a different or better job. Certainly, Mersey's critics have not been forthcoming in suggesting the names of judges who might have been chosen by the Lord Chancellor and who might have been likely to have succeeded where they believe Mersey failed.

In a sense those questions go to the core of the issues that we are examining. For some commentators it is clear that they believe that any inquiry established at the request of and under the management of the Board of Trade would have displayed the same characteristics as that led by Mersey. Others, however, point to the personality of the judge himself and his foibles as being the source of the problems. One senses that, in their view, had a more enlightened, more effective and less intransigent judge been appointed Commissioner then all would have been well. As in most complex situations with many interacting variables, the answer is unlikely to lie entirely with one view or the other.

We have touched on the question of vested interests and the possible influence that they may have had on the outcomes of the four inquiries that Mersey led and it is now time to consider what the principal interests were and, in general terms, the nature of any influence they may have had. Obviously, we will consider later the possible impact of vested interests in relation to specific issues as they concerned each of the captains. Broadly the interests that are normally suspected of influencing the process or outcomes of the inquiries can be divided into three groups: the Board of Trade itself; commercial interests; and other government interests, particularly the Admiralty in relation to the *Falaba* and *Lusitania*. We also have to be aware that these separate interests sometimes complemented each other and acted in concert, but sometimes competed and tried to obstruct each other.

The Board of Trade was the sponsoring government department for the three British inquiries, making all of the arrangements and meeting the quite considerable costs involved. The role of the Board in relation to maritime matters was as the regulator for the shipping industry, administering the legal framework within which British flagged ships carried out their business. That included such matters as the load lines that all ships were required to display on their sides and which governed the amount of cargo they could carry. The Board was also responsible for proposing any relevant new legislation to Parliament or the updating of existing legislation. It was in the interests of the Board that British ship owners continued to prosper and that Britain continued to dominate the world's maritime trade. When the *Titanic* inquiry was established, for example, the Board would have had two main concerns. It would have wished to avoid too much criticism of the fact that the legislation governing lifeboats was so appallingly out of date, its only defence being that the issue having been raised in Parliament two years previously, the wheels of government machinery were slowly grinding into motion just as the *Titanic* hit the iceberg. It would also have been concerned to avoid criticism of the White Star Line being too barbed in that it was an important element in the lucrative British transatlantic travel industry. However, the civil servants were conscious that White Star was American-owned and they might have been even more concerned to protect Cunard, had it been the company involved.

We noted in Chapter 2 how, in 1875, following the loss of the *Atlantic*, also a White Star ship (although at that time the company was British owned) lobbying by the owners had succeeded in persuading the Board of Trade to set up a second inquiry, which eventually exonerated them from negligence. It is often the case that agencies responsible for regulating industries in which large and powerful companies operate find it difficult to maintain not just the necessary separation of regulator from operator but also the appearance of independence. It is very difficult to get past the circumstantial level of evidence in order to determine the extent of a regulator's susceptibility to unreasonable influence by one or more of the companies it is responsible for regulating. Some commentators on the inquiries chaired by Lord Mersey have simply made the assumption that where there was motive there was influence. Obviously it was in the interest of the ship owners to ensure that they received as little criticism as possible but that of itself does not prove that, either by lobbying the Board of Trade or by getting directly to Mersey or his Assessors, they were able to achieve an outcome to the inquiry more favourable for them than might otherwise have been the case. Even if the findings of one inquiry seem to favour a ship owner more than scrutiny of the evidence at a later date might support, that is not of itself conclusive evidence that the inquiry was 'fixed'. At the same time a pattern of such discrepancies across a number of inquiries might suggest that not all was above board.

The type of criticism that ship owners wished to avoid concerned the safety of the ship's equipment, the competence of its navigation and the behaviour of the crew both before and during the incident. The latter two of those focused attention on the captain who was responsible for the navigation and who also carried ultimate responsibility while at sea for ensuring that the crew knew and understood their duties and carried them out effectively. The other principal commercial interest was the ship builders who wished to avoid any responsibility for loss of life being found to result from defective design or construction. That is not an aspect that is of particular concern in this book although it has been a matter of intense debate in the plethora of books and documentaries that have appeared since the wreck of *Titanic* was found in 1985. It has never been a significant factor in consideration of the loss of the other three ships, despite the speed with which two of them sank.

A state of war brings to the fore entirely different issues. The jingoistic attitude that prevailed in the warring countries in 1914 and 1915, before the awful slaughter on the Western Front and elsewhere took its toll of morale, infected every aspect of society. It would be quite unrealistic to expect those taking part in the courts of inquiry to be immune. But added to the patriotic desire to support the war interest of their own country was the potential for government actively to attempt to subvert the process in order to obtain quite specific outcomes, irrespective of whether or not those outcomes corresponded with the facts as the government knew them to be. In discussing Mersey's treatment of the four captains involved in the sinkings of the *Falaba* and the *Lusitania,* we will be trying to separate those different types of influence.

How cynical ought we to be in considering the extent to which Mersey was effectively doing the bidding of the various vested interests? Was he simply a pawn of the Board of Trade (or, in Canada, the Ministry of Justice), given a set of questions above the table and passed the expected answers below it? Was Baron Mersey in the pockets of the boardroom barons who ruled the shipping companies? Was he in effect an Admiralty agent in 1915 working to further the anti-German propaganda campaign? The United Kingdom has always prided itself on the probity of its public services. The civil service has had a reputation for professionally and impartially serving governments of every political persuasion. Unlike the USA, senior public servants are not replaced when an administration changes. Neither has the UK been associated during the nineteenth and twentieth centuries with levels of financial corruption which appear to have been endemic in some other countries. We have already noted, however, the ease with which communication was possible amongst the various players and the difficulty of ever knowing the nature of the communications that took place outside official channels. Also, the UK was not immune from scandals linking commercial and political interests. One person, whose name has already appeared, was at the centre of perhaps the most significant such scandal of the era leading up to the First World War and was also a key player in the *Titanic* inquiry.

Rufus Isaacs, who had prosecuted Whitaker Wright before the then Sir Charles Bigham, had prospered and progressed by 1912 to become Sir Rufus Isaacs, Attorney General. In May and June 1912 he appeared in the *Titanic* inquiry on behalf of the Board of Trade, an indication in itself of the seriousness with which the Board regarded the proceedings. Just a matter of weeks later the so-called Marconi scandal broke in which a number of ministers in the Liberal government, including Isaacs and Lloyd George, the Chancellor, were accused of insider dealing in Marconi shares based on a tip from Isaacs brother who was then Managing Director of the company in the UK. A parliamentary select committee eventually investigated the matter and, voting along party lines, exonerated the ministers, but in the view of many at the time and since, innocence was far from fully established. It is worth reflecting, in terms of Rufus Isaac's role in the *Titanic* inquiry, that the wireless operators on the ships concerned at that time were Marconi employees and their roles were under close scrutiny. Indeed Guglielmo Marconi himself was present on the first day of the American inquiry and gave evidence on two different occasions, one of them in relation to the sale of his employee's stories to American newspapers.

It would seem, therefore, that we do need to bring at least a healthy scepticism to the matter of influence on the inquiries, acknowledging that most of the major players on the government, legal and commercial sides regarded themselves as part of the same establishment club, with a strong sense of their mutual loyalty to that club, and that norms of behaviour were somewhat different to those which we attempt to enforce today. To what extent ought we to apply that scepticism to Mersey in person? One must assume that his loyalty to the establishment club was at least as strong as that of most of his contemporaries in similar positions. It is sometimes said that there are none so aware of their social standing as those who have recently improved it. Mersey had, through his own efforts, moved from a background in trade to the House of Lords and a well respected position in the judiciary. He is likely to have felt that he was a recently joined member of the club and wanted to consolidate that sense of belonging. He showed little appetite for any rebellious actions that would have labelled him a member of the awkward squad. Stepping out of line is often a sign of someone whose membership credentials are so well established that a little bit of rebelliousness will not jeopardise them.

That instinct to conform to establishment attitudes and not to rock the boat would almost certainly have infected to some degree any of the people that the Lord Chancellor could have appointed Commissioner of Wrecks. Mersey, however, had spent a lot of his career dealing with cases involving commercial interests. As we have mentioned that may have been seen by the Lord Chancellor as an advantage in that it gave him valuable insights relevant to what he was being asked to do. However, many people since have pointed to this experience as the origin of close links with people who had an interest in influencing the outcomes of the inquiries. He regularly attended the Annual Dinner of the Chamber of Shipping and on one occasion, proposing a toast to 'The Shipping Interest', he said: 'Those connected with the industry had to see that nothing was done by legislation or in other ways which would decrease the carrying power of this great country.'

Our scepticism should therefore extend to some degree to Mersey as someone who may have been susceptible to influence by vested interests, although it must be remembered that throughout his life he was never subject to any suspicion of impropriety in any matter, professional or otherwise. With the exception of the wartime pressure from the Admiralty, it is doubtful if he himself considered that he had deviated in the slightest from following his own lines of investigation and forming his own opinions based on the evidence that emerged, opinions which, in every instance, were endorsed by the expert Assessors who sat with him.

6

THE EIGHT CAPTAINS

The captains were Smith of *Titanic*, Lord of *Californian*, Kendall of *Empress of Ireland*, Andersen of *Storstad*, Davies of *Falaba*, von Forstner of U-28, Turner of *Lusitania* and Schwieger of U-20. The most famous of these was Kendall. That fame had nothing to do with the loss of his ship, however. Rather it related to his prior involvement in the celebrated Crippen murder case. Smith became infamous after his death, more so a century later than in the years immediately following the sinking, when to many he was a hero. Lord, for some, became the archetypal scapegoat, for others a disgrace to the British Merchant Navy. Turner achieved a certain notoriety resulting from the loss of the *Lusitania* but became a recluse. Of Andersen and Davies relatively little is known but records of U-boat operations were well maintained and we know something of both of the German captains. Von Forstner became a minor celebrity in the 1930s amongst those who take an interest in the existence or otherwise of mythical sea-serpents. Schwieger might have been treated as a war criminal at the end of the war, had he lived to see it. The only thing linking these eight men is that one man was called upon to pass judgements on their actions.

Edward John Smith did not come from a seafaring family. His father was employed in the potteries in Stoke-on-Trent and also ran a shop for a while. Born in 1850, he was educated at the local school to the age of 13 and then signed on at 18 as an apprentice on the sailing ship *Senator Weber* leaving Liverpool, owned by Gibson and Co. He seems to have taken to the life readily and progressed steadily up the promotion ladder. By 1880 he had moved to steam and joined White Star, the line with which he stayed for the rest of his life. He was Chief Officer of the *Cufic* for a while and then, in 1887, aged 37, he was appointed captain of the *Celtic*. He moved rapidly from ship to ship, acquiring newer and bigger ships as his reputation as a safe pair of hands was established. By the early 1900s he was the premier captain of White Star and he was given command of each of the new, large ships as they were built. He captained *Olympic* on her maiden voyage and then moved across at the age of 62 to take over the new *Titanic* as she emerged from her builders in Belfast.

Smith, referred to familiarly as 'EJ', was known as the 'millionaires' captain' because he had an excellent reputation amongst the wealthy first class passengers as a calm, reassuring, competent sea captain. He held the rank of Honorary Commander in the Royal Naval Reserve and, in consequence, the ships he commanded were entitled to fly the prestigious blue ensign in place of the 'red duster'. He was imposing in appearance with neatly trimmed white beard and immaculate uniform and he was clubbable, well able to hold his own in the dinner table conversations. It seemed that the wealthy, often aristocratic passengers who had the privilege of dining with him almost regarded him as 'one of us'. By association, the captains of the great liners became elevated onto a social stratum to which other sea captains could never aspire. One of the qualities that the major lines expected of their senior captains was that they should be able to acquit themselves well in the social dimension of their work, a dimension almost entirely limited to the first class passengers. Smith met that requirement in full and clearly must also have satisfied his managers on his competence as a seaman in order for them to trust him with their latest and most valuable ships.

In the seamanship department Smith appears to have had a strange combination of good and bad fortune up to the point where he took over *Titanic*. He had the good fortune to avoid any seriously threatening mishaps at sea and the bad fortune to experience a significant number of smaller ones. In a press interview, reported in 1907 in the *New York Times*, on the occasion of the maiden voyage of the *Adriatic*, Smith was reported as saying:

> When anyone asks me how I can best describe my experiences of nearly forty years at sea I merely say uneventful. Of course there have been winter gales and storms and fog and the like, but in all my experience I have never been in an accident of any sort worth speaking about. I have seen but one vessel in distress in all my years at sea, a brig , the crew of which was taken off in a small boat in charge of my third officer. I never saw a wreck and have never been wrecked, nor was I ever in any predicament that threatened to end in disaster of any sort.

On the face of it this seems a quite remarkable statement for someone who had spent the last three decades of the nineteenth century at sea, given the statistics of losses at sea and the catalogue of disasters on the Atlantic that we considered in Chapter 2. Journalists, of course are very good at putting words into people's mouths that are a little different to the way that they came out. It is also the case that the interview that Smith gave would have been part of the corporate public relations campaign that White Star mounted to encourage passengers onto their new ship and Smith would have been wanting to play up the message that only good things happen to people who go to sea. Perhaps what appeared in print was the result of a combination of those two influences. Factually, it appears at least to be correct in that Smith had never been on a ship that was wrecked or sunk and had never been rescued from an immediately life-threatening situation. To use the term 'uneventful', however, was perhaps a little rich.

In 1889 and in 1890 ships under his command had run aground but had been refloated and he had experienced fires on board in 1901 and 1906. His record of significant but non-fatal incidents continued after he gave the interview when the *Adriatic* itself grounded in the Ambrose Channel in November 1909, but the most serious was in September 1911 when the *Olympic* collided with a cruiser, HMS *Hawke*. This was not *Olympic's* first accident, having had a collision with a tug when berthing at New York just after entering service. The two collisions, it seems, were both the consequence of the difficulties that were being experienced manoeuvring these new, enormous ships in confined areas, particularly as their movements created much greater levels of suction than had previously been experienced. It was taking time for practitioners to adapt to the advances in technology and it would be unfair to single out Smith in this regard.

If Smith's career had indeed been as free of major incidents as he suggested in his interview, not having involved participation even as a third party in major life threatening situations, how well prepared was he for the situation that he faced on the night of 14/15 April 1912? The reassuring captain needs to be able to convince those under his care of his ability to avoid the worst happening but also needs to be able to deal with the worst if it should come about. In Chapter 2 we discussed the use of risk management techniques in business as a way of identifying major risks and ensuring that they do not materialise. Despite the best efforts of the best management teams, however, those risks sometimes do become reality and the wise businessman has prepared 'business recovery plans' to deal with the consequences and either get the business back into a good position, or, if that is not feasible, arrange for it to be wound up in as orderly a manner as possible. Each of the four captains of the ships that were sunk at some stage realised that they were in the position of having to manage the loss of their ship with the smallest loss of life possible. Smith was in a different position to the other three because he had by far the greatest amount of time to accomplish this objective. One of the issues that we will be looking at will be the manner in which he went about it.

The question of whether or not Smith planned to retire at the end of *Titanic*'s maiden round trip is of no consequence. Many believe that to have been his intention but others point to newspaper reports suggesting that he was planning to stay long enough to captain the third of the *Olympic* class ships (at that time possibly intended to carry the name *Gigantic* but subsequently it was decided to call her *Britannic*) by which time he would have reached the normal retirement age of 65. The fact was that he was approaching the end of a distinguished career. Like many in that position there may have been an element of coasting. The new big liners carried a large complement of well qualified officers, many of whom already held Master's or even Extra Master's certificates. One could see how someone in Smith's position might well become increasingly reliant on his immediate subordinates for the routine running and navigation of the ship. Indeed, that is probably how things should have been, up to a point. The increasing complexity of the electrical and hydraulic control systems on ships, the new wireless protocols that were to be observed and other recent developments all presented challenges that someone at Smith's stage in his career might well have found daunting. He may have largely relied on others to get to grips with these new-fangled gadgets while he got on with the more public face of captaining. While this might be a little speculative it does not seem at odds with what we know of his actions.

Captain William 'Will' Turner of *Lusitania* was in many respects in a similar position to that of Smith. He was Commodore of one of the other great Atlantic shipping lines and, in 1915, was coming towards the end of a highly successful career at sea. In almost every other respect, however, he was a very different character. Where Smith considered his time at sea to have been uneventful, Turner might have described his as having been punctuated by a seemingly never-ending series of dramatic episodes. Where Smith was the affable friend of the rich and famous, Turner was taciturn to the point of rudeness and disappointed his company as the public face of command in which Smith so excelled. It says something of the complexities of human relationships that the passengers whom Turner treated with such disdain clamoured to sail with him on the grounds, presumably, that if he was no good making small talk he must be an amazing seaman to hold down his job.

Turner was born in Liverpool in 1856 and did come from a seafaring background. His father Charles Turner was a sailing ship captain who took his young son to sea with him at the tender age of 7, signed onto the ship's register as 'cabin boy'. The ship was the barque *Grasmere*, and it was carrying 114 emigrants to New Zealand leaving Greenock on 14 December 1863. Slow progress because of contrary winds meant that she was off the Irish coast on the evening of 17 December, just south of the Copeland Islands. The *Grasmere* ran onto rocks off Ballyferis on the Ards Peninsula. All on board were rescued by the coastguards and were taken to Belfast but the ship was a total loss. At the subsequent Board of Trade inquiry Captain Charles Turner was censured for negligence in navigating his ship and his certificate was suspended for six months. So the Turners, father and son, lost ships for different reasons off the Irish coast and were both subject to scrutiny by Board of Trade inquiries.

Will Turner sailed with his father again as an apprentice on the *Queen of Nations,* again without much luck. The ship was badly battered by gales in the South Atlantic and had to jettison much of the cargo in order to stay afloat. She managed to make the Falklands and spent three months there under repair. He then sailed in a succession of sailing ships and having moved out of his apprenticeship was serving as second mate on *Thunderbolt* when he was washed overboard in heavy weather. Luckily the first mate reacted very quickly and threw him a lifebuoy on a line. He clung for over an hour before he was hauled back onboard. After that it was Will's turn to rescue others. In 1878 he left sailing ships with some regret to join the world of steam where the route to advancement now lay. Sailing as Fourth Officer on Cunard's *Cherbourg* on one occasion, the ship collided with a small barque *Alice Davies* in fog leaving Liverpool. The sailing ship sank but sufficiently slowly for a rescue party from the *Cherbourg* to rescue all but four seamen and the pilot. Will distinguished himself by saving a man and a boy from the rigging of the sinking ship. In February 1885 he distinguished himself again by jumping into the Alexandra Dock in Liverpool to rescue a young boy who had fallen in, a rescue for which he received the Silver medal of the Liverpool Shipwreck and Humane Society.

Turner returned briefly to sail in order to get experience of command, as Cunard only appointed captains with previous experience in the role, and on his return moved swiftly up the ranks. By 1897 he was Chief Officer of the *Catalonia*. On one voyage the ship came across a French schooner, *Vagne* , in a dismasted and sinking condition. Turner took charge of the rescue, which succeeded in saving all of the crew. For this he received an Illuminated Address to add to his Silver Medal. It was in 1903 that he was given his first command, the cargo carrying *Aleppo,* but he was quickly transferred onto larger passenger ships and in a remarkably short time was made captain of the *Lusitania*, the fleet's flagship, in 1908, on the recommendation of her retiring captain. In 1910 he was moved to her sister ship the *Mauretania* as Commodore of the Cunard Line and he also had the third of the trio, the *Aquitania,* for a while. It was on the *Mauretania* that he skilfully effected the rescue from a lifeboat of the captain and some of the crew of the *West Point,* a cargo ship that had sunk after a fire. For this he received another Illustrated Address from the Liverpool Shipwreck and Humane Society.

Following the loss of the *Lusitania* in 1915, Turner spent some time ashore recovering and was then appointed to a cargo ship, the *Ultonia.* Although a great come down from his previous role, Turner was glad of the opportunity to get back to sea and pleased also, no doubt, that Cunard had continued to support him. Towards the end of 1916 he was moved to the *Ivernia,* a troopship working in the Meditterannean. It was a short-lived appointment, as he was torpedoed for the second time, but once again he survived. That was the end of his sea-going career and he was awarded the OBE in 1918, formally retiring from Cunard in 1919. His retirement was overshadowed by the tragedy he had been part of and he became almost a recluse until he died in 1933.

Will Turner was therefore the tough old salt, gruff, strict disciplinarian and man of action. Smith was the urbane, elegantly presented senior sea officer. For all the contrast, however, they had much in common. Both became Commodores of their respective world class shipping lines, both received Transport Medals for their work on troopships taking men to the Boer War, both were Honorary Commanders in the Reserve and both were highly respected by their peers and by their paying customers. They had each begun their lives at sea in small sailing ships, little changed for hundreds of years, and ended them on liners attracting descriptions such as 'leviathans' and 'greyhounds of the seas', relying on sophisticated new technologies that had not even been conceived when they were young men.

The murder of Mrs Belle Crippen in February 1910 was an event that rivalled the horrors of Jack the Ripper in terms of worldwide press coverage. The Crippens were both Americans living in London and the story combined sex with ghoulish dissection, a transatlantic chase and the best forensic detection work available. That was a powerful mix, but what gave the story its unique twist was the fact that it involved the first use of wireless telegraphy to bring a major fugitive to justice. Once suspicion had been raised about the nature of Belle's disappearance some time after the event, Chief Inspector Walter Dew of Scotland Yard had Crippen's house searched and Crippen was interviewed but to no effect, despite the fact that his lover, Ethel Le Neve, was living with him at the house and using much of the missing wife's jewellery. Crippen, not realising that the detective had left empty handed, panicked and the couple fled to France and then on to Canada. Their flight triggered further investigations and parts of a corpse, subsequently identified as that of Mrs Crippen, were found buried in the basement. Crippen was such an incompetent criminal that, having left a trail littered with evidence, it was almost inevitable that the fugitives would be found. They were discovered on the SS *Montrose* en route to Canada by the ship's captain, Henry George Kendall, who recognised Crippen from a photograph issued by Scotland Yard despite his having removed his moustache. He also realised that Crippen's travelling companion was not the boy she was dressed as but his lover. A wireless message was sent which reached shore and Chief Inspector Dew was alerted. He took passage in the faster White Star liner *Laurentic* and arrived in Quebec a couple of days ahead of the *Montrose*. Dew arranged to be taken out to the *Montrose* as she came up the St Lawrence close to a place called Father Point. He was welcomed aboard by Captain Kendall and shortly afterwards Crippen and Le Neve were arrested, Crippen ostensibly relieved that it was all over.

Kendall's fame as the man who caught Crippen would be hard to overstate. The case had been on the front pages of newspapers all over the world for weeks and his photograph now accompanied the dramatic story of the arrest. It is a measure of how the Crippen case created celebrities and how short was the impact of the loss of the *Empress of Ireland* that, in November 1965 when Kendall died at the age of 91, the obituaries in newspapers recalled in detail the saga of the Crippen arrest and failed even to mention the deaths of more than 1000 people on the *Empress of Ireland*. A recent biography of Kendall by his great grandson, the motor racing journalist Joe Saward, is entitled *The Man Who Caught Crippen*.

Kendall's early life could have filled several issues of Boys' Own magazine. Although not from a seafaring background he went to sea at the age of 15 in steam on the North American run. Taken by the romance of sail he then spent some time as an apprentice on a barque from which he deserted as a consequence of a violent incident involving two other members of the crew. There followed a year on a small island off the north coast of Australia before an horrendous 197-day journey home in a small, leaky, poorly provisioned sailing ship carrying bird manure fertiliser. Despite all of that Kendall continued his career at sea, taking his certificates and progressing onto the promotion ladder on steamships, beginning as Fourth Officer of the *Lake Superior*. The Canadian connection was to stay with him for the remainder of his time at sea as he served with Canadian Pacific up to the outbreak of the First World War and his wartime service was on an Allan Line ship taken up as an Armed Merchant Cruiser.

Kendall was just 40 in May 1914 and in some ways he was a cross between younger versions of Smith and Turner. He was quite a tough character who had been physically and mentally tested in fairly extreme situations, but he was also an excellent conversationalist who enjoyed mixing with passengers and telling stories of his own adventures. Much later in life he was to write an autobiography called appropriately enough *Adventure on the High Seas*, although one hesitates to apply the term 'adventure' to something as unremittingly horrible as the sinking of the *Empress*.

Shortly after the disaster war broke out and he found himself in Antwerp as German troops advanced through Belgium. Along with the British Consul he organised the escape of two Canadian Pacific ships then in the port, one being his old *Montrose* and the other the disabled *Montreal*. He took command of the *Montrose* and towed the other ship, along with 600 refugees, back to England. Kendall was called up as a reservist with a commission in the RNR and spent the war as second in command of the Armed Merchant Ship *Calgarian* until it was torpedoed and sunk by U-19 near Rathlin Island off the north coast of Ireland in March 1918. A total of 49 men died but he got away and was picked up. There followed a period as a Convoy Commodore and that was the end of his seagoing career; after the war he was shore-based in jobs connected to the shipping industry.

Smith, Turner and Kendall were the three captains of large liners, each of whose losses resulted in over 1000 deaths, all in a period of just three years. In his treatment by the press, Smith was either a hero or a villain, depending on the newspaper; Kendall remained largely untouched by the disaster, being exonerated by the inquiry and remaining the Crippen celebrity; Turner felt the criticism he received both in the inquiry and in the press very deeply and never recovered. However, the man who received the worst criticism of all, both through the work of Mersey and in press reports was a captain who suffered no loss or damage to his ship. Captain Stanley Lord of the *Californian* protested that he had been badly treated by the *Titanic* inquiries for a year or two after the event but then settled into a highly successful second phase of his career and put the matter behind him. However, when he was an old man, the controversy blew up again with the publication of the book *A Night to Remember* and the release of the film based on it, from which spun out the entire *Titanic* industry. The story told in *A Night to Remember* relies almost entirely on the findings of the British inquiry as its factual basis. Compared to later film productions this one was a straightforward telling of the story, without fictional sub-plots, and in many respects was well done. The producer, Bill McQuitty, was inspired to make it because as a child he had watched *Titanic* being launched and then sailing out of Belfast along the County Down coast. Unfortunately, the film not only repeated the story of the *Californian's* close proximity to *Titanic* and its supposed failure to save lives, it also embellished the story by implying that Stanley Lord slept through the night of the disaster having had a couple of drinks. Lord, like Henry Kendall, was entirely teetotal at sea.

As a result of the hurt that this caused him Lord began again to try to clear his name, swearing out a lengthy affidavit in 1959 and asking the Board of Trade to re-open the matter. They refused to do this on the basis that no new evidence had become available. This was correct procedurally but missed the point that it was the interpretation of the evidence available in 1912 that was being questioned. Lord died before anything further could be done but others, including his son, carried on the campaign. When the wreck of the *Titanic* was found, some distance from where Mersey had believed her to be, the Board of Trade did eventually relent and a further inquiry was held into the particular circumstances relating to the *Californian*. The outcome was partial exoneration of Lord, but there was a significant caveat to which we will return.

Stanley Lord had achieved command at the early age of 29 and was only 35 at the time of the *Titanic* disaster. His record with the Donaldson Line, which owned the *Californian*, was exemplary and the company's management wanted to retain him even after the criticism of the inquiries emerged. It was the Board of Directors who asked for his resignation on PR grounds. They felt that his continued association with the company would not be good for business. He was recruited by the Lawther Latta Line and given a command a short time later and he remained with them until, at the early age of 50, he retired, partially on grounds of poor eyesight but also because he was in a financial position to do so. He received a glowing testimonial from his employers, describing him as one of the finest commanders ever to have served them. The only question mark against his competence as a captain in his entire career was his actions, or lack of them, on one particular night.

Those are the facts about the man's career, but what sort of person was he? This question is perhaps more important in his case than in those of the other merchant ship captains because much of the controversy that swirled around Stanley Lord was not just to do with his ability as a seaman, but with his integrity, his leadership style and his bravery. Those most ill-disposed towards him have portrayed him as an inveterate liar, an intimidating martinet and a coward. One recent writer even used the term 'sociopath'. On the other hand, to those who feel that he was gravely maligned by the inquiries, Lord was as upstanding and brave as the honest British seaman ever could be. It is now very difficult to discern the real Stanley Lord through the fog of war between the obsessive pro and anti factions. Those who met him in his later years, including some of his detractors, found a courteous, affable and even humorous old man quite different to the sour and bullying captain they might have expected. It would seem that either he had had a personality transplant sometime in middle age or else the view that his critics had formed of him was based on unreliable half truth and innuendo. As often is the case, however, the alternatives are probably not as wholly incompatible as they might seem.

Quite a number of people present quite different sides of their personality in a position of authority at work and relaxing at home. It is not unusual to be invited to a social occasion at your boss's house and to meet there an entirely different person to the ogre you have learned to know and loathe in the office. As a young captain of a hard working freighter on the North Atlantic, Stanley Lord would have been keenly aware of the need to impose strict discipline in a harsh environment populated by some quite tough characters who would have taken any informality as a sign of weakness. In that respect he would have been little different to the great majority of his peers and much the sort of person that junior officers would have been used to dealing with. Even if it were to be shown that the criticisms of his behaviour on the night of 14/15 April 1912 were justified, there seems no need to indulge in excessive character assassination for which there is little if any evidence from other periods in his life.

The unfortunate Fred Davies who died when his ship the *Falaba* was sunk has left little with which to build up a portrait. He served the Elder Dempster Line, sometimes described as an artery of the Empire, and his ship was one of the class of medium-sized passenger/cargo ships that carried people and materials back and forth to the colonies in West Africa. He had been with the company for 20 years, giving excellent service and was described as a quiet and unassuming man, well respected by his peers. Unlike others of our group of eight commanders, his actions at the time his ship was lost were not seriously questioned at the inquiry and there has been little said since that would call into doubt his competence or the courage with which he faced what turned out for him to be his demise. There is some confusion about the manner of his death. It appears that he was rescued alive from the sea as the ship took its final plunge but passed away shortly thereafter. One newspaper report said that he had struck his head on the gunwale of a boat as he jumped from the ship and it was this that killed him. In another report, however, the Quartermaster of the ship claims to have pulled him out of the water using a boathook but makes no mention of a head injury.

The ship that collided with the *Empress of Ireland* is usually described as a 'collier'. While accurate, that description may be a little misleading because the term collier has come to be associated in many people's minds with the image of a small coaster taking coal into little ports around the country. The *Storstad* might more properly now be described by the more modern term 'bulk carrier', as she was a sizeable ship for her time at 6000 tons and was used to transport a variety of bulk cargoes. It just so happens that the cargo she was carrying, fully loaded, at the time of the collision was coal, almost 9000 tons of it. Being built for northern, ice-ridden waters she had a strengthened bow making her just about the worst possible ship to ram a passenger liner. Her captain was Thomas Andersen and, like Davies, we only have a limited idea as to what he was like. He has been described as brusque, a typical tramp ship captain, again (like Davies) quiet and unassuming. We know that he and his wife were close. She frequently sailed with him and was on board at the time of the collision. Indeed, she played a significant role in helping rescued survivors and issued her own statement about the accident on arrival in port.

In none of the other cases have we introduced any of the other ship's officers, although some will feature later. However, the particular circumstances of the collision involving the *Storstad* require that we do mention the Chief Officer, Alfred Toftnes, a tall 33-year-old, recently promoted and holding his own master's certificate. The reason for bringing him onstage at this time is that it was his actions rather than Andersen's that were subject to the most intense scrutiny in the inquiry, as he was officer of the watch when the accident occurred and Andersen was not on the bridge until just before the ships collided. This meant that, when the stories coming from the two ships to explain the tragedy differed, the two people going head to head were the rather famous captain of a prestigious liner and the mate of a Norwegian tramp. Toftnes seems to have been quite a strong character who stuck firmly to his story. Both he and his captain continued on their careers afterwards with no apparent ill effects from the inquiry outcomes. The *Storstad*, with Captain Andersen still in charge, was torpedoed and sunk off the Irish coast in March 1917, all of the crew surviving.

It will hardly surprise the reader that two captains who did not come well out of Mersey's deliberations were von Forstner of U–28 and Schwieger of U–20. It is doubtful if either of them could possibly have conducted themselves in such a fashion as to please our learned Judge in the circumstances then pertaining. As the 'von' implies, Forstner was of aristocratic lineage, his full name being Georg-Günther Freiherr von Forstner and he had taken command of the submarine the previous year when it had been completed. The *Falaba* was by no means either the first or the last ship that he had attacked. The previous day he had sunk two ships, one called *Aguila*, killing several people by gunfire when she refused to stop. He retained command of the submarine until July 1916 and U–28 had several subsequent commanders before being lost in September 1917 when the munitions ship it was attacking exploded and took its attacker down with it. Von Forstner was appointed to a training role and survived the war.

In 1917 von Forstner published a journal that included a lot of material about how submarines worked and how U-boats went about their business. The journal was translated into English and published in Boston in November that year. It makes fascinating reading, remembering of course that it was obviously produced as a piece of German propaganda, probably to counter the growing antipathy in America to the war being fought by German submarines. Von Forstner refers in the journal to a number of the actions in which he had been involved as the captain of U-28, actions in which he claims to have made every attempt to abide by the Cruiser Rules. He describes in some detail the capture of two ships carrying food cargoes, which he escorted into German-held Belgian ports and also the sinking of another ship, the *Vosges,* like the *Aguila,* sunk the day before the *Falaba.* We will return to that incident later when considering the verdict that Lord Mersey arrived at in relation to his actions during the attack on the *Falaba.* We will also consider a report that appeared in the *New York Times* carrying a story by the doctor on the White Star *Iberian,* which was sunk by U-28 on 30 July 1915.

In his journal von Forstner makes no mention of the *Falaba,* nor does he record any strange sightings when the *Iberian* sank. However, twenty years later he wrote an article claiming that as the *Iberian* went down there was an enormous explosion, probably caused by the cold water hitting her boilers, an explosion that was confirmed in the report by the ship's doctor shortly after the event. As the mass of debris rose into the air von Forstner said that he and several other members of the submarine's crew saw a vast sea serpent rising up with it. Unfortunately at this stage none of the other members of U-28's crew whom he named were alive to corroborate the sighting, but his story became very well known amongst that strange group of people who continue to be fascinated about the possible existence of as yet undiscovered sea monsters. Needless to say there is no reference to the sea serpent in the report in the *New York Times.* Von Forstner died in 1940 just as the second round of U-boat warfare was getting under way.

One thing which von Forstner and Walther Schwieger of U-20 had in common was concern for the welfare of their crews. Schwieger in particular was known to avoid running unnecessary risks while always being prepared to press home an attack. Originally from Berlin, he was tall and fair haired. His thirtieth birthday came just a month before the sinking of the *Lusitania.* It seems that he and von Forstner differed, however in their mode of operation. While von Forstner clearly made some attempt to stick to international conventions, Schwieger seems largely to have ignored them. It appears, if differences between these two captains are typical, that there was no coherently imposed strategy by the German naval command as to the manner in which their submarines operated, at least in the early stages of the war. The lack of a consistent policy may have reflected tension between an aggressive naval hierarchy and a slightly less hawkish civil administration.

Walther Schwieger, like von Forstner, was a career naval officer having joined as a cadet in 1903, moving to submarines in 1911. His first command was U-14 and he took over the more modern diesel powered U-20 just four months after the war began. His concern for his crew was reflected in their respect for him. Conditions aboard submarines remained pretty grim until the large modern nuclear boats emerged after the Second World War. In the early boats that we are concerned with here they really were horrible with appalling sleeping conditions, limited washing facilities and obnoxious sanitary arrangements. In a boat that had been submerged for some time it was common for the atmosphere to become so thick and barely breathable that men would vomit when exposed to fresh air. Schwieger tried to make life as bearable for the men under his command as possible, although in the exposed seas off the west of Ireland or in the heavily patrolled waters around the English Channel he would have had little scope to offer relief. After U-20 was lost by stranding, Schwieger took command of U-88. He continued as a successful and well respected captain (in Germany) until September 1917 when, shortly after leaving harbour, U-88 hit a mine and all aboard were lost.

Now that we have been introduced to the eight men and seen a little of their stories, we need to consider briefly what was expected of a captain. Against what criteria should these men have been judged? Once away from land a captain is a sort of dictator because the law allows for no superior authority aboard a ship. Even the Chairman of the shipping line does not outrank a captain when at sea. Because he is the person who must always have the final say, the captain can, at least in theory, be held responsible for everything that happens while a ship is at sea, irrespective of whether or not he is directly involved. He can delegate authority but not responsibility. The practice of holding the man at the top accountable for everything that happens in an organisation has become increasingly the norm over the last thirty years or so. Chief Executive Officers of big companies justify their extremely large salaries with the mantra 'the buck stops here'. Ministers are called to account for the actions of quite junior civil servants in a way that would not have been thought reasonable a century ago. One of the issues we will want to consider is the extent to which our captains should or should not have been blamed for the shortcomings of members of their crews.

Once a ship docked, the merchant ship captain's role changed. He reverted to being an employee of the shipping company who had to fit into the management structure in his appropriate place. That meant reporting to the Superintendent, the manager responsible for the running of the fleet of ships, and also being amenable to the requirements of the senior management of the line and the Board of Directors. For some captains this transition from dictator to employee and back to dictator as the ship moved from port to port was not an easy one, particularly when management decisions limited the resources that were available to them when going to sea. If the calibre of the crew that the captain was permitted to recruit was poor, to what extent could he then be blamed for their failings? If the equipment on the ship was below standard, how could he be blamed for the consequences of its inadequacies?

There was also the matter of the policies that management laid down to which the captain was expected to adhere. These might indicate routes to be followed, speeds to be maintained, expected turn-around times etc. No captain could afford to ignore these, but they did have the right to put the safety of the ship first; indeed they were required to do so by law. If a conflict arose between what the company expected and what reasonable caution required then the captain should always choose the latter. No captain could excuse the loss of his ship on the basis that he was required to follow company policy.

The two submarine captains, however, were in a different position. In the Board of Trade inquiries into the loss of the *Falaba* and the *Lusitania* von Forstner and Schwieger were not being judged on their competency as captains. They were being judged solely as the agents of a foreign power with which Britain was at war. So far as we can tell they were both excellent seamen who were also good at the difficult job of commanding a highly complex type of ship with a very high level of risk in its operation. The question that was asked of them in the inquiries was whether or not the manner in which they employed this innovative technology in warfare was acceptable.

In the next section we will look at the stories of each of the incidents that became the subject of the inquiries and at the issues that these presented so far as the actions of the captains were concerned. After that we will review the judgments that Mersey arrived at on the actions of the eight captains and consider whether or not they stand up to scrutiny against the evidence with which he was presented. We will also want to see how they rate in those instances where evidence has come to light that Mersey did not have.

7

IMPROBABLE THINGS DO HAPPEN

Quite simply, the sinking of the *Titanic* should not have happened because the odds against such an event occurring were startlingly high. Some people have said the opposite; that the disaster was an inevitable consequence of the hubris and arrogance which, they claim, characterised Edwardian society to an exceptional extent. Perhaps there is a philosophical point that the author is missing here, but surely it is rare for societal attitudes to be connected in quite such a mechanical manner to specific events. We are dealing after all with the twentieth century and not the Bronze Age world of the Old Testament.

Given the manner in which some aspects of technology had progressed so rapidly since around 1880 (size, speed, complexity of ships, communication) while others had largely stood still (navigation, ability to see ahead), it was likely that some incident would occur that would draw attention to the developing discrepancy between what it was possible to do and what it was safe to do. However, it was not probable that the incident would take the form that it did. What were the chances that the incident would involve the largest ship in the world at the time; that it would happen on that ship's first voyage; that it would take the form of a collision with an iceberg rather than with land or another ship; that the collision with the berg would be precisely such as to open sufficient of the ship to the sea to make its sinking inevitable; that it would happen when legal requirements for lifeboats were out of synchrony with the size of the largest ships; that, despite the use of wireless, no other ship would come to its aid before it sank? Multiply those chances together and the odds against the entire event happening in the way it did are very, very large.

That improbability is one of the factors that has caused the *Titanic* disaster to exercise its peculiar fascination for so many people over such a prolonged period. Few readers will therefore lack familiarity with the basic story but it is repeated here as a necessary framework to what follows, partly also to separate the historical facts from some of the subsequently manufactured accretions. This is the 'stripped out' version including only what is, to the best of the author's knowledge, generally agreed to be beyond reasonable doubt; as is the description of the sinking of the *Empress of Ireland* which follows it. Perhaps we need to clarify the issue of reasonable doubt by stating unequivocally that the ship which sank in the early hours of 15 April 1912 was the *Titanic* and not her sister ship, *Olympic*. The preposterous notion that the two might have been switched is well beyond 'reasonable'; that would have required tens of thousands of shipyard workers to be complicit in a vast and successful conspiracy of silence. Nobody who knew Belfast shipyard workers would suggest that such a thing was remotely possible, to point up just one of the more absurd aspects of the hypothesis.

The *Titanic* was launched from the Harland and Wolff shipyard on 31 May 1911. Her fitting out was completed in time for trials to be held on the morning of 2 April 1912 and she left Belfast that same evening for Southampton. It is worth pointing out the brevity of the sea trials and the short time between them and the commencement of the maiden voyage. While many of the crew had had experience on similar ships (including a significant number on *Olympic*) there was very little opportunity to weld the crew into an effectively functioning team and, for the considerable number for whom this was their first experience of a large passenger liner, little chance to familiarise themselves with their new role and surroundings.

The ship departed Southampton at 1215 on 10 April on her maiden voyage and travelled to Cherbourg, arriving that same evening. Here a small number of passengers left the ship, having booked only that leg of the journey and a rather larger number joined. They embarked on the ship by means of two steam tenders, *Nomadic* and *Traffic*, each a small scale passenger ship in her own right. Unlike *Titanic,* the *Nomadic* was to have a long career, one which still continues. Having spent many years as a stationary quayside restaurant on the Seine in Paris, she has now been taken back to Belfast where she is being restored as a public exhibit. Not only is *Nomadic* an interesting part of the *Titanic* story, she is now the only example to be seen in the city of the enormous output of Harland and Wolff and other Belfast shipbuilders over a century and a half.

Titanic also stopped to drop off and take on some passengers at Cobh (or Queenstown as it was then known) in County Cork, transfer being effected by the tenders *Ireland* and *America*. Amongst the passengers leaving the ship was a trainee priest by the name of Brown, who was a keen amateur photographer. His photographs and those of a friend called McLean who was with him, in particular one taken from the tender looking up at Captain Smith peering over the side of his bridge, have become world famous. *Titanic* left Cobh at 1330 on 11 April and headed out into the Atlantic for the first and last time. On Sunday 14 April she began to receive ice warnings from some ships that were ahead of her. Some of the ice was reported to the north of her track but at least two messages mentioned ice that straddled her route. Both low lying field ice and large bergs were mentioned. Not all of the messages reached Captain Smith; one from the *Mesaba* was not passed to the bridge and one from the *Californian* a short time before the collision was excluded by the *Titanic's* wireless operators. The speed of the ship was not altered in response to the ice warnings.

The night of the 14/15 April 1912 was one of the calmest that anyone with experience of the North Atlantic could remember. There was no moon, just starlight, and it was clear with good visibility. The look-outs in the crow's nest saw the iceberg first at around 2340 and called the bridge by telephone. Officer of the watch, First Officer Murdoch, ordered the helm put to starboard in order to turn the ship's head to port. He also ordered the engines to go full astern, although this was by no means immediate in a ship with steam reciprocating machinery. As her head swung to port, the starboard side slid along the edge of the iceberg, opening six of her compartments to the sea. There is some doubt about how far the ship travelled before stopping and in what direction she was pointing when she did so. It took about twenty minutes to ascertain the nature of the damage, from which it was clear to the captain that she would sink. Orders were given to prepare the lifeboats and hoist them out ready to be filled.

Titanic's wireless operators had been very busy that evening sending personal messages on behalf of passengers. Now they were asked to send urgent calls for assistance. Anyone responding to such a call had to be told where the ship was and Fourth Officer Boxhall calculated the ship's position by dead reckoning and this position was broadcast. He made an error in his calculation and we now know, from the position in which the wreck was found in 1985, that he placed the ship between 10 and 13 miles almost due west of where she was. Preparations to load the lifeboats went ahead slowly and with some difficulty because for a time the noise created when the engineers released the high pressure steam from the boilers was such as to make any conversation on the boat deck almost impossible. Around 0030 the first sighting of another ship was reported and about 10 to 15 minutes later the first lifeboat was launched. It contained only 28 people instead of its full complement of 65. Captain Smith was reported to have advised those in the lifeboats to row to the ship whose lights had been seen and return for more people.

Around the time that the first lifeboat was leaving, the firing of rockets from the bridge began as a further attempt to attract assistance, in recognition that, in 1912, many ships were not equipped with wireless or did not operate it on a 24-hour basis. For the same reason attempts were made to contact the ship whose lights had been seen by morse code using one of the ship's large signal lamps. No response was seen. The evacuation continued with lifeboats leaving the ship at intervals, most of them containing fewer people than they were built to take. The last rocket was fired at around 0140 and the last lifeboat cleared the ship just after 0200. A final distress message was sent by the wireless operators a few minutes later and the ship sank at approximately 0220.

The wreck of the ship lies in two pieces on the sea floor at a depth of around 13000 feet. Arguments have raged over the years as to when the ship came apart. Some say that the split happened while the ship was still on the surface and was seen by a number of witnesses; others that it occurred just under the surface as the forward part submerged, and there is some witness evidence for this point of view as well. Given that the scope of this book is limited to the actions of the captains involved, the matter is not one that need concern us. What is of interest is the response that the distress calls elicited from nearby ships. There were a number of responses but none gave those on board *Titanic* assurance that a rescue ship would arrive before it was too late. Their best hope lay with the *Carpathia,* but only if *Titanic* stayed afloat for an unlikely four hours. Having made her best possible speed, *Carpathia* found the lifeboats at around 0400 and began to rescue the pitifully small number still alive. The number saved was 705, the number lost was 1522.

Some distance to the north and slightly west of where the *Titanic* collided with the iceberg the *Californian* lay stopped. Having encountered substantial field ice, Stanley Lord decided to wait until daylight before pushing on through it on his way to Boston. He put the engines on standby and the single wireless operator closed his set down for the night shortly after broadcasting the ice message that was excluded by the operators on *Titanic.* Normal watches were maintained by bridge officers and lookouts during the night. A short time after the ship had stopped another ship was seen approaching and it stopped with its masthead and navigation lights visible. An hour or so later a rocket was seen from the bridge of the *Californian* that appeared to come from this ship. The sighting was reported to Stanley Lord, who had retired to the chartroom for a rest after having been on duty for the entire day. He suggested that an attempt should be made to contact the ship by morse lamp. This was done without response and subsequently a number of further rockets were seen, again interpreted by those observing as coming from the nearby ship. Finally, the lights of the ship were observed to change in a way that the officer of the watch, Second Officer Stone, believed indicated that the ship was steaming off to the south west. Captain Lord was informed of these developments both by voicepipe and by a visit from the junior watch officer, Apprentice Gibson, to the chartroom. Arguments have continued ever since as to how much Lord did or did not understand of these messages in his sleep befuddled state. No instruction was given to investigate the matter of the rockets other than by attempting to signal to the ship from which they were thought to be emanating. The wireless operator was not roused to see if there was anything being broadcast that would shed any light on the reason for the rockets being fired. The fact that they had been seen only came to light when some members of the crew, in particular a donkeyman named Gill, spoke to reporters on the ship's arrival in Boston.

It was at 0600 that *Californian* received a wireless message to say that the *Titanic* had sunk. She got underway immediately and pushed through the ice field towards the position that had been given in the distress calls. On arrival there she found another ship stopped but no sign of wreckage or survivors. Discovering that the *Carpathia* was completing the rescue of survivors some distance to the south east, Lord again traversed the ice field to get to that position and arrived at approximately 0830. The *Californian* assisted the *Carpathia* until nothing more could be achieved and then resumed her passage to Boston. This is a very brief outline summary of events that took place in the space of two and a half hours that morning, the details of which have proved highly contentious. Witness evidence on movements and sightings by the different ships is confusing and contradictory to the point that no resolution is now possible, despite the many kilograms of paper and litres of ink that have been consumed fruitlessly in the attempt.

Of the 1522 people who died on *Titanic*, 832 were passengers. That was 8 fewer than the number of passengers who died when the *Empress of Ireland* sank just two years later in May 1914. Where the gradual foundering of the *Titanic* on a crisp clear April night was a protracted drama full of pathos, the sinking of the *Empress* was a brief, ugly convulsion shrouded in fog. If the sinking of the *Titanic* was highly improbable, that of the *Empress* was merely unlikely. As we saw in Chapter 2, collisions between ships in fog were a major risk, both in terms of the likelihood of them occurring and the seriousness of the consequences when they did. Even the coming of radar and GPS based navigation has not eliminated the risk. Ships still regularly collide in fog, particularly in crowded waterways. Mostly the ships affected are cargo ships and, unless there are serious environmental after effects such as oil spills, the accidents attract little publicity. But some have involved passenger ships. Amongst the most famous since the loss of the *Empress* have been the sinking of the *Egypt* in 1922, leading to one of the most exciting gold salvaging episodes ever, and the collision in 1956 off the eastern coast of the of the USA between the Italian liner *Andrea Doria* and the Swedish cargo vessel *Stockholm*. Forty six people died in the collision and the liner sank the following day.

What was unlikely about the accident that occurred in the St Lawrence in May 1914 was the fact that of all the possible combinations of ships and collision geometries, few would have been such as to lead to the enormous loss of life which occurred. A heavily loaded bulk carrier, with ice strengthened bow, striking a large passenger ship almost at right angles, in the area of the big open space of the engine room was a scenario for a major tragedy and so it proved.

When the *Empress* left Quebec in the late afternoon of the 28 May 1914 she was carrying 1057 passengers and 420 crew. Amongst her passengers, as well as a small number of people who were then well known in the theatre or business, there was also a large party, totalling 171, from the Salvation Army. This was the Canadian contingent on their way to a major International Conference being held by the Army in London. Included in the group was the full membership of the Territorial Staff Band from Toronto. The first part of the journey out into the Atlantic required the services of a pilot and, shortly after 1.00am on the 29th, he was dropped off at the usual disembarkation point for pilots at Father Point. As mentioned in the last chapter, it was at Father Point that Inspector Dew from Scotland Yard was taken out to the *Montrose* in order to arrest Crippen. The greatest triumph in Henry Kendall's life and the most harrowing tragedy were enacted in exactly the same place.

Just 10–15 minutes after moving off out into the seaway, which is approximately 30 miles wide at this point, the lights of another steamer were seen a few miles away, coming in the opposite direction. This was the *Storstad* and the officers on her bridge also saw the lights of the *Empress* at about the same time. A short while later each ship lost sight of the other as a bank of fog rolled across and what happened over the following ten minutes became obscured not only for that period of time but has remained so ever since because two entirely different versions emerged from the two ships. Probably all that we can be sure of is that, just before the fog reduced visibility, the *Empress* turned to starboard to come onto her course out to sea. Worried about the proximity of the other ship, Kendall, at some point, ordered the *Empress* to be stopped by putting the engines astern, although the timing of that order taking effect is in doubt. Also at some point, although again the timing is not certain, the *Storstad* stopped her engines and her helm was put over which may, or may not have had the effect of turning her to starboard. Suddenly those on the *Empress* saw the *Storstad* heading directly for the starboard side of the ship, already too close to prevent a collision. It was only a minute or two earlier that the Chief Officer of the *Storstad*, Alfred Toftnes, had called Captain

Andersen to the bridge. As the bow of the *Storstad* plunged into the side of the *Empress,* Kendall gave the order to close watertight doors. In many cases there was neither time nor access to enable the order to be carried out.

Briefly the two ships were locked together. Kendall called across to Andersen to ask him to put his engines full ahead in order to keep the ships together so that the collier would act as a plug in the wounded liner's side and limit the inflow of water. Andersen claimed afterwards that he did so. Kendall maintained that he did not because the two ships separated, the bow of the *Storstad* being heavily twisted in the process. Into the cavernous hole that was opened in the hull of the *Empress* the water surged with terrible force. Immediately she began to keel over to starboard. Although efforts were made to get lifeboats away, those on the port side were soon useless and within a few minutes more those on the starboard side were being forced under water on their davits. As one reporter described it, with a graphic but unpleasant simile, the ship rolled over 'like a hog in a ditch'. Just 15 minutes after the collision, the *Empress* disappeared leaving a mass of wreckage and people floating and struggling in the bitterly cold water.

Two tenders from Father Point and a tug did most of the rescue work, assisted by the crew of the *Storstad,* but only 465 people were pulled from the St Lawrence alive. Of these, just 217 were passengers; only 4 out of 158 children aboard survived. On the other hand almost 60 per cent of the crew were saved. The relatively large proportion of crew members compared to passengers surviving resulted from the circumstances of the accident. It took place when almost all of the passengers were in bed while a significant proportion of the crew were on duty. As the ship had only started her voyage a matter of hours before, the passengers had not had a chance to familiarise themselves with the ship while members of the crew knew their way around. This was critical because the electricity failed within a minute or two of the collision and the ship was in total darkness. The events in the passenger accommodation during the sinking must have been horrendous beyond description. Captain Kendall was amongst those rescued. He ended up aboard the *Storstad* and confronted Andersen with 'You sank my ship, Sir'. Both Captain Andersen and his wife worked tirelessly to try to bring some comfort, including dry clothes, to the distressed survivors brought onto their ship by the lifeboats the crew had lowered.

So, two very different accidents to Atlantic passenger liners had claimed the lives of 2534 men, women and children. One eventually became the symbol of all man-made disasters; the other was largely forgotten as the world went to war a few weeks after Lord Mersey completed his report and the newspapers began to carry stories of carnage on an even greater scale.

8

MEN OF STEEL

Earlier we discussed the international agreements that governed the use of raiders attacking merchant ships in wartime, informally known as the Cruiser Rules. Given their genesis at a time when knights still took part in jousts, it is hardly surprising that they have a whiff of an earlier age of chivalry about them. Events were to prove that they were entirely inadequate to deal with the type of warfare that commenced in August 1914. Initially it seemed as if the principal impact of the new submarine technology would be in devastating the ranks of surface warships, much as naval commentators had predicted. The first ship ever to succumb to a torpedo fired by a submarine was HMS *Pathfinder*, a light cruiser attacked by U-21 on 5 September in the Firth of Forth with the loss of around 250 men. The explosion of the torpedo set off one in the forward magazine that resulted in her sinking almost instantly.

Just over a fortnight later came an incident that not only demonstrated very clearly the power of the new underwater raiders but seriously embarrassed the British Admiralty. Early on a calm, autumn morning in the North Sea, Otto Weddingen in the primitive U-9, outmoded even by 1914 standards, torpedoed and sank the three old armoured cruisers *Aboukir*, *Hogue* and *Cressy* one after the other. The statement issued by the Admiralty sets out very clearly the nature of what happened and their attempt to cover their embarrassment.

> The sinking of the *Aboukir* was of course an ordinary hazard of patrolling duty. The *Hogue* and *Cressy*, however, were sunk because they proceeded to the assistance of their consort and remained with engines stopped endeavouring to save life, thus presenting an easy and certain target to further submarine attacks. The natural promptings of humanity have in this case led to heavy losses which would have been avoided by a strict adherence to military considerations. Modern naval war is presenting us with so many

new and strange situations that an error of judgement of this character is pardonable, but it has been necessary to point out, for the future guidance of his Majesty's ships, that the conditions which prevail when one of a squadron is injured in a minefield or is exposed to submarine attack, are analogous to those which occur in an action, and that the rule of leaving disabled ships to their own resources is applicable, so far, at any rate, as large vessels are concerned. No act of humanity, whether to friend or foe, should lead to a neglect of the proper precautions and dispositions of war, and no measures can be taken to save life which prejudice the military situation. Small craft of all kinds should, however, be directed by wireless to close on the damaged ship with all speed.

The loss of nearly 60 officers and 1400 men would not have been grudged if it had been brought about by gunfire in an open action, but it is peculiarly distressing under the conditions which prevailed. The absence of any of the ardour and excitement of an engagement did not, however, prevent the display of discipline, cheerful courage, and ready self-sacrifice among all ranks and ratings exposed to the ordeal.

The sense of the naval leadership struggling to come to terms with new technological developments that were turning their nicely ordered world upside down is evident in the statement, as is the view that what was happening was somehow a sneaky, underhand form of warfare. To say that the loss of so many men would 'not have been grudged if it had been brought about by gunfire in an open action' and to refer to the 'absence of any of the ardour and excitement of an engagement' displays an attitude to warfare into which submarines simply do not fit. The statement that no act of humanity or measures to save life should 'prejudice the military situation' is one with which the German authorities would have concurred in directing the use of their U-boats against merchant ships.

The mirror image of the Admiralty's attitude can be found in a book *Raiders of the Deep* written by an American, Lowell Thomas, published in 1928 and containing accounts of the exploits of U-boats provided to him in interviews after the war by their ex-crews. The book, like the Admiralty statement, exhibits a gung-ho, isn't war a jolly jape sort of attitude, but this time from the perspective of the men of steel who fought in these new-fangled and dreadfully dangerous contraptions beneath the waves. As Thomas puts it:

In setting down this account of the submarine war, straight from the lips of the U-boat commanders, I have disregarded all controversial ground, or at any rate have attempted to. The right and wrong of undersea war is not discussed here. The tales I have to pass on are tales of sheer adventure. Stranger than fiction? Aye! And tales, I believe, such as no other chronicler will have a chance to set down in our time. At any rate, we all hope the world has learned its lesson, and may there be peace among men for generations to come.

Setting aside the horrible irony of the latter part of the quote, the first part illustrates how the submarine itself had the potential to become the vehicle for tales of derring do and many accounts of the actions of British submariners in Gallipoli and the Baltic and elsewhere also appeared after the war ended.

Relatively few of the submariners' exploits, however, involved attacks on warships. The initial flurry of cruiser sinkings flattered to deceive and U-boats were relatively ineffective weapons against battle fleets during either world war. Just two days before the sinking of the *Falaba*, Otto Weddingen died in U-29 when attempting to attack the British battle fleet; his boat was rammed by HMS *Dreadnought*.

Gradually the focus of U-boat actions in late 1914 and early 1915 turned to attacks on merchant ships. The pace of such attacks increased significantly in February 1915 when the German government issued a statement to say that, from the 18th of that month in a designated area around the British Isles, all enemy ships would be sunk on sight. The statement went even further by indicating that the difficulty in determining the nationality of ships from some distance in a submarine was such that neutral ships could not expect to be spared in the designated area. The number of ships that were torpedoed without warning increased significantly but, at the same time, there were also examples of other ships being stopped and their crews getting away before the submarine opened fire. Although this German announcement of what was described by others as 'unrestricted submarine warfare' was rescinded later in 1915 as a result of pressure from neutral nations, principally the USA, it was in place at the time of the two sinkings in which we are interested.

The *Falaba* was a nine-year-old Elder Dempster liner used on the run from Liverpool out to West Africa. On her last voyage she left Liverpool on the evening of 27 March 1915 carrying 147 passengers and a crew of 95 and heading for Sierra Leone as her first stop. All but seven of the passengers were men, mostly colonial administrators and businessmen along with some soldiers joining or re-joining their regiments. One passenger who was to feature in the aftermath of the drama was a 31-year-old mining engineer from Massachusetts called Leon Chester Thrasher (spelled Thresher in many British publications, possibly because that was the spelling given in the published proceedings of the inquiry). In addition to the passengers she carried a general cargo and amongst it, her manifest recorded, were 13 tons of cartridges and gunpowder 'for government use'.

Chief Officer Walter Baxter was the officer of the watch the following morning when, about 1140, the conning tower of a submarine was spotted several miles away. Captain Davies joined him immediately on the bridge and ordered the ship's head to be turned directly away from the submarine and the engines to be brought up to full speed from the 13-knot cruising speed, actions that were in line with the instructions from the Admiralty. The submarine, now fully on the surface and showing a German flag, chased the fleeing *Falaba,* hoisting code flags calling on her to stop. The flag hoist was changed to one saying 'stop or I will fire' and some witnesses said that a flare was sent up to emphasise the threat. There followed a discussion on the bridge of *Falaba* as to the correct course of action. The officers were aware that the Admiralty wished them to try to save the ship by fleeing if possible, but the submarine had almost caught them up. Davies decided that to continue to attempt to flee would place the passengers in too much danger and he stopped the ship. He instructed the wireless officer to send a message reporting that the ship had been stopped by a hostile submarine and that he expected to be sunk. Two messages were sent in plain language, the latter requesting the assistance of a warship. The wireless station at Land's End confirmed that the message had been passed through to naval command.

Kapitanleutnant von Forstner in U-28 called across by megaphone to the *Falaba* and ordered Davies to abandon the ship as he intended to sink her. He may also have ordered all wireless transmissions to cease but this is not certain. Davies immediately ordered the evacuation of all of the passengers and crew. Some of the lifeboats had already been swung out the previous evening as a precaution and were ready for immediate use, but others were still on their chocks. Given the brief interval promised by von Forstner there was obviously a degree of haste that spilled over into near panic as the evacuation proceeded. It did not go well. The lowering of several lifeboats was mishandled or obstructed by jammed ropes that caused them to crash into the sea with their passengers. A couple of other lifeboats were not watertight by the time they were lowered and filled with water. The crewing of some boats was largely left in the hands of passengers and organisation was poor. Just as the final boat was being lowered towards the stern, U-28's torpedo hit amidships. The resulting explosion caused the last lifeboat to fall into the sea and the ship to sink very rapidly. The torpedo may have caused munitions in the ship's hold to explode although there is no clear evidence of this. Davies and Baxter were both picked up from the sea but Davies died shortly afterwards, possibly from a head wound. There was no evidence given at the inquiry as to how

Davies died. U-28 circled briefly and then submerged. The survivors were picked up by a couple of steam drifters and taken to Milford Haven. A total of 104 people died in the sinking, one of them being Leon C Thrasher.

A number of survivors told their stories to newspaper reporters and these were circulated to newspapers around the world. They had a number of features in common. One was complaint about the lack of organisation in the lifeboats and also the condition of the boats themselves and their equipment. But the one that had a big impact on headlines was a report from a number of sources that while the evacuation of the *Falaba* was taking place, the German sailors had lined the casing of the submarine and laughed and jeered at people struggling in the water. Survivors also claimed that von Forstner had fired his torpedo only five minutes after giving his warning, far too short a period to enable a proper evacuation of the ship. Such stories had enormous propaganda value, of course, and there was no attempt to prevent them appearing.

Once von Forstner had returned home the Germans felt obliged to respond and issued a statement giving their version of the event. In their version, U-28 actually allowed the British ship a total of 23 minutes before firing the torpedo as the evacuation had not been nearly completed after the 10 minutes which the Germans claimed had been given. The statement also denied absolutely that there had been any jeering or laughing by the submarine crew while this was going on. The torpedo had been fired, it was said, only because a warship had been seen approaching and it was considered too dangerous to wait any longer.

Leon Thrasher was the first American citizen to have died as a result of the actions of a German submarine. There was a bizarre postscript to his death. The body was not one of those recovered at the time of the sinking. Instead, it was washed up on the south coast of Ireland along with others from the *Lusitania*. Before its identity had been confirmed, Cunard had paid for the funeral as part of the mass burial of the *Lusitania* dead. It was reported that they tried subsequently to recover their costs.

It was the habit of the German authorities (and indeed the British ones) to use sympathetic Americans to seed supportive stories into the American popular press and this seems to have happened in this case. A cotton broker, J J Ryan, who had visited Germany on business, apparently met a gentleman called 'Commander Schmidt' who claimed to have been the captain of U-28. In fact it seems likely that Schmidt was von Forstner's second in command. Schmidt claimed that the German sailors had actually been crying when watching the distress of the passengers in the water and expressed regret at having to sink the ship. According to the report that appeared in the *Evening Press* in New York he went on:

I warned the captain of the *Falaba* to dismantle his wireless apparatus and gave him ten minutes in which to do it, and also to get out his passengers.

Instead of acting upon my demand, he continued to send out messages to torpedo boats that were less that twenty miles away to come to his assistance as quickly as possible.

At the end of ten minutes I gave him a second warning about dismantling the wireless apparatus and waited twenty minutes.

Then I torpedoed the ship, as the torpedo-boats were getting close up, and I knew they would go to the rescue of the passengers and crew.

The only ships which are known to have been within sight of the submarine at that time were the little steam drifters that were later to pick up the survivors. It is inconceivable that these could have been mistaken for torpedo-boats by the German look-outs, but it must be remembered that the incident took place in well populated waters with frequent Royal Navy patrols and that the *Falaba* had put out a wireless message requesting armed assistance. It is understandable that von Forstner was very nervous sitting for any length of time on the surface in those conditions, and even a smudge of smoke on the horizon may well have been interpreted as a hostile warship.

Walther Schwieger avoided this problem by remaining submerged when he sank the *Lusitania*. The two incidents were quite different in almost every other respect as well, not least in the scale of the human cost. The story of the *Lusitania* has become so overlaid by conspiracy theories that it is difficult to burrow underneath them to the fairly simple events that took place off the coast of Ireland on the morning of Friday 7 May 1915, six weeks after the destruction of the *Falaba*. Those readers who wish to believe that First Lord of the Admiralty, Winston Churchill, deliberately set the *Lusitania* up to be sunk, as bait to lure America into the war, need not feel threatened by the following. We can be sure that, whatever Churchill was up to in the spring of 1915 (and it would seem likely that his main preoccupation was in the Eastern Mediterranean), he did not take Will Turner and Walther Schwieger into his confidence. Their concerns were not with geopolitical strategy but with carrying out their duties. Had the actions of either of those captains been even slightly different that morning, none of Churchill's Machiavellian plans, if such there were, would have materialised.

Lusitania left New York just after midday on Saturday 1 May carrying 1257 passengers and 702 crew. Despite the appearance of adverts in the American East Coast press that morning warning passengers on ships leaving for Europe about the policy of the German government announced the previous February, the atmosphere on board was not particularly tense. Everyone knew that there was little chance of running into a surface attack in mid-Atlantic and that the submarine threat only became significant once the Irish coast was approached. At that time submarines had not ventured out into mid-Atlantic. As we have already noted, the Admiralty had issued advice to captains of merchant ships as to how the likelihood of a successful attack could be minimised. Advice was also provided as to how they should act in the event of being attacked by a submarine. This was updated at regular intervals and there was some confusion at the inquiry as to which specific communications Turner had seen. Because submarine warfare was so new and because the Germans were varying their tactics as they experimented with the new weapon, the initial advice issued by the Admiralty was sometimes contradicted by later updates. In the very early stages in 1914, captains were told to keep close to land as submarines would not operate in sight of the shore. That advice was quickly countermanded and ships were then advised to avoid coming close to shore, headlands in particular. Part of the difficulty that captains experienced was the sheer volume of material that was issued. Turner later described it as sufficient to paper the walls of his cabin.

Although what the Admiralty issued was formally regarded as advice, there were sanctions available to ensure that it would be obeyed. As normal marine insurance did not cover acts of war, the government had set up arrangements to indemnify owners who lost vessels to enemy action. Claims under those arrangements were made dependent on the ship that was lost having followed the Admiralty advice. The company whose captain recklessly ignored that advice could not expect to receive the same level of compensation.

By the end of April 1915 the advice that had been issued told masters that, in areas with a significant threat of submarine attack, they should not steer a straight course but should zigzag; they should stay well clear of headlands and stay out from land in mid-channel; they should keep speed up to the safe maximum, especially in the vicinity of ports; they should time their arrival at the port that they were sailing towards so that they did not need to linger outside it for tidal or other reasons. The advice, perhaps deliberately, was quite vague. While it was issued in confidential form, much of it was repeated in wireless messages that the Admiralty suspected were being decoded by the Germans.

The British were also decoding a substantial amount of the German wireless traffic and were able to tell in which area submarines were operating and, in many cases, identify the submarines concerned. As well as issuing generalised advice the Admiralty also issued specific warnings to ships in particular areas that there were U-boats operating. Such information was also available, of course, as a result of the attacks that were taking place. Although no convoy system was in operation arrangements were occasionally made to provide

naval escorts for particularly valuable ships passing through areas where submarines were known to be active. On a previous voyage in March a destroyer
escort had been provided for *Lusitania* as she approached the south coast of
Ireland but had failed to meet up with her. It was the view of the Admiralty,
with limited justification, that the best protection for a ship was speed as no
ship travelling at high speed had yet been torpedoed.

In the 24 hours prior to the sinking, the *Lusitania* had received warnings
of submarine activity off the south coast of Ireland and Will Turner was in
no doubt that he was steaming into an area of heightened risk, just as Smith
was in no doubt on *Titanic* that he was travelling towards ice. One warning which proved to be of particular significance in later investigations was
received shortly after 1100 on 7 May, reporting submarine activity about 20
miles south of Conninbeg lighthouse, at that time about 120 miles ahead of
the ship. Early in the morning of 7 May there was fog and Turner reduced
the speed of his ship to 15 knots until it cleared when he went back up to 18
knots. At the time the ship was running with one of her boiler rooms closed
down because the company had seen a reduction in coal consumption as
their only method of retaining profitability on the route. This limited her top
speed to 21 knots instead of the pre-war 25 knots, but Turner deliberately
kept her to 18 knots that morning because he wished to time his arrival at the
Liverpool Bar such that the ship would not have to hang about but would be
able to go straight in to port as the Admiralty advised. Also early that morning,
Turner had the ship's lifeboats swung out and provisioned ready for filling and
launching quickly if required. A further precaution entering the danger zone
was an order that all portholes be closed so that, if the ship was damaged, it
would not take on additional water through openings. It was an oral instruction only that was not followed up to ensure compliance. Finally, to limit the
movement of any water in the ship, the watertight doors were closed except
for those that had to stay open for operational purposes such as the ones used
by trimmers going back and forward with coal for the boilers.

Turner was concerned that navigation by dead reckoning was not sufficiently precise in these circumstances, particularly as the fog might return at
any time, so he decided that he needed to get a good position fix by taking
bearings on recognisable features on land. He altered course to port, therefore,
to get closer to the Old Head of Kinsale. He had been keeping around 25
miles from land but this new course brought him in to about 12 miles. Even
then, he was much farther out than would have been normal peacetime practice where, in clear weather, the ship would have passed the headland at only
one to two miles distance. Having come into where the fix could be taken,
the ship was then turned to starboard back onto its original course. In doing

so, Turner was not heading out to the 'mid-channel' area that the Admiralty had advised him to stay in but was running roughly parallel to the coast. It is doubtful whether the term 'mid-channel' had any meaning when the nearest land other than the coast of Ireland was over 100 miles away. Indeed, the Admiralty may only have meant the advice to apply in narrow waterways such as the English Channel or the North Channel between Ireland and Scotland where 12 miles out would have been mid-channel in both cases.

Walther Schwieger was also approaching the end of his voyage having left Germany on 30 April. Despite urgings to use the shortest route by his superior prior to setting out, he had cautiously brought U-20 down the west coast of Ireland rather than through the narrow and dangerous North Channel. The early part of his patrol had been unproductive and by 5 May he and his crew were becoming frustrated, their only attempted attack having failed as a result of a malfunctioning torpedo. That evening he sank the small schooner *Earl of Latham* by gunfire, her crew getting away in a boat but having a ten-mile row to the shore. The following morning matters improved from his point of view though not for the crews of the two Harrison Line ships he sank. U-20 attacked the *Candidate* on the morning of 6 May, initially by gunfire. The ship tried to flee but shell hits caused it to stop and the crew got away in boats in something of a panic as Schwieger lined up the torpedo shot that was the coup de grace.

Before encountering the second of the Harrison Line ships, the *Centurion*, Schwieger narrowly missed an opportunity to fire at the 16,000 ton White Star Liner, *Arabic*. Had she passed a little closer to U-20 and had visibility not been limited by fog, it is clear from Schwieger's war diary that he would have made an attempt to sink her with a torpedo. The *Centurion* came into view shortly afterwards in a favourable position and he sank her using two torpedoes, the crew succeeding in leaving in the lifeboats. This was by no means the first ship that Schwieger had torpedoed without warning. In January of that year he had sunk three merchant ships close to Le Havre without any warning and the following month had missed the hospital ship *Asturia* with a torpedo, claiming afterwards that he thought that she was a troop transport despite the white paint and red crosses. Schwieger's reputation, both leading up to the sinking of the *Lusitania* and after it, was that he was one of the more ruthless of the U-boat commanders, one who made the most aggressive interpretation possible of his orders while, at the same time, exercising considerable caution in their execution.

The sinking of the two Harrison Line ships on 6 May resulted in the warning that *Lusitania* received just after 1100 on 7 May to the effect that there were submarines active in the area twenty miles south of the Conninbeg

Lightship. The warning was vague and did not inform Turner that two ships had been sunk, nor that these attacks had taken place the previous day. The fog up to about 1100 that morning caused Schwieger to stay submerged to avoid being run down and when he came up to periscope depth he saw the cruiser *Juno* heading back into Queenstown. Travelling fast and zigzagging, the *Juno* gave him no opportunity to take a shot at her. It was at 1340, U-20 now on the surface, that the smoke, masts and funnels of the *Lusitania* were first spotted. Schwieger took his boat back under and looked to see if a shot would be possible. At first it seemed not, as the liner's course would not have brought her close enough to the submarine, which could only move slowly underwater. Then, as Schwieger watched through the periscope, he saw the liner's head swing to starboard as Turner brought her back parallel with the coast. Now coming broadside on at 700 metres the *Lusitania* presented a very hittable target despite her speed of 18 knots. Schwieger sent a torpedo off from one of his bow tubes and he and his crew waited in silence for the 35 seconds it took for it to reach its target. It is worth noting that the torpedo was fired not from the landward side of the liner but the seaward side and U-20 had actually come closer to the land in order to get into position to fire it.

On *Lusitania* the bubble track of the torpedo was spotted both on the bridge and by some of the passengers on the deck, but not with time for any evasive action to be effective. It struck the starboard side just abaft the bridge with an explosion that flung wreckage and water to a height well above the funnel tops. This was closely followed by a second explosion, the cause of which has remained contentious ever since. It was not caused by a second torpedo, nor by the explosion of munitions, either included on the cargo manifest or not. We know that it was not a second torpedo partly because Schwieger sent a wireless message back to HQ later that day informing them that he had sunk the *Lusitania* with a single torpedo. At that stage, before any second explosion had been mentioned, he had no reason to falsify his account. Also, all of the torpedoes aboard U-20 can be accounted for on her patrol. The signal sent by Schwieger was intercepted and decoded by the British Admiralty, who therefore knew that only one torpedo had been fired.

The second explosion was not the result of the torpedo setting off the munitions listed on the ship's manifest as these consisted of shell parts and small arms ammunition, neither of which would explode. If there were another secret cargo of explosives, as has sometimes been alleged, it would not have been stored close to the place where the torpedo struck. Furthermore, if such a 'contraband' cargo had exploded, it would have caused damage to the ship which Dr Robert Ballard did not find when he scrutinised the hull in 1993. The most likely explanation for the second explosion was the fracture of one of the large steam pipes taking steam from the boilers to the engines. Another possibility is that the torpedo set off a mixture of coal dust and air in the now nearly empty coal bunkers. The effect of the torpedo combined with the second explosion on the ship was immediate and dramatic. Electric power failed within a few minutes, the engines lost power and she developed a significant list to starboard. The loss of engine power frustrated Turner in two ways. His first thought after the ship was hit was to try to beach her. The absence of a response from the engine room quickly made him abandon this idea so that his next and only remaining option was to evacuate the ship. She needed to be stopped first and there was no power to put the screws astern and bring her to a halt. Witnesses were agreed that the *Lusitania* was still moving forward as her bows touched the bottom in the final stages of sinking eighteen minutes later.

The scenes that ensued, once the realisation caught hold amongst passengers and crew that the ship was sinking rapidly, were amongst the most distressing ever reported from a maritime disaster. The slow foundering of the *Titanic* evoked panic in some, but many remained calm and events happened relatively slowly and in a comparatively controlled manner. The speed of the *Empress's* sinking, the darkness and the fact that so few passengers even made it to the deck shortened the horror and limited the extent to which surviving witnesses could report what had happened. On the *Lusitania*, in the middle of a calm sunlit May day, the frantic and often unsuccessful attempts to get lifeboats away amid crowds of terrified passengers, many separated from their loved ones, created an awful experience for all involved. The list made it nearly impossible to get the lifeboats down the port side and a number of people were killed and injured when boats swung in against the ship or fell to the sea. On the starboard side the boats hung out from the side of the ship and it was difficult to get them loaded. In one case the forward movement of the ship caused one lifeboat to land directly on top of another that had just been released.

As the ship gradually fell over on her starboard side and disappeared those lifeboats that had been successfully launched, many nowhere nearly filled, were left surrounded by a large amount of wreckage and a vast number of people struggling in the water. Most people going into the water had lifebelts, although some had not. There was an ample supply on the ship but some people had been unable to access them in time. In many cases they had been incorrectly fitted and caused injury or death when the wearers jumped from the ship. Many of the lifeboats made every possible effort to pull people who were still alive out of the water; some did not do so out of fear of being swamped. Rescue was not immediate. There were a few small fishing boats in the vicinity which got there as quickly as they could and started to take people on board. They could only take limited numbers and the boats that had left Queenstown on hearing of the sinking did not begin to arrive for over an hour. People were still being pulled from the water more than three hours after the liner had sunk.

Of the 1257 passengers on board, 785 were lost as well as 413 of the 702 in the crew. Undoubtedly the sheer magnitude of the disaster would have caused major headlines around the world, even while the terrible events of the Western Front were getting into their stride. However, it was the deaths of the 128 Americans amongst the passengers that gave the sinking an entirely different dimension. It is not within our scope here to consider the political implications of those deaths, but we will analyse the extent to which that outcome was the product of the particular personalities and actions of the captains of the submarine and the liner in a later chapter.

These then were the events that took place between April 1912 and May 1915 into which Lord Mersey and his teams of assessors were asked to inquire. What were the issues that the inquiries examined as they affected the captains – and the issues that they might have inquired into but chose not to?

9

ISSUES

There are two ways we can approach the identification of the issues that faced the Mersey inquiries as they concerned the eight captains. One is simply to take the sets of questions each inquiry was given as its brief and select those that raised matters relevant to their actions. The second is to consider from first principles what the job of a captain entails and see where those responsibilities sit in relation to the events. The latter would seem to be the more profitable if we wish to pick up on matters that might have been looked at in the inquiries but which did not in the event surface to any significant extent. In the following chapters the answers that Mersey produced to the questions that he was asked can be set against the issues which seem, from this perspective, to be the ones that matter so far as our eight captains are concerned.

Any captain was only as good as the resources he had at his disposal. So what was he expected to do with those resources? The captain was expected to bring his ship safely from port to port in good time and to arrive with the ship, passengers and cargo intact. He was expected to do this without any cost to the company beyond what had been budgeted for and he was required to avoid any bad publicity reflecting on the company. He was required to ensure that the treatment of passengers was such that they would wish to travel with the company on future occasions and to deal with cargo agents in a way that encouraged them to continue to trust their cargo to his company. Should any problems arise he was expected to use his expertise to overcome them so as to minimise their impact. That meant doing what was required to complete the voyage as close to time and budget as he could manage. If the problem were such as to prevent completion of the voyage he should try to keep the costs of any salvage or insurance claims to the minimum. If the problem threatened the survival of the ship, or of any of those on it, he was expected to do all in his power to save the ship and preserve the lives of those on board. Should he come across another ship experiencing a problem, he was required to offer assistance, especially if life was endangered, but without, in the process, running unnecessary risks to his own ship or incurring unnecessary expenditure. In short, the captain was a company man always subject to the crucial proviso that no expectation that the company laid on him could justify the taking of unreasonable risks with the safety of passengers or crew. Some commentaries on incidents at sea treat the captain of a ship as if he were a free agent able to set his own agenda and treat company requirements as of little import. Shipping companies were in business to make money and the ship captain, tasked with pursuing the company's interests, was no different to any of their other employees, except in one respect.

The role of the ship master differed from that of other company employees as a result of the Merchant Shipping Act. The Act gave him particular responsibilities that were laid on him personally because of the post that he held; they did not accrue to the company for which he worked. He was required to maintain discipline aboard, both amongst passengers and crew and was empowered to take such action as was needed in order to do so. This might include restraining a crew member who refused to obey orders and detaining him if necessary to prevent violence. If a crime was committed on board he was entitled to arrest a suspect and hold that person in detention until they could be handed over to port authorities. When death occurred on board he was permitted to order burial at sea, especially where retaining the corpse on the ship might present a health hazard. In these types of matters the captain was effectively the agent of the state of registry of the ship rather than of the company. He needed to be able to ensure that one role did not conflict with the other, although, in general, the Act itself had been designed so as to support captains in their work and not make life more difficult for them.

Moving away from the purely contractual and legal aspects of the job, the one quality that was most expected of a captain was that of leadership. He may have the guidelines of company policy as to how the crew were to be managed and he may have the sanctions of law to back him up, but he needed the ability at the personal level to guide, to motivate and to inspire confidence. Each of the six merchant captains we are focusing on was selected by his company as someone whom they believed to have that quality. Smith and Turner were more than that; they were Commodores, in effect the role model for other captains in the fleet. Kendall and Lord had shown leadership qualities early in their careers and were young for their roles.

There is a difference, of course, between the role of the merchant ship captain and that of the man who leads a warship. Where, for the captain of a liner or cargo ship, the safety of the ship and those on board is his single most important consideration, for the captain of a warship it is the achievement of his war objectives. He may be expected to sacrifice the safety of the ship and all on board if necessary in the pursuit of those objectives. Military discipline gives him even greater powers to enforce his decisions on his crew than the terms of the Merchant Shipping Act. Herman Wouk's novel *The Caine Mutiny* and the film made of it with Humphrey Bogart explore the limits of a warship captain's power in the US Navy, when a captain shows signs of serious mental instability. The message that emerges is that only in the most extreme circumstances can the power of a captain be successfully challenged. The responsibility that goes with such unlimited power is the obligation to demonstrate leadership at a very high level and under life threatening conditions.

When a warship is operating as one unit amongst others in a fleet under the control of a senior officer, that officer will take the big decisions that govern how the fleet acts. For the captain of the lone-wolf submarine on patrol, there is no such relief; all of the decisions must be his and his alone. Submariners then, and still today, tend to be young men. When navies began the submarine arms of the services in the first years of the twentieth century, those who volunteered for officer roles tended to be young, ambitious and action orientated, rather like the first pilots who became the dare-devil air aces over the Western Front. The actions of the air fighters, however, were not under the same ethical scrutiny as those of the submariners, although that was not true of their colleagues who dropped bombs away from the war zones. But fighter pilots flew on brief sorties either alone or with just an observer. A submarine captain had to lead thirty to forty men on an isolated patrol lasting for a couple of weeks and, as we have already noted, not only was their work dangerous, their living conditions were appalling. There can be few roles that have tested the ability of one man to lead others to such a degree. The two young men who led out U-20 and U-28 passed that leadership test, by all reports, but that is not the only criterion against which they must be judged.

Bringing a ship safely from port to port meant setting the correct courses and speeds and this could only be achieved if the position of the ship were known to an acceptable degree of accuracy. Deciding what was the appropriate course and speed, even in the largest ship, usually remained in the hands of the captain and was rarely delegated to a more junior officer, even one with an Extra Master's Certificate. An officer of the watch could change either course or speed if required, especially if safety were involved, but would usually be under orders to notify the captain immediately. Navigational decisions were important in each of the sinkings with which we are concerned, speed in particular. Was the *Titanic* travelling too fast as she headed towards the ice that had been reported? Did the reversal of the *Empress*'s engines to take speed off her make the risk of collision greater rather than less? Did the speeding up of the *Falaba* when the submarine was spotted excuse a more belligerent approach by the submarine? Was the 18 knots at which the *Lusitania* was travelling critical to the success of the attack?

The direction in which each of the ships was going was also crucial. The *Titanic* deviated slightly from the normal track, running just a couple of miles farther south. However that did not take her clear of the area in which the ice had been reported. Should Smith have taken the ship a greater distance south in order to avoid the area altogether? Having dropped off the pilot and moved out into the St. Lawrence, Kendall turned his ship to starboard onto her course out into the Atlantic. Was that change of course executed properly, or did the ship yaw about and confuse those on the bridge of the *Storstad* just as the fog closed in? Did the *Falaba*'s turn away from the submarine, like her increase in speed, aggravate the situation? Was the *Lusitania*'s steady course about 12 miles or so from land, without the zigzagging that the Admiralty had recommended, a fatal mistake?

Each of these questions is really asking the same thing. Did the captain in question prioritise correctly the risks with which he was presented and take the right actions? We know now, of course, that, in each case, one or more of those risks did materialise, with dreadful consequences, so we must identify the issues which relate to the way the captains tried to limit those consequences. Some of the actions that were needed to reduce the danger to life actually had to be taken well before the incidents occurred. How well equipped and prepared was each ship to face the emergency that developed? How much of that preparation was the responsibility of the company rather than of the captain? It would not make sense to hold Smith to account for the fact that the *Titanic* lacked sufficient lifeboats. We have already observed that the brief interlude between leaving the builders and starting her maiden voyage left little time to work up the *Titanic*'s crew into coherent teams in the different departments. However, did Smith do all that might reasonably be expected to prepare the ship and the crew in the time available to deal with an emergency? The same question might also be asked of Kendall, Davies and Turner. Kendall had only been in charge of the *Empress* for a month but Davies and Turner had both had charge of their ships, or their sisters, for some time and the ships were in mid-life. On the other hand, both of them suffered from the difficulties of recruiting and retaining good quality, experienced seamen during wartime.

Preparing passengers to deal with an emergency was part of the captain's remit. Although the captain had the power to give passengers orders so as to preserve good order and could instruct them to undertake lifeboat drill, for example, it is clear that many captains found some conflict between the need to deal with safety matters and the desire to give passengers the sort of pleasant experience that would tempt them back on a future occasion. Too much emphasis on preparing for nasty things to happen might not be good for business. Associated with that was the reluctance of passengers to engage with safety issues. This was evident even on the *Falaba* and *Lusitania* when the threat of German attack was quite explicit. One passenger claimed to have been quite relaxed when he saw a German submarine only 100 yards from the *Falaba;* he thought that the Germans just wished to come aboard to inspect the papers. All of us have a remarkable capacity to deal with threats by ignoring them in the hope that they will go away.

Good preparation might be important, but the crucial factors when disaster has struck are organisation and discipline. The captains of each of the four ships that sank faced the same problem, albeit in very different circumstances. They each needed to ensure that the evacuation of their ship was carried out in such a way that as many people as possible were safely into lifeboats that were equipped and manned. That objective could only be achieved if the crew knew what they had to do, were in a position to do it and did not panic. Furthermore, the passengers needed clear instructions as to what they should do, with order maintained. The situation on *Titanic* differed from that on the other three ships because of the relatively long period of time between the collision and the ship sinking. It is possible as a result to ask more meaningful questions of Smith as to how well the 2 hours 40 minutes were used on *Titanic* compared to the 14 minutes on the *Empress* or the 18 minutes on the *Lusitania*. On *Falaba* the amount of time is shrouded in controversy, but that incident differed from the others in that, for most of the time that the evacuation was taking place, the ship was undamaged, it was daylight and there was no list or other factor complicating the process. Could any of the captains have done things differently, in a way that would have resulted in the death toll being lower?

It is not just the actions of each of captains, but their manner, their composure and their assertiveness that might well have made a difference. In Chapter 2 we saw how the calm, clear voice of Captain Sealby when the *Republic* was sinking provided real leadership and was so reassuring to his passengers. Was there any indication of that kind of leadership being displayed by Smith, Kendall, Davies or Turner? Was that even a matter on which an inquiry such as the ones Mersey chaired could have commented upon? Would a judge in his seventies, his life spent in the court room, appreciate the impact that such qualities might have in the midst of the drama of a sinking ship?

While the general expectations on Stanley Lord and Thomas Andersen as captains of merchant ships were the same as for the other four, their roles in the incidents that we are examining were different so the issues concerning their actions are also different. Lord was unique amongst the eight captains in that neither he nor his ship was present when the incident took place. Exactly how far away the *Californian* was from the sinking *Titanic* is unlikely ever to be known with certainty, but we do know that rockets were seen from her bridge at around the time when they were being sent up by Fourth Officer Boxhall on *Titanic*. For Stanley Lord that was the start of something that was to have almost as great an impact on his life as on many of those who succeeded in the struggle to stay alive that was taking place just over the horizon. Leaving aside for the moment the question as to whether or not the rockets that Second Officer Stone and Apprentice Gibson saw on *Californian* were actually those fired by Boxhall, the issue for Mersey was whether they should have been treated as distress signals irrespective of which ship they had emerged from. If they should have been treated as distress signals, then why did Lord not take action? Was it a failure of communication or of will? If of communication then was Lord at fault in the way he led his officers such that communication was ineffective? If of will, does that raise an issue about Lord's duty to come to the assistance of another ship in difficulty? There would then be implications as to Lord's character.

Once the *Californian* had received the news of the sinking of *Titanic* Lord then moved his ship. Did he do everything possible to get to the scene as quickly as possible and did he do as much as he could have done once there? Given that the *Carpathia* had already brought all of the survivors from the lifeboats aboard, it may be that there was no further reason for the *Californian* to remain. There is one further issue that concerns Stanley Lord's actions and how they were dealt with by Mersey. It has often been alleged that Lord attempted to cover up the facts of what had taken place on his ship prior to the inquiry and gave evidence that was, at the very least, less than the full truth. While the opinions of many witnesses at the four inquiries have been challenged and the memories of others doubted, Lord is the only one who has subsequently been accused of deliberately attempting to mislead Mersey on matters of fact.

Chief Officer Toftnes called Thomas Andersen to the bridge of *Storstad* a bare minute or so before his ship rammed the side of the *Empress of Ireland*. Andersen had given instructions that he was to be called in the event of fog. Should Toftnes therefore have called him when the fog came down rather than when an emergency was developing? Was Andersen at fault for not ensuring that his instructions were sufficiently clear and for failing to impress on his officers the need for them to be obeyed to the letter? We touched on the question earlier as to the extent to which a captain should be held accountable for the failures of his subordinates and this is a case in point. There are echoes here of the sinking of the *Atlantic* in 1873 described in chapter 2. Her captain also was not called as he had he instructed but was subsequently found guilty of negligent handling of his ship.

Once the *Storstad*'s bows had disappeared into the side of the *Empress* Andersen's first consideration was for the safety of his own ship and crew. He did not immediately know the extent of the damage that *Storstad* had received and thought that she might sink. Once satisfied that she was not in immediate danger, did he do enough to minimise the impact of the collision on the *Empress?* Kendall maintained that Andersen should have put his engines full ahead in order to keep his ship embedded in the hole that it had created, thus reducing the flow of water into the *Empress.* Was that the right thing to do and, if so, did Andersen make the attempt with sufficient determination?

Once the ships had split apart, Andersen was again pre-occupied with ensuring that he could rely on the *Storstad* staying afloat. Had she been in real danger, fully loaded as she was, of slipping under, there would have been little point in bringing people from the *Empress* on board just to undergo a second evacuation. He satisfied himself that she was safe and then went back to use his own boats to bring survivors on board from the rapidly sinking *Empress.* One of them was Kendall who was clearly upset and confrontational towards Andersen, whom he blamed for the collision. This was the only face-to-face meeting between any of the captains. The overarching question for the sixth merchant ship captain was simply whether or not he did all in his power to save life.

Mersey had no interest in the competence of von Forstner or Schwieger either as seamen or as captains of their ships. He was concerned with one issue only and that was whether or not they had behaved in an acceptable manner in wartime. This issue could be sub-divided. Were the ships they attacked legitimate targets? Were the methods they used in their attacks justifiable under the international conventions then in force? The first question can actually be dealt with now because it did not surface in the inquiries either as a question asked of Mersey in his brief nor in the outcomes. It was simply assumed that *Falaba* and *Lusitania* were legitimate targets. We mentioned in Chapter 3 that the propaganda war on both sides during the First World War, as it related to the use of submarines, was carried out with shameless hypocrisy. Hypocrisy is only effective, however, if you have at least some semblance of cover for your own sins. For Britain to claim that either of these ships was not a proper target would have lacked any credibility given the activities of her own submarines in promoting the blockade against Germany and in attacking Turkish shipping in the Dardanelles.

The second question, as to the methods the two U-boat captains had used, was a valid one. Britain had not sunk without warning a large passenger liner carrying civilians and so, in the case of the *Lusitania*, could take the high moral ground. In the case of the *Falaba* the issue was more about the detail of the attack, because a warning had been given, and in most respects the sinking was not that different from the types of attacks being carried out by British submarines. The timing of Mersey's appointment is germane here. He was appointed for the second time as Wreck Commissioner on Monday 3 May 1915 when the *Lusitania* was in mid-Atlantic on her final voyage. On the Tuesday the Board of Trade announced that it required an inquiry to be conducted into the loss of the *Falaba*. Mersey was in the process of preparing for the opening of that inquiry when, late on the Friday, news came through of the sinking of the *Lusitania*. The *Falaba* inquiry held its hearings on 20, 21, 27 and 28 May. It is difficult to know how much the appalling stories of the suffering that those on the *Lusitania* had experienced, which were on every page of every newspaper throughout the run-up to the *Falaba* hearings, influenced Mersey in his approach to the earlier sinking. How much his view of the behaviour of von Forstner was influenced by what he now knew of the actions of Schwieger?

10

E.J. SMITH

The British inquiry into the loss of the *Titanic* lasted from 2 May 1912 to 3 July with sittings on 37 days during that period at two different venues. The report was read by Mersey at a final session on 30 July. By any standards it was a long and detailed inquiry at which a total of 97 witnesses gave evidence. The cast list was impressive, with the Attorney General Sir Rufus Isaacs appearing for the Board of Trade and Butler Aspinall KC for the government. We have already mentioned the Marconi connections of the former and the fact that his client, the Board of Trade, was the sponsoring department of government for the inquiry. Butler Aspinall was to be almost as much of a fixture in these inquiries as Mersey himself, appearing for Canadian Pacific in the *Empress* inquiry, for Elder Dempster in the *Falaba* inquiry and for Cunard in the *Lusitania* one.

We touched on the possible impact on the *Falaba* inquiry of the timing of the sinking of *Lusitania*. In the case of the *Titanic* we need to be aware of the timing of the American Senate hearings as they preceded the British inquiry and attracted considerable publicity on both sides of the Atlantic. The Senate Sub-Committee began to hear witnesses on Friday 19 April, just four days after the tragedy and completed its sessions on Saturday 25 May. Its final report was issued just three days later on 28 May. There was, therefore, quite a long period of overlap as both inquiries heard testimony. Because almost all of the witnesses were in America at the start of the process, the pattern was almost always that those who testified at both appeared first in front of the Senators. Not all who appeared at one testified at the other; the American inquiry had much more evidence from passengers, for example, than Mersey heard. It is impossible to gauge the extent to which the evidence given at the sessions in New York exerted an influence on any of those taking part in the ones in London. It may be that Mersey himself or the lawyers representing the different interests were prompted by what they knew of the proceedings in America to ask some additional questions. Bruce Ismay, of White Star, amongst others, was questioned by the Attorney General on differences between his answer to a question in New York and his answer to the same question in London. In one case he had quoted Chief Engineer Bell as saying that he 'thought' the pumps would cope with the inflow of water while in the other he had used the word 'hoped'. Rufus Isaacs thought that the difference might have been significant; Ismay blamed it on his unreliable memory. When we come to consider how the *Californian* incident was dealt with, however, the overlap might be thought to have impinged on more than quibbles about words.

The American and British press not only reported the proceedings of the two inquiries, they also commented on their very different styles and approaches. To the American press the Senate hearings were purposeful, direct and effective, with nobody given any favour. Their description of the British inquiry, however, from the very beginning, was of a carefully staged white-wash in which the people really to blame were being given an easy ride. Senator Smith was perceived as a persistent terrier, chasing down the cul-prits who had caused the deaths of 1500 people. Mersey, on the other hand, was regarded as a rather curmudgeonly old duffer, more concerned with maintaining proper protocol than finding any real answers. There were also echoes of that type of thinking in some the British press as well, including the *Spectator*, but most British newspapers regarded the American hearings as a bizarre form of theatre, lacking in the dignity that such a solemn undertaking warranted. There was confidence that the more measured judicial approach of the British inquiry would produce a better considered outcome. The antipa-thy towards the American inquiry was heightened by the openly anti-British tone of much of what was emerging in New York. No-one was in any doubt that, so far as the Senators were concerned, all responsibility for the disaster resided firmly on the eastern side of the Atlantic.

Senator Smith launched his report with a barnstorming speech blam-ing, in the most extravagant language, Captain Smith for speeding into an iceberg, the Board of Trade for not requiring sufficient lifeboats to be car-ried and Captain Lord for not bothering to save those who died. Any other fault lay entirely with White Star. The British press mostly responded with an anti-American rant which, if it did not include the word hillbilly, it was certainly implied. Perhaps not surprisingly, over the years, respect has grown for what that the Senate Sub-Committee achieved. People have seen through the bluster to a process that, although rushed, was a genuine seeking after truth. Senator Smith may have shown some lack of nautical understanding, but he was direct and focused and he did not display any softness towards big

business or government agencies. To recognise the value of the work of the
inquiry in New York, however, is not to endorse its findings uncritically.

The written report of the Senate Sub-Committee (as against the Chairman's
speech launching it) implied criticism of the speed at which *Titanic* was travelling when the accident happened but did not make criticism of Smith explicit
and did not include any specific recommendations about the speed of ships in
the vicinity of ice. Mersey went into this in rather greater detail and included
amongst his witnesses other captains with experience of this route in the
North Atlantic. They were asked to describe their normal practice when close
to ice. The following is an extract from the evidence of Captain Edwin G
Cannons of the Atlantic Transport Company.

The Attorney General: There is only one further question I want to put to
you. When you do sight an iceberg do you reduce your speed or do you
keep your speed?
– I keep my speed.
What is the speed of the vessel?
– Sixteen knots.
You keep your speed – that, of course, is, I suppose, in the day or it might
be at night?
– Both day and night.
The question I put to you, and you have answered, is when you have sighted
an iceberg?
– Yes.
Then you have time, I suppose, from what you said, to get clear of the ice-
berg going at the speed at which your vessel then is?
– I have never had any difficulty to clear when I have met ice ahead.
Does that mean that you see the ice some distance ahead?
– Yes.
How far as a rule?
– Well, I have seen it over three miles and at less distances.
Are you speaking of the day or night?
– At night.
Do you mean you would see it further in the daytime?
– Yes, decidedly, in clear weather.
At night you have seen it at three miles and sometimes less?
– Yes.
And supposing that your look-out is properly kept and that the night is
clear is there any difficulty in your sighting an iceberg at sufficient distance
to enable you to steer clear of it?

– None whatever.

And supposing you received reports of icebergs in a latitude and longitude which you would expect to be crossing during the night would you take any precaution as regards speed?

– I should maintain my speed and keep an exceptionally sharp look-out until such time as I either had the ice-blink or some sight of ice ahead or in the track of the vessel.

This evidence was broadly consistent with those of the other captains although there were differences in terms of the numbers and positions of lookouts. Cannons was also asked about the visibility of ice in different sea states, most particularly when there was a calm sea with no swell, something very rarely seen in the North Atlantic. In his view this would make no difference – ice would still be visible from a distance that would permit easy avoidance even at night. He did admit never to having seen 'black' ice, that is a berg that had recently overturned. It is also worth emphasising that 'maintain speed' for Cannons meant keeping to 16 knots, not the 22 knots at which *Titanic* was travelling.

Second Officer Lightoller, the senior surviving *Titanic* officer, had the watch prior to Murdoch's on the evening of 14 April, which ended at 2200. At about 2100 Smith joined him on the bridge and they had a conversation about the ship, the weather and the ice warnings. In light of Cannon's evidence it is worth recalling what Lightoller remembered of that conversation. On the subject of the weather they agreed that the night was so clear that no additional precautions were necessary but that if any problem should arise (if it became hazy, for example) Smith was to be called immediately. Lightoller was also asked if he spoke to Smith about the sea being so calm:

The Solicitor-General: Had not you better tell us as accurately as you can what passed between him and you when he came on the bridge at five minutes to nine?

– I will.

If you please.

– At five minutes to nine, when the Commander came on the bridge (I will give it to you as near as I remember) he remarked that it was cold, and as far as I remember I said, 'Yes, it is very cold, Sir. In fact,' I said, 'it is only one degree above freezing. I have sent word down to the carpenter and rung up the engine room and told them that it is freezing or will be during the night.' We then commenced to speak about the wind. He said, 'There is not much wind.' I said, 'No, it is a flat calm as a matter of fact.' He repeated it;

he said, 'A flat calm.' I said, 'Yes, quite flat, there is no wind.' I said something about it was rather a pity the breeze had not kept up whilst we were going through the ice region. Of course, my reason was obvious; he knew I meant the water ripples breaking on the base of the berg.

You said it was a pity there was not a breeze?

– Yes, I said, 'It is a pity there is not a breeze,' and we went on to discuss the weather. He was then getting his eyesight, you know, and he said, 'Yes, it seems quite clear,' and I said, 'Yes, it is perfectly clear.' It was a beautiful night, there was not a cloud in the sky. The sea was apparently smooth, and there was no wind, but at that time you could see the stars rising and setting with absolute distinctness. And also...

Then you both realised at the time, did you, that since it was a flat calm it would be more difficult to see the ice?

– As far as the base of the berg was concerned, yes, it would be more difficult; naturally you would not see the water breaking on it if there were no wind; and so you would not have that to look for.

Also included in the conversation was a reference to 'blue' ice. Ice that has no frost crystals on it because it has recently been immersed in water is sometimes referred to as blue and sometimes as black ice. Cannons, of course, had testified that he had never encountered this phenomenon although he had spent many years on the North Atlantic.

> *Lightoller:* We then discussed the indications of ice. I remember saying, 'In any case there will be a certain amount of reflected lights from the bergs.' He said, 'Oh, yes, there will be a certain amount of reflected light.' I said, or he said; blue was said between us – that even though the blue side of the berg was towards us, probably the outline, the white outline would give us sufficient warning, that we should be able to see it at a good distance, and, as far as we could see, we should be able to see it. Of course it was just with regard to that possibility of the blue side being towards us, and that if it did happen to be turned with the purely blue side towards us, there would still be the white outline.

So just two and a half hours before the collision with the berg, Smith discussed with one of his senior officers the peculiar effects of the exceptional calmness of the sea that night on the visibility of icebergs and the possibility that 'blue' ice might be more difficult to see. Lightoller confirmed, however, that the only specific mention of speed in the conversation was Smith saying that were the visibility conditions to change it would be necessary to slow the ship. We do not know whether or not the iceberg that the ship struck was one that had recently inverted and was showing blue ice. The chances of that being the case are low, but we do know from the timings given at the inquiry that it was only seen at less than a thousand yards distant. The expectations of other captains giving evidence was that, even at night under the conditions existing on 14 April, a berg should have been seen at well over a mile, possibly two and, therefore, should have been easily avoidable. There were lookouts both in the crow's nest and the bridge and they had been warned to be especially vigilant. It seems unlikely that the reason for the late sighting of the berg was negligence on their part.

Captain Rostron of *Carpathia* provided another insight into this question when he was asked about bringing his own ship past icebergs on the way to rescue the survivors. He reported seeing about six bergs on the journey. All of them, except the last, were spotted at a distance of one to two miles. The last was seen less than half a mile away and he had to make an emergency swerve to avoid it. He was questioned as to why he had seen this berg so late when he had had ample warning of the earlier ones. This is the relevant passage from his evidence.

The Commissioner: You cannot account to me for your seeing some of these bergs a couple of miles away, but not seeing this particular one till it was about a quarter of a mile away?

– No.

You cannot account for it?

– No.

It happened to yourself?

– I cannot account for it at all.

It did happen to yourself?

–Yes, it did happen.

The Attorney-General: That would seem to indicate a considerable risk in going through the ice region, does it not?

–Yes.

The Commissioner: Is that a common experience, that when you are amongst icebergs you will detect one two or three miles away and another not till it is within a quarter of a mile? Is that within your experience?

– No, I do not think it is common experience. I think it is rather uncommon, as a matter of fact.

The Attorney-General: Rather uncommon?

– I think so.

I want to understand this a little more if we can. If I correctly followed you, you said you only saw this one at about a quarter of a mile distance from you by the streak of a star upon it?

– No, the first one I saw was about one and a half to two miles away; that was the one we saw at about a quarter to three with the streak of the star. That was the first one we picked up; it was a large one.

That one we understand, but this last one that you saw about 4 o'clock when you were getting ready to pick up the boat on the port side, was there anything at all special about the colour of that iceberg?

– No, but I suppose it must have been because of the shadow or something of that kind that we could not make it out before. I cannot account for it.

Rostron clearly believed, as he made clear in answers to subsequent questions, that the failure of the men on *Carpathia* to spot that particular berg was because of some characteristic of its shape that prevented starlight being reflected. Sides that fell precipitously or which had a concave shape, he felt might have made the berg less visible than others. It should be stressed that the berg he saw so late was quite a low one and therefore not the one with which *Titanic* had collided earlier. Rostron had clearly found the experience quite disturbing as it was so abnormal. In his evidence to the British inquiry, Second Officer Lightoller was quite sure that the berg with which *Titanic* collided was one that had recently capsized and did not, therefore, reflect starlight in the usual way. He described that factor, combined with the complete absence of swell and the fact that there was no moon as a combination of circumstances that would only arise once in a hundred years.

Mersey's conclusions on the basis of this evidence were possibly amongst the most sensible of the opinions he arrived at in all four inquiries. This is what he said in his report.

Why, then, did the Master persevere in his course and maintain his speed? The answer is to be found in the evidence. It was shown that for many years past, indeed, for a quarter of a century or more, the practice of liners using this track when in the vicinity of ice at night had been in clear weather to keep the course, to maintain the speed and to trust to a sharp look-out to enable them to avoid the danger. This practice, it was said, had been justified by experience, no casualties having resulted from it. I accept the evidence as to the practice and as to the immunity from casualties which is said to have accompanied it. But the event has proved the practice to be bad. Its root is probably to be found in competition and in the desire of the public for quick passages rather than in the judgment of navigators. But unfortunately experience appeared to justify it. In these circumstances I am not able to blame *Captain Smith*. He had not the experience which his own misfortune has afforded to those whom he has left behind, and he was doing only that which other skilled men would have done in the same position. It was suggested at the bar that he was yielding to influences which ought not to have affected him; that the presence of Mr. Ismay on board and the knowledge which he perhaps had of a conversation between Mr. Ismay and the Chief Engineer at Queenstown about the speed of the ship and the consumption of coal probably induced him to neglect precautions which he would otherwise have taken. But I do not believe this. The evidence shows that he was not trying to make any record passage or indeed any exceptionally quick passage. He was not trying to please anybody, but was exercising his own discretion in the way he thought best. He made a mistake, a very grievous mistake, but one in which, in face of the practice and of past experience, negligence cannot be said to have had any part; and in the absence of negligence it is, in my opinion, impossible to fix Captain Smith with blame. It is, however, to be hoped that the last has been heard of the practice and that for the future it will be abandoned for what we now know to be more prudent and wiser measures. What was a mistake in the case of the *Titanic* would without doubt be negligence in any similar case in the future.

When we considered peacetime risks in Chapter 2 and discussed the different types of risk, we identified collision with icebergs as one of those with very serious potential consequences but very low probability of occurrence. That type of risk we thought presents problems because there would be insufficient experience to establish just what type of avoidance measure would be needed. That, in effect, is what Mersey acknowledged and so he decided that Smith had not been negligent. There was one aspect, however, that he omitted to mention. He spoke of how it was usual practice to maintain normal speed in the vicinity of ice. He did not draw attention to the fact that, over the previous decade or so, 'normal' speed for the large liners on the North Atlantic route had gradually risen from around 16 knots to 22 or even 25 knots. *Titanic* was not the fastest, but she was amongst that group of very fast liners. Had Smith slowed *Titanic* to what had recently been 'normal' speed of 16 knots he not only would have missed that particular berg (it would have drifted south of his track by the time he reached it), he would also have been judged by his officers to have been unnecessarily cautious. Captain Rostron of the *Carpathia* was praised by Mersey for taking the risk of keeping his speed up to his maximum of 16 knots as he approached the ice field in the race to save the *Titanic* survivors. The words 'full speed' or 'keeping up speed' did not refer to an absolute value.

Mersey not only exonerated Smith as to *Titanic*'s speed, he also exonerated the management of White Star. There was never anything but the flimsiest hearsay evidence to suggest that the Chairman of White Star, Bruce Ismay, had pressurised Smith into maintaining a higher speed than he otherwise would have done. It makes perfect sense that Smith, as Mersey suggested, was simply sticking to normal practice by maintaining speed despite the ice warnings. His colleagues in other similar ships were doing exactly the same thing in identical circumstances. He had no need of a Chairman whispering in his ear to persuade him to do so. And, as we noted earlier, the captain is the supreme authority on a ship whether the Chairman of the Line is there or not. Smith was the archetypal company captain in some respects, but in matters of seamanship he appears to have been his own man.

It took about 20 minutes to half an hour after the collision to establish how seriously *Titanic* was damaged. There is relatively little information about what was happening on the bridge during that time because hardly anyone present survived. We know that various people, including the carpenter and the Chief Engineer, were reporting back the extent of the damage and it seems that shortly after midnight Smith knew that the ship would inevitably sink and that her time afloat was limited to about two hours. We will not detail the events of those two hours —many other people have already done so — but focus on the one man who had the ultimate responsibility of ensuring that the maximum number possible of those on board stayed alive.

The order to begin readying the lifeboats was given at 0005 and the first distress call, with Boxhall's incorrect position, was sent at 0015. Taking this latter point first, it is only since Dr Robert Ballard discovered the wreck of *Titanic* in 1985 that we have had conclusive evidence of the mistake that Boxhall made. During both the American and British inquiries there was evidence given that cast some doubt on the the the accuracy of his calculation but, in both cases, it was accepted as gospel. Mersey, in particular, seemed reluctant to entertain any doubt about a position computed by a White Star officer holding an Extra Master's Certificate. That being the case, he was in no position to ponder as to whether Smith had been sufficiently careful in using a quick calculation by one officer as the sole basis for the position given on the distress calls. The history of the ship's navigation that evening was that, at about 1930, Lightoller took some stellar sights with his sextant. He gave the results to Boxhall who worked out the position and noted it in the chart room. At about 2200 the captain asked about the position and Boxhall gave him the piece of paper on which he had written the 1930 calculation. Smith himself then marked it on the chart. It was that position that Boxhall used later at about 0010 to calculate the position sent out by the Senior Telegraphist in the first CQD message. Boxhall testified that, having worked it out, he showed it to the captain and then took it to the wireless room himself. The surviving Junior Telegraphist, Bride, however, testified that Phillips was given it by Captain Smith. Where exactly in the chain of events from the taking of the stellar observations by Lightoller to the transmission by Phillips the mistake occurred is unknown and forever will remain so. In retrospect it might have been prudent for someone to have checked Boxhall's figures, but in the event the error probably did not materially alter the outcome.

Smith's final task, on what he must have realised was likely to be the last night of his life, was to manage the evacuation of the sinking ship in the knowledge that there was lifeboat accommodation for fewer than half of those on board. No one from what might be described as the senior management team on the ship survived and we are therefore very reliant on the evidence of the officers Lightoller, Pitman, Boxhall and Lowe, who did. While many other crew members were involved in getting people off the ship and in seeking help, it is the evidence of these men that provides the most valuable insight into how the process was organised. The inquiry transcripts contain such a wide range of evidence, much of it contradictory, from so many different people that, like the Bible, one can always find supporting quotes for almost any proposition. It seems reasonable, therefore, in considering the role of Captain Smith during the last two hours of his life and the life of his ship, to focus principally on the evidence of his senior surviving officers, evidence that shows what they were thinking, seeing and doing during that time.

Second Officer Lightoller began his posting to *Titanic* as First Officer, but a last minute change of crew, the insertion of Wilde as Chief Officer, had moved him down to Second. He had held an Extra Master's Certificate since 1902 and had been with White Star for over twelve years. He had had an adventurous youth experiencing shipwrecks, fires, gold mining, riding North American trains as a hobo and working as a cowboy before settling down as a career merchant navy officer. It was a pattern that repeated itself throughout his life. During an eventful period as an RN officer in the First World War he was awarded a DSC and Bar. More peaceful times between the wars were spent mostly ashore running guesthouses and farming chickens. In May 1940, at the age of 66, he was asked to hand his motor yacht over to the navy for use at Dunkirk. He refused and took the boat across himself with his son and one of his son's friends. They brought more than 120 troops back to Ramsgate under continuous threat from German aircraft. Lightoller spent the remainder of the war helping with the navy's small boats. He died in 1952.

Charles Lightoller is frequently described as the hero of the *Titanic*. He certainly seems to have been one of the most clear headed and purposeful crew members that night and it was his part that the male lead, Kenneth Moore, played in the film *A Night to Remember*. He impressed as a witness in both inquiries giving relatively straightforward and consistent answers over long periods in the witness box. He was called on three separate occasions by Mersey. He has been accused of being somewhat defensive of his senior officers and his employers, whether out of loyalty or conviction it is difficult to be sure. It may be that he felt that it was not his place to be critical of them; it may also be that those questioning him did not make sufficient attempts to elucidate that criticism. While it is worth bearing that concern in mind, it does not devalue the detailed recall of events that he provided. Lightoller and his wife were clearly deeply affected by the tragedy and both were present at all 37 sessions of the British inquiry

We have already seen something of his testimony about the conversation he had with the captain prior to the collision. He had gone off watch and retired to bed when the collision happened. He went on deck to see what had happened, could see nothing unusual, spoke to Third Officer Pitman who knew no more than he did, saw that there appeared to be no alarm on the bridge and returned to his cabin. He was lying down for between 20 and 30 minutes, he reckoned, when he was awoken by Boxhall. At this point Smith gave the orders to uncover the lifeboats, swing them out and prepare to load them with women and children. Lightoller detailed the available crew members to begin undoing the covers on the lifeboats on both sides, using hand signals to do so because of the deafening noise from the escaping steam. Then, at Wilde's request, he took charge of the boats on the portside (even numbered) beginning with number 4. When boat 4 had been prepared he had it lowered to A-Deck in order to fill it with passengers from there. When he discovered that the closed windows of the promenade on A-Deck prevented that being done he ordered that the passengers be told to come back up to the boat deck, left boat 4 and got boat 6 ready to load from the boat deck. He was quizzed about the time taken up to that point, partly in order to establish how soon he noticed that the ship was down by the head. This is the relevant extract from his evidence.

The Commissioner: At what point of these events did you notice that the ship had begun to be down by the head or to have a list?
— It was when I was at No. 6 boat, My Lord.
As I understand, that would be about half-an-hour after you had come on deck?
— I think it is longer than that.
Well, let us say three quarters of an hour?
— Yes, perhaps three quarters of an hour.
You had been half-an-hour in your bunk before you came on deck at all?

– I said approximately half-an-hour.

So this would be an hour or an hour and a quarter after the collision. And was it then for the first time you noticed the vessel had a list?

– At whatever time that was, My Lord. However, it works out it was about when I was at boat No. 6.

The Solicitor-General: What you had been doing in the interval was, you had been getting No. 4 unstripped; you had been getting her swung out, her falls cleared and let down as far as the A deck, and there you had ascertained that it was not possible to open the windows and get the people through?

– Not immediately, and therefore rather than delay I did not go on with it.

The questions in this part of the evidence were designed to try to establish the timetable of events on board the ship and not to cast doubt on the way that the process was managed. It did not seem to strike anyone during Lightoller's evidence that the time taken to perform the various operations he described was longer than it might have been. Nor was any criticism implied regarding the way Lightoller went about them. One wonders what the reaction from Mersey might have been had the *Titanic* been the fourth of his quartet of inquiries rather than the first. The crews of *Empress*, *Falaba* and *Lusitania* each had 20 minutes or less to evacuate their ships. None of them fully succeeded, but each managed to launch some of the lifeboats and, in the case of the *Falaba* an attempt was made to lower all of them. At the *Empress of Ireland* inquiry the report of a Board of Trade inspection conducted on the liner in Liverpool was submitted in evidence and it included a report on an exercise in getting out the lifeboats. The following is an extract:

> As soon as the muster was over the bugle was sounded and all hands repaired to the boat deck when the order 'out all boats' was given. All the boats under davits, sixteen in number, were at once swung out. Two sailors were in each and they shipped the thole-pins, passed the ends of the painters out and shipped the rudders, the rest of the boats' crews setting up the guys and clearing away the falls. From the time the order was given to the time the boats were ready for lowering about four minutes had elapsed.

Those on *Lusitania* and some of those on the *Falaba* had been uncovered and swung out before the emergency arose, but, even so, the timetable followed on *Titanic* seems remarkably slow. Lightoller was asked about this at the American inquiry and his response was that 'there was no urgency'. Later in his evidence he was asked at the British inquiry about the time taken to lower the boats and this was his response:

Mr. Lewis: I want to know the general methods adopted by the company as far as this Witness knows. (To the witness.) With regard to particular life-boats, I understood you to say in your evidence that it took about an hour and a half to two hours to prepare and lower the boats upon which you were engaged, is that so?

The Commissioner: Yes, he has said it, and I know it, you know.

Mr. Lewis: Do you consider that under the circumstances of the case, when the ship was sinking rapidly, that that was a reasonable time to take?

– Yes.

What is the object of a boat list and boat drill?

– It is rather obvious; it is to teach the men to know their stations.

In the event of danger is not the object to be prepared to lower the boats simultaneously?

– Not necessarily.

If, for instance, the accident was even worse, if it is possible to conceive, and you had knowledge that the ship was to sink in an hour, obviously it would be desirable to get the boats down speedily, would it not?

– Yes.

Is not the object of having boat stations in order that you may station men at the different boats to lower them at once if necessary?

– No.

What is the object of having firemen and stewards on the boat list?

– To know their stations.

Is it not a fact that you ran a risk by proceeding from boat to boat to lower those boats of having several boats left?

– They were not left.

Is it not the fact that you did have boats left, collapsible boats or rafts that you could not get off in time?

– No.

The Commissioner: Now what is the real object of your questions. They are not helping me at all. Is your real object that you think more men belonging to your Union ought to be employed? These questions do not assist me one bit.

Finally, on this topic, Lightoller was asked:

You considered that everything was done that was reasonable with regard to the launching of the boats?

– Yes.

These questions were asked by one of the lawyers representing the Seamen's Union and Mersey here is seen at his peremptory worst, dismissing them as self serving when he should have been considering the issue seriously.

We need to take stock here of the picture that Lightoller has painted and then consider how Mersey dealt with that picture in his report. As Second Officer Lightoller apparently had no designated emergency role but did as he was detailed to do on the night by the Chief Officer. He assigned men to work on the boats irrespective of their actual stations, if indeed they knew them. He did not know which deck lifeboats were filled from, sending number 4 down to the Promenade deck and only then finding that it could not be loaded from there and recalling the passengers. There was another major factor that became clear from some of the evidence given by the Second Officer. He thought that lifeboats should only have a small number of passengers in them when they were lowered and should receive the remainder of their quota once they were in the water because they would not be strong enough to carry the weight of a full load going down on the falls. He told how he had despatched the Boatswain to open the forward gangway doors low down on the ship in order for passengers to go down ladders into the boats after they had been launched. He never saw the man again and did not know whether or not the doors had been opened. If they had been the large additional openings low down would almost certainly have shortened the life of the ship. No passengers were ever instructed (so far as we know) to go down below to the gangway doors to embark on the lifeboats.

Lightoller also insisted that it was correct to lower the boats sequentially rather than simultaneously and this clearly was the order that he and Murdoch on the starboard side had been given. We really need to remind ourselves that this was a highly competent seaman with over twenty years experience at sea but one who clearly had little training in emergency procedures on this ship or any other. The idea that passengers might climb down ladders from the gangway doors into the floating lifeboats is quite bizarre even on a night as calm as 14/15 April 1912.

The idea that it might not be safe to lower a lifeboat with its full complement of 65 people was not just Lightoller's. Fifth Officer Lowe testified that the same approach was being adopted for a while on the starboard side under Murdoch's supervision until eventually the later lifeboats were filled. He also thought that there was a plan to add more people into the boats through the gangway doors and had heard that someone had been sent down to open them. He knew nothing of any passengers being directed to leave the ship by that means. Third Officer Pitman was sent away in a boat by Murdoch quite early in the evacuation as the officer to take charge of the lifeboats so he had relatively little to offer about events on the ship. He was told by Murdoch to keep close to the ship and to stay within reach of the aft gangways although he said that he was not told why. When asked he expressed the view that the filling of lifeboats by ladders from the gangways was not a practical proposition.

So what was Smith's role in this process? The only mention of the captain was a reference by Lightoller to having heard Smith call out to the boats through a megaphone. This is what he recalled.

> *The Solicitor-General:* After these boats had been launched and left the side of the ship, did you hear any orders or call given to any of them?
> −Yes.
> By whom?
> − By the Commander.
> Through the megaphone?
> −Yes.
> Did that happen more than once?
> − More than once, yes.
> What was the order?
> − To come back.
> Was he hailing any particular boats?
> − No. I heard the Commander two or three times hail through the megaphone to bring the boats alongside, and I presumed he was alluding to the gangway doors, giving orders to the boats to go to the gangway doors.
> *The Commissioner:* When was this?
> − During the time I was launching the boats on the port side, I could not give you any definite time.
> *The Solicitor-General:* You heard the orders given and you heard the orders repeated; could you gather at the time whether they were being obeyed or not?
> − No.
> You did not know one way or the other?
> − I did not know anything at all about it.

Lightoller indicated that the last interaction that he himself had with Smith was when he was at the early stages of getting the port side boats organised. He wanted confirmation that he was to begin loading and lowering them.

> *The Solicitor-General:* What was the order?
> − After I had swung out No. 4 boat I asked the Chief Officer should we put the women and children in, and he said 'No.' I left the men to go ahead

with their work and found the Commander, or I met him and I asked him should we put the women and children in, and the Commander said 'Yes, put the women and children in and lower away.' That was the last order I received on the ship.

So far as can be estimated, this conversation took place between 0030 and 0045. The last order that the Second Officer received from any of his seniors was at least an hour and a half before the ship sank.

After Boxhall had helped to estimate the extent of the damage he went to help on the boat deck. He appeared to be 'floating', helping out as he was needed. At some stage after the order to get the boats prepared he spoke to Smith and asked him if the situation was serious. Smith told him that he had been advised that the ship would only stay afloat for an hour or an hour and a half. Boxhall assumed that this advice had come from the ship's designer, Thomas Andrews. He went back onto the bridge and began firing off the distress rockets, having cleared that with the captain. He, Smith and others on the bridge watched the lights of a ship which he judged to approach to within about 5 miles and then to turn and head away. He was asked to try to contact her by Morse lamp which he did without detecting any reply. Boxhall was certain that the ship was within signalling range and the captain appeared to be of the same opinion. Those were the only interactions that he reported with Smith and he did not include in his evidence any other steps taken by the captain.

The other person who reported significant interaction with Smith during this time was Junior Telegraphist Harold Bride, Phillips having been lost. In his testimony he mentioned that Smith had come to the wireless room to give the order to send the distress calls and give the position. Bride had taken responses to the calls for help to Smith on a few occasions and he reported that on one of those the captain had been on the boat deck supervising the lowering of boats on the starboard side, that is the side for which First Officer Murdoch was responsible. At a late stage the captain came back to the wireless room to tell the two operators to leave and save themselves. That was the last time Bride saw him.

What then did Mersey make of this evidence as to the organisation of the evacuation? Too much and too little would appear to be the answer. In his comments he deplored the fact that so many boats went away with less than their full complement, in some cases by a very large margin. The following is an extract from the report of the inquiry.

Many people thought that the risk in the ship was less than the risk in the boats. This explanation is supported by the evidence of Captain Rostron, of the *Carpathia*. He says that after those who were saved got on board his ship, he was told by some of them that when the boats first left the *Titanic* the people 'really would not be put in the boats; they did not want to go in.' There was a large body of evidence from the *Titanic* to the same effect, and I have no doubt that many people, particularly women, refused to leave the deck for the boats. At one time the Master appears to have had the intention of putting the people into the boats from the gangway doors in the side of the ship. This was possibly with a view to allay the fears of the passengers, for from these doors the water could be reached by means of ladders, and the lowering of some of the earlier boats when only partly filled may be accounted for in this way. There is no doubt that the Master did order some of the partly filled boats to row to a position under one of the doors with the object of taking in passengers at that point. It appears, however, that these doors were never opened. Another explanation is that some women refused to leave their husbands. It is said further that the officers engaged in putting the people into the boats feared that the boats might buckle if they were filled; but this proved to be an unfounded apprehension, for one or more boats were completely filled and then successfully lowered to the water.

Mersey jumped to the conclusion that Smith had been responsible for the idea that passengers should join lifeboats already in the water from the gangways and that he had ordered lifeboats to come back to the gangways for that purpose. The only evidence for that was Lightoller's supposition as to the reason for Smith calling lifeboats back towards the ship. In this, Mersey was making too much from too little.

The inquiry evidence presented two different explanations for lifeboats leaving half full or even less. One was the reluctance of passengers to get into the boats. The other was the extraordinary belief amongst at least some of the officers (which may or may not have been shared by Smith) that it was unsafe to lower lifeboats with a full load of passengers. Which of these reasons was the more significant? If the officers loading the boats were of this view, how hard did they try to persuade passengers to get into the boats on the boatdeck? Mersey was clearly perplexed that so many lifeboats went away with fewer on board than should have been the case and he suggested that perhaps they should have been held longer before lowering, or that men should have taken the place of women reluctant to leave husbands, or that the gangway doors should have been used to fill the boats. If this is criticism it is mild indeed and not directed at anyone in particular. So far as the conduct of the officers was concerned he said that: 'The officers did their work very well without any thought for themselves.' He added that: 'The discipline among passengers and crew during the lowering of the boats was good, but the organisation should have been better, and if it had been it is possible that more lives would have been saved.'

Coming from someone with a reputation for rushing to judgment, this is a considered, cautious understatement. So were the recommendations that he made based on these conclusions, which were as follows:

Manning the Boats and Boat Drills

13. That in cases where the deck hands are not sufficient to man the boats enough other members of the crew should be men trained in boat work to make up the deficiency. These men should be required to pass a test in boat work.

14. That in view of the necessity of having on board men trained in boat work, steps should be taken to encourage the training of boys for the Merchant Service.

15. That the operation of Section 115 and Section 134 (a) of the Merchant Shipping Act, 1894, should be examined, with a view to amending the same so as to secure greater continuity of service than hitherto.

16. That the men who are to man the boats should have more frequent drills than hitherto. That in all ships a boat drill, a fire drill and a watertight door drill should be held as soon as possible after leaving the original port of departure and at convenient intervals of not less than once a week during the voyage. Such drills to be recorded in the official log.

17. That the Board of Trade should be satisfied in each case before the ship leaves port that a scheme has been devised and communicated to each officer of the ship for securing an efficient working of the boats.

The last recommendation is the only one with any bearing on the training of officers in how to deal with emergencies. The remainder deal with the role of the 'men'. In 1912 any reference to 'men' automatically excluded the officers. It was not the 'men' who failed the passengers on *Titanic;* it was the lack of understanding of the officers of the nature of the emergency that they were dealing with and their lack of skill in the processes involved in evacuating their ship. How much of that inadequacy on the part of the officers should have been laid at the door of the ship owners and how much was the responsibility of Smith?

When we come to the ship owners, we are obliged to consider industry norms as we did with speed. What was normal industry practice and to what extent was White Star following those norms? If Smith could be exonerated for maintaining speed despite the ice warnings because that was normal industry practice, then White Star likewise could claim that their officer training in matters of safety was no worse than anyone else's. It seems quite likely that White Star was not an exception in this area.

Mersey tacitly acknowledged that ship owners and ship builders have to be coerced into dealing with matters of safety as they see their self-interest as being better served by skimping where they can get away with it. His final recommendation, however, went some way to taking the matter more seriously. Under the heading 'General' he recommended that an International Conference be called to agree a common line of conduct in a number of areas affecting safety at sea. The conference was called in 1913 and was chaired by Lord Mersey himself. It was the first of a series of such conferences that continue to the present day and which have had a considerable influence on the construction of ships, the provision of safety equipment and the training of crews. Perhaps we should temper our concern at his understated response to the inadequacies of the evacuation of the *Titanic* with some acknowledgement that he initiated a process that, over time, has led to a substantial improvement in maritime safety.

There is one matter, however, that we have not yet explored so far as Smith is concerned and that is the quality of his personal leadership. While one can understand a reluctance to speak ill of the dead, it does seem wrong that the lack of leadership during the sinking of *Titanic* was not the subject of comment in the report. Smith knew by midnight that his ship would sink in around two hours or so and yet it was a further 45 minutes before the first lifeboat left on one side of the ship and almost an hour before the first one left on the other side. Clearly there was no sense of urgency, as Lightoller admitted at the American inquiry. Why not? There were only two ways in which the number of deaths could have been substantially reduced given the shortage of lifeboats. One was to transfer people to a rescue ship and the second was to create more floats or rafts to support people and keep them out of the water. Smith was well aware of exactly what had happened when the *Republic* sank five years previously. He knew how long it took to transfer passengers and crew by lifeboat to another ship. While wireless messages had not given any promise of a ship arriving before *Titanic* sank, there was always a possibility of a ship appearing, given the number still without any wireless or with

only part-time operation. To facilitate a rapid transfer the first requirement
was for *Titanic's* lifeboats to be off the ship, full and roped together. That way
they could be emptied and sent back as quickly as possible to re-load. Smith
had men available, massive amounts of wood and substantial quantities of tools
to work with. It would never have been possible to construct rafts to hold all
who needed them, but many more might have been saved nonetheless.

The picture that emerged from the evidence at the inquiry was of the crew
all working as best they knew how, but without any clear strategy from above.
It could be that this absence of strategy was a result of Smith's own lack of
experience of emergencies – his 'uneventful' career – or that Smith's one central strategy was to avoid panic. Trying to speed up the launching of the boats
and coerce into them reluctant passengers, while at the same time breaking
up furniture and panelling to make rafts might have induced a state of disor-
der amongst passengers or crew that would have been difficult to deal with.
Perhaps Mersey should have reflected on how captains ought to lead in this
type of situation in such a way that the risk of panic can be managed and set
against the potential gains of urgent action. It seems doubtful that the right
answer was the laissez faire policy that Smith adopted and that resulted in
1500 people losing their lives.

11

STANLEY LORD

The controversies surrounding Stanley Lord are such that it would be better, in this instance, to start with the conclusions that Mersey reached and work back, rather than trace the evidence through to the report. Mersey dedicated a complete chapter in the report to '*The Circumstances in Connection with the S.S. Californian*' although the original set of questions forming the inquiry brief had not included one about the actions of other ships. On 22 May, the thirteenth day of the inquiry, Sir Rufus Isaacs proposed and Lord Mersey agreed that the Board of Trade should be asked to add an additional question to the brief and question 24(b) was adopted: 'What vessels had the opportunity of rendering assistance to the *Titanic* and, if any, how was it that assistance did not reach the *Titanic* before the SS *Carpathia*?'

Although the question was added six days before the report of the American inquiry was published, it came after Stanley Lord and other members of his crew had given evidence to Mersey as well as in New York and after it had become clear that the Senators were in no doubt as to his culpability in failing to come to the assistance of those on the sinking ship. The phraseology of the question clearly reflected the concerns that had developed in the press as the blame game gained momentum. It is hardly surprising that the answer of the Mersey inquiry to the question that it had asked of itself was brusque and to the point:

> The *Californian*. She could have reached the *Titanic* if she had made the attempt when she saw the first rocket. She made no attempt.

There followed a recommendation to the effect that:

> The attention of Masters of vessels should be drawn by the Board of Trade to the effect that under the Maritime Conventions Act, 1911, it is a misdemeanour not to go to the relief of a vessel in distress when possible to do so.

If the conclusion in the report avoids any specific criticism of Lord in person, the recommendation could scarcely be more pointed. Mersey explained in the discursive chapter on the *Californian* exactly how the evidence led him to his findings. Irrespective of one's views as to what actually happened that night one can admire the judicial style of Mersey's summary of the evidence.

> There are contradictions and inconsistencies in the story as told by the different witnesses. But the truth of the matter is plain. The *Titanic* collided with the berg 11.40. The vessel seen by the *Californian* stopped at this time. The rockets sent up from the *Titanic* were distress signals. The *Californian* saw distress signals. The number sent up by the *Titanic* was about eight. The *Californian* saw eight. The time over which the rockets from the *Titanic* were sent up was from about 12.45 to 1.45 o'clock. It was about this time that the *Californian* saw the rockets. At 2.40 Mr. Stone called to the Master that the ship from which he'd seen the rockets had disappeared.
>
> At 2.20 a.m. the *Titanic* had foundered. It was suggested that the rockets seen by the *Californian* were from some other ship, not the *Titanic*. But no other ship to fit this theory has ever been heard of.
>
> These circumstances convince me that the ship seen by the *Californian* was the *Titanic*, and if so, according to Captain Lord, the two vessels were about five miles apart at the time of the disaster. The evidence from the *Titanic* corroborates this estimate, but I am advised that the distance was probably greater, though not more than eight to ten miles. The ice by which the *Californian* was surrounded was loose ice extending for a distance of not more than two or three miles in the direction of the *Titanic*.' The night was clear and the sea was smooth. When she first saw the rockets the *Californian* could have pushed through the ice to the open water without any serious risk and so have come to the assistance of the *Titanic*. Had she done so she might have saved many if not all of the lives that were lost.

Eloquent it might have been, but Mersey's summary was a triumph of conviction over objectivity. No jury, having heard a summary such as that, could have returned any verdict other than 'guilty as charged'; except of course that Lord had not been charged. We saw earlier how the rules for inquiries permitted anyone who was liable to be subject to criticism in an inquiry to be represented by an attorney. Even after the formulation of the extra question, Mersey refused Stanley Lord the right to be represented. Furthermore, despite the reference to a 'misdemeanour' and despite also some subsequent clamour in the press, Lord never was charged with any offence nor was action taken against him to remove or suspend his certificate. Perhaps the most inaccurate sentence (of many) in Mersey's summary was the assertion that the truth of the matter was plain. A century later it is still not possible to make that assertion with the confidence that Mersey displayed.

Following years of controversy, much of it conducted in a spirit of animated hostility, the government decided in 1990 to ask the recently formed Marine Accident Investigations Branch to carry out a reappraisal of the evidence. In March 1992 MAIB produced a report that was distilled from a strange mixture of opposing opinions. The initial work was done by an Inspector who came to the conclusion that a substantial southerly current had brought the *Californian* much closer to *Titanic* than the position in which she had stopped. Thus he believed that the two ships had seen each other and so he broadly concurred with Mersey's findings. The MAIB Chief Inspector was unhappy with his conclusions and asked his Deputy to review the evidence again. He came to the view that the two ships were much farther apart and that it was most unlikely that either could have seen the other. The Chief Inspector endorsed his Deputy's views and, in March 1992, submitted a report to that effect. The report was accepted by the government and now replaces Mersey's original findings as the 'official' position. It is the only example of any of Mersey's conclusions being officially overturned.

The MAIB report, notwithstanding the internal disagreements that preceded it, is quite a contrast to most of the other literature on the subject. When one has perused the sometimes dense and turgid polemics that characterise much of what has been written, the MAIB report appears brief, logical and clear. There is no need to repeat here what the MAIB investigators did twenty years ago. There is no new evidence; the position of the wreck is the main piece of evidence that has emerged since Mersey completed his work and that was known to the MAIB. We shall therefore use the 1992 findings as the basis for evaluating the earlier inquiry and then reflect on what that tells us about Stanley Lord and how he was treated in 1912.

The MAIB report concluded that *Californian* was between 17 and 20 miles North by North West of the *Titanic* as she was sinking. This means that, in normal circumstances, the ships would not have seen each other's lights. The Chief Inspector acknowledged that a phenomenon known as 'super-refraction' might have made it possible for one ship to have seen something of the other even at that distance, but he did not consider this likely and advanced a number of reasons for ruling it out. These included the impossibility at that distance of distinguishing coloured navigation lights even with super-refraction. Witnesses on both *Titanic* and *Californian* testified to seeing the navigation lights of the ship that they were observing. This question of the distance at which navigation lights are visible in clear conditions was also raised at the inquiry into the loss of the *Empress*. The Chief Officer of the *Storstad* was asked how far the ship's sidelights were visible and he replied about four or five miles. The MAIB report, therefore, endorses the view that the ship seen by the *Californian* was a third ship, identity never likely now to be known. The ship seen from *Titanic*, as reported by a number of witnesses, including Boxhall, was either that third ship or some other unidentified vessel.

On the matter of the relative position of the two ships, the MAIB report therefore agrees with Lord's view, to which he stuck for the rest of his life, that the ship seen by *Californian* was not the *Titanic*. However, Lord also maintained, again consistently, that the rockets that his officers had observed, and which appeared to come from that ship, were not the rockets that Boxhall fired from the bridge of *Titanic*. Here, the 1992 report agrees with Mersey. No-one, in all of the time since the disaster, has found any evidence of any ship sending up rockets that night other than *Titanic* and, much later, the *Carpathia* as she raced towards the lifeboats. One of the justifications that Lord gave for believing that the rockets could not have come from *Titanic* was the fact that the direction in which they were observed from *Californian* was different to that of the *Titanic's* radioed position. Mersey perhaps ought to have taken that fact rather more seriously than he did, but he was convinced of Lord's guilt and had discounted almost all navigational evidence from *Californian* as a result. He was also more than a little confused as to the distinctions between bearings, headings and directions. The position of the wreck, discovered by Ballard in 1985, both helps to confirm Lord's navigational evidence while, at the same time, removing the substance of his argument. We now know that the direction in which the rockets were seen from *Californian* was the direction in which *Titanic* lay stopped at the time. It now seems clear that the white rockets that were seen by Second Officer Stone and Apprentice Gibson were indeed the distress rockets fired from the sinking *Titanic*.

Two questions now remain. Firstly, why were the rockets not properly recognised as distress signals and appropriate action taken? The second is something of a 'what if' question that historians generally dislike. If Lord had acted in response to the rockets, could the *Californian*, as Mersey maintained, have substantially reduced the death toll? In beginning to answer the first question, we should note that Lord himself did not see any rockets. Just before the first rocket was seen he had retired to the chartroom for a rest having been continuously on the bridge since early in the day. The only people who gave evidence as to the rockets that were seen were Stone and Gibson.

The regulations about the use of rockets as distress signals at sea at the time, give a simple description: "Rockets or shells throwing stars of any colour or description, fired one at a time at short intervals.' Mersey himself read this out to the inquiry after a vast amount of time had been spent questioning witnesses as to the interpretation they placed on the rockets observed having been white. The various lawyers had pressed Gibson, Lord and Stone (in that order) as to what they believed at the time the rockets had signified, largely on the assumption that informal company signals would have been coloured while white signals meant distress. The important words in the regulations were the last ones, 'one at a time at short intervals'. 'Short' has been interpreted by some as meaning intervals of a minute or less but the regulations themselves did not specify this. It seems that the ones fired by *Titanic* were at fairly irregular intervals but rather longer than a minute.

Without going into the details of the long and confused interrogations of the three *Californian* officers, all of which have been analysed *ad nauseam*, the following sequence seems reasonably certain, although timings are approximate.

- Just before he went to sleep in the chartroom, at about 0040, Lord spoke to Stone by voice tube. Stone assured him that the steamer that had come up and stopped close to them was still there, that he had tried to contact her by morse lamp and that no reply had been received.

- At 0115 Stone called Lord on the voice tube to report that the ship had fired five rockets and was now steaming away to the South West although Lord's memory of this conversation is that only one rocket was mentioned. Lord questioned Stone about the colour of the rockets and was told that they were white. He then instructed Stone to watch the other ship, continue trying to morse, and to send Gibson down to report to him when he had any news.

- Gibson went down to the chartroom to report to Lord just after 0200. He told him that the ship had fired a total of 8 rockets and was now disappearing in the South West. Lord asked him about the colour of the rockets and asked Gibson the time. Gibson then left and went back to the bridge. Lord said that his only memory was of Gibson opening and closing the door some time between 0115 and 0430.

- At 0245 Stone again called Lord by voice pipe to report that the steamer had now disappeared to the South West and again mentioned that the rockets were white. Lord claimed to have no memory of that conversation whatsoever.

When pressed as to their interpretation of the meaning of the rockets both Gibson and Stone denied that they had ever believed them to have been distress signals. The idea that they might have been calls for assistance only occurred to them the following day when they knew about the sinking of *Titanic*. However, they had no other rational explanation for what they saw. They spoke of company signals but admitted they had never before seen company signals of this nature. Stone also admitted that they met the description that he had been taught to look for in distress signals, except for two features. They were much lower in the sky than he would have expected of distress signals fired from a ship he estimated to be only about 5 miles away. Secondly, the ship they were apparently being fired from was moving while firing them, her bearing gradually changing, he claimed, from around South East to South West. This second observation is a rather puzzling one to which we will return later. Stone and Gibson both testified to a discussion between them on the bridge about the rockets during which they agreed that whoever was sending them up must have some good reason for doing so. They also reported observing that the lights of the ship that they were watching behaved oddly as she was steaming away. Here the inquiry descended into farce at times, a frustrating exercise in semantics in which the questioners tried desperately to get the witnesses to use a form of words that could be interpreted in line with what someone might have seen if what they had been observing was the *Titanic* sinking.

Notwithstanding the points about the apparent lowness of the rockets, the moving ship and the oddness of the lights, the MAIB report concluded that Second Officer Stone should have interpreted the rockets as being in all likelihood distress signals. That being so, he should have been more forceful in bringing them to the attention of his captain. In particular, when Gibson returned from the chartroom to say that the captain had not indicated that any further action should be taken, Stone should have left the bridge to inform him in person exactly what had been observed. It was a serious matter for the officer of the watch to leave the bridge, even when the ship was stationary; but, in the view of the Chief Inspector of MAIB, the circumstances warranted that course of action. There may be two reasons why Stone did not do so. One, of course, is that it genuinely did not occur to him that what he had seen was a call for assistance. That indeed is what he testified in the inquiry; his inability to provide a convincing alternative, however, at least leaves him open to doubts as to his competence.

The second possible reason is that he was scared of Lord's reaction if he had appeared in front of him in the chartroom. Lord was asked about what Stone should have done if he had believed the rockets were distress signals. This is the relevant section of the proceedings.

Mr. Dunlop: You were surprised about the *Titanic*. Did you question your
Second Officer as to why you had not been called?
– I did.
What was his explanation to you?
– He said that he had sent down and called me; he had sent Gibson down,
and Gibson had told him I was awake and I had said, 'All right, let me know
if anything is wanted.' I was surprised at him not getting me out, consid-
ering rockets had been fired. He said if they had been distress rockets he
would most certainly have come down and called me himself, but he was
not a little bit worried about it at all.
If they had been distress rockets he would have called you?
– He would have come down and insisted upon my getting up.
And was it his view that they were not distress rockets?
– That was apparently his view.

Lord therefore testified to his expectation that Stone would have come to
him in person had he felt the need to do so. Some commentators have stated
that in doing so Lord was, at best, disingenuous. He appears to have been
something of a martinet and must have been aware at least of the possibility
that his second officer might have been very wary of waking him in that way,
if it turned out that there was insufficient reason to do so. At the same time, if
we take Stone's testimony at face value, we cannot then set Lord's aside without some evidence.

The background and personality of the captain have been brought into
this discussion, but not that of the other two actors who, together with him,
determined how the *Californian* reacted. Second Officer Stone was described
by Lord in testimony as being reliable, but was also described elsewhere as
being somewhat unimaginative. Although he did not suffer any consequences
because of his association with the sinking of *Titanic*, in his subsequent
career he was not a high flyer. Stone continued to serve for some time with
the Leyland Line rising to become Chief Officer and he served as a Sub-
Lieutenant in the RNR in WWI. He worked on Harrison Line ships after
the war until he suffered some form of breakdown in 1938 after which he
worked in Liverpool docks as a supervisor.

Apprentice Gibson, who appears to have been viewed as a bright young
lad in the context of the inquiry, progressed even less well in his career at
sea. He only passed his exams for his Masters' Certificate 28 years later, in
1940, and rose no higher than third officer, spending time as an AB, a Bosun
and a Quarter Master as well as an officer. He was described by one captain as a 'positive menace on the bridge'. These post-*Titanic* histories of the

two junior officers do not lead us, directly or indirectly, to any specific conclusions about what happened that night. They are presented only for the purpose of completeness.

In accepting the MAIB's conclusions, we are therefore suggesting that Stone (and Gibson, but the responsibility lay with Stone) should have recognised the rockets as distress signals and should have ensured that Lord was aware of that. Before considering the second of our questions, however, we do need to make some reference to the 'moving ship' issue. If the rockets that Stone saw were being fired from the (stationary) *Titanic*, how could he have observed the compass bearing of their point of origin changing during the time that they were fired? There appear to be only two answers. Either he was entirely mistaken and had failed to take bearings on the compass but had noted the change visually, a change that had actually resulted from the *Californian* swinging round while stopped. That seems by far the more likely explanation despite Gibson's assertion in evidence that he understood Stone to have taken bearings. Gibson himself did not claim that the ship sending up the rockets had been moving while doing so, but did not argue with Stone's evidence. During the period when four of the first five of the rockets were sent up, Gibson was not on the bridge. The other possibility, at least in theory, is that the *Californian* and *Titanic* were each being moved by significant (but different) currents. While that eventuality cannot be ruled out, the scale of the movement that Stone reported seems beyond the capacity for currents alone to cause within the timescale of his observations.

Our second question is an important one because of Mersey's wholly unsubstantiated assertion that, had the *Californian* responded to the rockets, she could have rescued some, or even all, of those on *Titanic*. The MAIB report is clear on this matter also. Even had Lord been awakened and action taken at the point when Stone should have realised that the series of rockets represented a call for help, the *Californian* could not have reached the scene of the sinking in time to prevent the loss of any lives. There was of course the confusion over the *Titanic's* position. If Lord had woken Evans, his Marconi operator, and received the CQD signal with the wrong position where would he have headed? In the direction of the ship which was still in sight and which Stone had reported as firing rockets, or in the direction of the position given by *Titanic*? The MAIB report suggests that Lord would have recognised the significance of the discrepancy and sent a wireless message to *Titanic* querying the position being broadcast. Presumably then either Phillips or Bride would have gone from the wireless room along the boat deck to the bridge and told Smith (or Boxhall?) that the position was being queried by a ship that reported seeing the rockets. The position might then have been checked, the error discovered and a correct position broadcast. Lord would then have known where to head. There is a considerable element of speculation in that chain of events and a rather large number of possible breakdown points. However, even if Lord had set off in the right direction at a safe pace through the ice field surrounding the *Californian,* it is most unlikely that he could have been at the disaster site before *Titanic* had sunk. As the survival time of those not in the boats was very short the *Californian* might only have succeeded in gaining the kudos that, in the event, went to the *Carpathia* as the ship that found the lifeboats.

In Chapter 9 we posed the question as to whether the failure of the *Californian* to take action in response to the rockets was a failure of communication or of will. On balance the MAIB report comes down on the side of communication, preferring to believe Lord when he said that he was not properly awake when Stone and Gibson spoke to him and did not appreciate the significance of what he was being told. Undoubtedly Lord was very tired when he went for a rest. He had been on duty for over 15 hours and had experienced an ice field for the first time in his career. That having been said, one of the characteristics of the sailor that is often spoken of is the ability to take short periods of sleep and awaken from them immediately if called. It is also worth remembering that the voicepipe that Stone used twice to speak to Lord was not in the room beside him where he was resting but was in the neighbouring room. Lord therefore had to walk from one room to the other to take the call. The nature of what he was told, however, was not such as to give rise to concern instantly, as Stone was at pains to stress that the ship he was watching was moving away and at no time did he use the word 'distress' or even hint that he thought someone was in trouble. The tone of the messages was reassuring rather than rousing and it is certainly quite possible that, in his sleepy state, that is exactly how Lord interpreted them. There is no need to paint Lord as a paragon of ship-mastery (as his more fervent supporters do) in order to accept that the failure to take action was not a failure of will on his part. The description of him as a sociopath, coming from the anti-Lord camp, surely falls into the category of what the MAIB report itself describes as 'scurrilous'.

In the last chapter we decided that Mersey was fair in his treatment of Smith on the speed issue but was not as critical as he should have been of his lack of effectiveness during the period between the collision and the ship foundering. We can draw mixed conclusions here also. Mersey was mistaken in supposing that the two ships were in sight of each other but he was right in believing that the *Titanic's* rockets were seen. The confusion that was apparent in the minds of the officers of the *Californian* over what sort and colour of rockets constituted a distress signal should have been the subject of more direct comment and, indeed, should have led to a recommendation about the better standardisation of practice. The claim that the *Californian* could have rescued many of those in danger on the *Titanic* showed little understanding, amongst other things, of the logistics of transferring a very large number of people between ships at sea in the dark, especially when one of those ships is sinking rapidly by the head. The barbed recommendation about masters being reminded of their obligation to go to the relief of a ship in distress was, at the very least, unwarranted by the evidence.

12

HENRY KENDALL AND THOMAS ANDERSEN

The inquiry into the loss of the *Empress of Ireland* was quite different to any of the other three inquiries over which Mersey presided. The reason for the difference was not the fact that it took place in Quebec, three thousand miles from London, or that it took place under Canadian rather than British jurisdiction. It was different because of the adversarial legal battle it fore-shadowed. Within minutes of the *Empress* sinking, when Kendall was fished out of the water and brought aboard the *Storstad*, accusations of blame began as he confronted Thomas Andersen. By the time the inquiry commenced reciprocal law suits had already been filed and the inquiry itself became the cockpit within which claim and counter-claim were made. It was understood by all concerned that whatever emerged from the inquiry would, in all probability, determine the outcomes of the lawsuits and, in fact, that is exactly what happened.

Thus the *Empress* inquiry resembled a criminal trial more than an investigation into a horrible tragedy. It was a trial with two competing defendants. If one was found guilty the other must be innocent and vice versa – or so it was played out. The lawyer representing the Canadian Pacific Railway acted as defence lawyer for his client and, in effect, also as prosecutor of the Dominion Coal Company who had chartered the *Storstad*. The lawyer for the Dominion Coal Company played the opposing two roles. Caught somewhere in the middle, rather uncomfortably, were the lawyers representing, amongst others, the Canadian government and the Union of Seamen. We must not forget also that the inquiry was not a 'one man show', with Mersey as the only judicial presence. This inquiry was a tribunal. Mersey sat, as President, with Sir Adolphe Basile Routhier, a retired Chief Justice of the Superior Court of Quebec and the Honourable Ezekiel McLeod, Chief Justice and Judge in Admiralty for New Brunswick. The Canadian Government was represented by Edward L Newcombe who, as well as being a lawyer, was the Deputy Minister of Justice.

The role played by Newcombe was a slightly controversial one. Before the inquiry began he arranged for the existing Canadian Commissioner of Wrecks, a Captain Lindsay, to take preliminary statements from all potential witnesses and to advise as to which ones should be called to testify. This was a process which greatly helped the inquiry to focus on those who had the most information about the tragedy, but it did open the Ministry to accusations of self-interest. In the event these accusations do not seem to have been of any substance and there were witnesses called who had not been included in the list drawn up by Lindsay and Newcombe. The process exposed Newcombe to some sharp exchanges with Mersey, who was less than happy with a few of the outcomes. One does wonder if Mersey would have spoken with quite the same asperity to a Home Office minister in London, had one appeared in front of him in a similar role.

Butler Aspinall KC, whom we met previously representing the Board of Trade in the *Titanic* inquiry, was the lawyer for the CPR. An establishment figure with experience in maritime matters, he also had a killer instinct for exposing what he considered to be weaknesses in the opposition case. For the most part he and Mersey communicated in a relatively relaxed manner; appropriate deference was always shown to the bench and apologies for over-stepping the mark were suitably profuse. When Aspinall argued the toss with Mersey, he always took care to point out at the start that his lordship would win anyway. Aspinall was persistent in following issues through. Witnesses cross-examined by him were worn down through multiple probes, rather than being demolished by a masterstroke. While he clearly did have an under-standing of nautical terminology and his knowledge of ship construction was quite impressive, there were occasions when he failed to appreciate the sig-nificance, or the implications, of the testimony from the sailors involved.

We have already noted the comments of the British press about the different styles of the American and British *Titanic* inquiries. Those differences owed something to the fact that the American one was composed of a committee of politicians while the British one was judicial in character. But the differ-ences reflected as well a less formal and rather more theatrical approach that characterised American courtroom procedures. The lawyer for the Dominion Coal Company, representing the *Storstad* interest, brought something of that approach to the *Empress* inquiry. Charles Sherman Haight was a well known New York lawyer specialising in Admiralty cases who had a reputation for daunting courtroom performances. He had a relationship with Mersey that was much less relaxed; the two came from quite different backgrounds and

legal traditions so it would only be expected that there might be some fireworks. It is probably to the credit of both that the fireworks did not burn the
house down and Haight certainly had all the latitude he desired to present his
case in his own way. In the event, his client might have been better served had
he been somewhat more restrained.

Our two captains were both present throughout the inquiry sitting in close
proximity. We do not know what words, if any, were exchanged between them
during the nine days of testimony and the two days of summing up. They lis-
tened to the testimony of 60 witnesses in addition to each other's. Kendall was
recalled to the stand twice, but Andersen only testified once. At the start of the
inquiry Kendall was obviously suffering from his ordeal and walked hesitantly
using a stick, despite which he refused a seat when giving evidence. Kendall
knew that he had more to lose than Andersen. He had been on the bridge of
the *Empress* throughout the entire incident and was personally responsible for
every order given on the bridge. Andersen had been resting below as the two
ships approached and was only called a minute or so before the actual collision. While he might have to answer for the fact that he was not on the bridge
when the fog came down, he could not be so directly criticised for the orders
given by his officers.

Because the inquiry had the appearance of a criminal trial but not the
reality, the lawyers involved were not restricted by the protocols that would
normally prevent collusion between prosecuting and defence counsel. There
was clearly frequent contact between Aspinall and Haight during the inquiry
and there appears to have been agreement between them at least as to the
ground that they would fight over. They agreed that the navigational evidence from both ships was so imprecise as regards timings, positions and
speeds as to be nearly worthless. The story told by those on the *Empress* was
wholly incompatible with that coming from the crew of the *Storstad*. For this
reason the two lawyers agreed that no collision would have taken place unless
one of the two ships had altered her course while in the fog, despite firm
denials from all involved. Therefore, one crew was lying to the court. Their
only disagreement was about which crew had conspired to commit perjury.
When, in their summings up, both Haight and Aspinall had described their
respective positions, Mersey challenged Aspinall as to whether there might
be another possibility.

Lord Mersey: If your story is right it follows logically that the witnesses for
the *Storstad* are either telling deliberate lies – and I don't think you can
escape from saying it – if on the other hand Mr. Haight's story is right it
follows as he says that the witnesses from the *Empress* must be deliberately

1 Viscount Mersey.

2 (Below left) Captain Stanley Lord of the *Californian*.

3 (Below) Captain E.J. Smith of the *Titanic*.

4 The *Titanic* at Queenstown.

5 A depiction of the sinking of the *Titanic* in the *London Illustrated News*.

6 The *Californian* photographed from the *Carpathia* on 15 April 1912. (Courtesy of The National Archives at New York City)

7 Captain A.H. Rostron and under officers of the *Carpathia*, 29 May 1912. (Library of Congress)

8 (Top) The *Empress of Ireland*.

9 (Above) The *Storstad* with her damaged bow.

10 Captain Henry Kendall of the *Empress of Ireland*.

11 Captain Thomas
Andersen of the *Storstad*.
(Courtesy of the artist,
John Andert)

12 Victims of the sinking of the *Empress of Ireland*. (Library of Congress)

13 (Top) Captain Kendall giving evidence to the *Empress* inquiry.

14 The *Falaba*.

15 (Below left) Kapitanleutnant Walther Schwieger of U-20.

16 (Below) Captain Will Turner of the *Lusitania*.

17 The *Lusitania* passing the Old Head of Kinsale. (Courtesy of the Peabody Essex Museum)

18 An artist's depiction of the moment the second torpedo hit the *Lusitania*. (Library of Congress)

19 The body of a victim of the sinking of the *Lusitania* is unloaded from the *New York*. (Library of Congress)

20 An anniversary parade to mourn the sinking of the *Lusitania* marches towards Marble Arch bearing a model of the stricken vessel.

putting forward a story which they know is untrue. That seems to me to be the position involved by the pretensions of the two sides. What I am asking is this, is it according to your view possible that there may be a middle course involving both sides in blame?

Mr Aspinall: As your Lordship says of course it is possible, but what I submit is the manner in which your Lordships will approach the consideration of this case will be, your Lordships will consider the evidence, and I submit that in a court of law that the court is slow, and properly slow to arrive at a conclusion which neither party to the dispute invites the court to come to, and to which conclusion neither party has addressed its evidence.

Lord Mersey: Of course you must remember that this is not a suit.

Mr Aspinall: I admit that.

Lord Mersey: This is an inquiry.

Mr Aspinall: That is clear, but nevertheless I submit I am entitled to put forward this contention, that where you find two ship-owners represented, if I may say so, by counsel who know their business, if in accord with this view that it is one to blame, and not both, and when it is remembered that the evidence on both sides has been massed so to speak to arrive at that conclusion, that whether it be a tribunal which is inquiring, or whether it is a tribunal which is determining liability, that that tribunal would be slow to say that they propose under these circumstances to arrive at a middle course.

Judge McLeod: What this commission wishes to do is not to try the case between the *Empress* and the *Storstad* but to satisfy ourselves and, if we can, satisfy the public, just how this accident happened, and if coming to that conclusion we have to find that both are to blame we are entitled to do it.

This is really quite an extraordinary passage. Aspinall is speaking not only on his own behalf but also that of his opponent and his rather weasel attempt to pin the tribunal down to an interpretation of its role with which both lawyers would be happy was very sensibly rejected by McLeod.

Newcombe was the one who summarised the evidence as he saw it from a perspective not governed by a financial imperative to find any particular party at fault. He suggested that the middle way which Mersey had identified was the correct answer. He argued that there had been mistakes on both ships, mistakes which he considered might amount to negligence, but that it was not necessary to assume anyone was lying in order to envisage how a collision was possible. His belief was that the *Empress* had inadvertently stopped across the path of the *Storstad* but that the *Storstad* had not reacted sufficiently to the signals from the *Empress* telling her that she was stopping. It was a brave attempt, but he was not able to square enough of the evidence with this explanation to make it wholly convincing to the tribunal and, in the end, Aspinall won the day so far as the report was concerned. It is worth noting, however, that there is no suggestion in the inquiry report that the crew of the *Storstad* deliberately conspired to mislead the court and no witnesses were ever charged with perjury.

Reading the transcript of this inquiry and thinking back to the *Titanic* one, it seems as if some of the informality that Haight brought to the proceedings rubbed off on the judge. Mersey remained as gruff as ever, but here one can sense a hint of a smile behind some of his bearishness, as when he called to a witness: 'Speak up man, I'm old and deaf!'

Mersey made no secret of his dislike for one witness and it is unlikely that he was alone in that reaction as he does seem to have been quite an annoying character. He was a man called Galway and he was the Quartermaster on the *Empress* who had had the watch prior to the one in which the collision took place. Some of his testimony was flatly contradicted by the colleague who took over the wheel after him and also by the pilot who was on the bridge with him. One of the sources of Mersey's annoyance was Galway's habit of repeating each question he was asked before beginning to answer it. Perhaps he was just putting into effect in the courtroom the training that he had had on a ship's bridge. All quartermasters are drilled to repeat each order that they are given parrot fashion before executing the order and then reporting it done. Mersey was not amused by that, but he was amused by a phrase which Galway used more than once in which he described a ship's steering mechanism as its 'principal asset'. When it turned out that Galway had given a lengthy newspaper interview without referring to the ship's steering, Mersey quipped: 'So the principal asset was left out.'

The words that the court reporter put on paper no doubt give a very accurate record of exactly what was said by witnesses, by counsel and by those on the bench. They only occasionally provide insights into what the atmosphere was like and how different witnesses reacted to the sometimes robust cross-examinations to which they were frequently subjected. One such insight came in a remarkable attack in the summing up by Haight on two of the witnesses from his own ship. (Incidentally, it is slightly odd to read how both Aspinall and Haight had acquired first person ownership of their respective ships. Each spoke of 'my ship' and 'our captain' etc.) Haight had a problem in that the engine room log from the *Storstad* did not entirely back up the story being given by the bridge personnel. Haight wanted to make sure that it was the bridge story that carried credibility. This is how he lashed into the ship's Chief Engineer and the engineer in charge in the engine room at the time of the collision.

Lord Mersey: Was the chief engineer there at that time?

Mr Haight: He was in his bed, my Lord, but as I saw him on the stand he might as well have stayed in his bed all the time.

Lord Mersey: Does that mean that you do not care about him, or what does it mean?

Mr Haight: It was an inadvertent expression of my contempt for the man who went to the lifeboats instead of going below to be on the scene of action with his assistant engineer; perhaps I should not have allowed myself ...

Lord Mersey: Do you mean that he came up on the deck instead of going to his engine room?

Mr Haight: I do, my Lord. The engineer who was in charge of these engines stood before your Lordships a pitiable exhibition of absolute terror. Your Lordship may remember it; drops of cold perspiration formed on his forehead, ran down his face and dropped from his chin. He stood there for 15 minutes, the most pitiable exhibition of terror that I ever saw.

Mersey's response to this tirade was cryptic and, surprisingly for him, possibly even an attempt at tact: 'My eyesight is getting bad.'

There was another difference between this inquiry and the other three. A considerable number of the witnesses were not native English speakers. Captain Andersen, Chief Officer Toftnes and a few other crew members from *Storstad* were questioned in English but others required the assistance of a Norwegian interpreter.

There was one moment of light relief when a seaman from the ship failed to respond to the interpreter. Only then was it discovered that he was a Russian Finn. Luckily the interpreter was able to cobble together sufficient Finnish for his evidence to be heard. The pilots on the St Lawrence and some of the shore staff involved in the rescue were French Canadian but their English was sufficient for them to manage without an interpreter, although with a little difficulty in the cross-examination.

One witness, Third Officer Saxe of *Storstad,* posed problems when it was found that he was a German speaker who was struggling to cope with questions in English. Mersey himself came to the rescue by asking him questions in German to which he responded in kind, resulting in the following record of the proceedings;

Lord Mersey Let us go step by step. What does one long blast mean?

– (No answer).

Do you speak German?

– Jawohl, mein Herr.

(At this point Lord Mersey asked a few questions of the witness in the German language, and was answered in the same tongue).

Lord Mersey: The witness answers that one long blast means: I am going straight on my course.

The third day of the inquiry saw the worst of the blow-ups between Haight and Mersey. The context was Galway's evidence and the flare-up probably owed something to Mersey's resentment that Haight had foisted such an objectionable witness on him. Galway was a late addition to the list of witnesses because he had come forward about a supposed problem in the *Empress's* steering very late in the day, so late, in fact, that Haight had interviewed him in his hotel room just the night before. That was the cause of the row as Haight persisted in asking the witness to repeat what he had said the night before instead of giving his evidence directly to the court. After all, a witness could truthfully repeat in court lies that he had spoken the night before without committing perjury. This culminated in the following passage.

> *Mr Haight:* You said on your cross-examination that you had heard about their wanting you to go home on the *Caligarian* today. When did you hear about that?
>
> – I heard about it last night.
>
> From whom?
>
> – From the office lad,
>
> Did you make any statement to me last night on this subject?
>
> *Lord Mersey:* This is becoming a most curious examination. In all my life I have never heard any counsel ask a witness to repeat the statements that he made to him in private.
>
> *Mr Haight:* I thought that having been cross-examined by the other side as to what he had said –
>
> *Lord Mersey:* It is becoming to my mind, so utterly irregular that I really cannot interfere – you must finish it in your own way.
>
> *Mr Haight:* I do not care to press the question.
>
> *Lord Mersey:* If we were to pursue this to the end we should have you in the witness box and have you cross-examined and that, at all events, I am not going to allow.
>
> *Mr Haight:* It would not be a matter that I would object to. If anybody wishes to cross-examine me I would be willing to submit to it.
>
> *Lord Mersey:* Well then, you are a very odd man.

Both men having had time to reflect overnight, the fourth day began with apologies and statements of mutual respect. Haight said that: 'If I had had an opportunity to choose my words with a little more care I should have expressed myself quite differently.' Mersey responded:

> Mr. Haight, your conduct in this case hitherto, in my opinion, has been quite irreproachable. You have done your best, and in my opinion you have acted in the wisest way in the conduct of the cause which has been entrusted to you here. It may be – let me say it – that in my conduct of the inquiry yesterday I became a little heated because I did not like one of your witnesses, but do not attribute my observation to anything you said or did for whatever you said or did was done with proper care and in the best interests of the people you represent. I am glad you have given me an opportunity to say that.

We noted that during the course of the *Titanic* inquiry the Board of Trade had been asked to alter the terms of reference so as to include an additional question which then provided the basis for castigating the inaction of the *Californian*. The *Empress* tribunal agreed to a similar request to the Canadian Government, on this occasion to permit them to include a significant type of evidence omitted from the original set of questions. It related to the whistle signals that each of the ships had sounded while in the fog, signals that were of great importance in attempting to piece together the movements of the ships as they approached each other. Clearly, if a situation arose in which an inquiry felt, on the basis of testimony that it had heard, that the questions which it had been asked to follow up did not cover all of the relevant issues, it was entitled to draw this to the attention of the government and have the matter addressed. The change in the *Titanic* inquiry's terms of reference has been interpreted as part of a sinister conspiracy to attack Stanley Lord, but in procedural terms it was unexceptional.

In evaluating the findings of the tribunal one must be conscious that the inquiry had available the assistance of a team of expert assessors who brought to the tribunal's work knowledge of the conditions in the St Lawrence and an understanding of steamship handling that cannot now be replicated. With that caveat in mind it is now intended to approach the evaluation with a discussion of the issues as devoid of nautical terminology as possible.

We take up the story of the events of the early hours of 29 May 1914 given in Chapter 7 at the time that the *Empress* dropped her pilot about a mile off Father Point. She headed out from shore into the St Lawrence and between 15 and 20 minutes later the lookout reported the masthead lights of the

Storstad. Both of the surviving officers on the bridge at that time estimated
the distance at about 6 miles. The night was then clear and it seems that the
crew of *Storstad* spotted the masthead lights of the *Empress* at about the same
time. They gave a similar estimate of the distance. Having made the necessary
offing from the shore Kendall then turned the *Empress* through about 30°
onto her course down the St Lawrence. Shortly afterwards he observed the
Storstad carefully, measuring her compass bearing and noting that he could
now be sure that the *Empress* would pass her right side to right side. First
Officer Jones confirmed that he also believed this to be the position.

The evidence of the bridge personnel on the *Storstad* at this stage now
diverges. They observed the *Empress* change course, but were convinced from
their observations that the ships would pass left side to left side. As Aspinall
kept emphasising in his summing up, despite the difference in their observations of each other, neither crew seems to have had any concern about the
possible risk of collision at this stage. However, all then saw a fog bank rolling
out from the shore and very soon the lights of each ship gradually became
obscured from the other. One has to take all timings given from this point on
as being quite unreliable because there are no reference points, up until the
collision itself, to calibrate them. Human memories are very unreliable in esti-
mating time, even in situations where the memory is not being reconstructed
on the other side of a highly traumatic incident.

Henry Kendall decided, shortly after visibility had seriously deteriorated,
to stop his ship. He did so as quickly as possible by putting the engines into
reverse for around three minutes, although there is some doubt as to whether
this was sufficient to bring it to a complete halt. In the witness box he
explained his action as being one of caution, but he was not entirely convincing as to the reason why he considered such a dramatic act to be necessary
in a situation where the ships were on courses that would allow them to pass
each other in safety. Haight at the time and some later commentators have
questioned the legitimacy of his action in terms of the regulations governing
the avoidance of collisions at sea. Mersey ruled that it was acceptable in those
terms and was not unseamanlike, although he did question its wisdom. The
regulations advised captains to maintain existing courses and to proceed with
caution in fog, but there was also a catch-all clause that allowed a captain to
take whatever action was necessary in order to avoid a collision. What the regulations did require, however, was that any change in the situation of a ship in
fog should be clearly signalled using the ship's whistle. Kendall did this, blowing three short blasts on two occasions to indicate that his engines were in
reverse. There was little agreement amongst witnesses as to the whistle signals
that were blown by the two ships when in the fog, except so far as these two

sets of three short blasts were concerned. Everybody agreed that the *Empress* had made these signals, although the timing varied depending on the witness.

Alfred Toftnes, Chief Officer of *Storstad,* was in charge of the bridge when the *Empress's* signals were heard. Despite orders to call the captain in the event of fog he had not yet done so. Thomas Andersen was generally supportive of his Chief Officer in the witness box but he did agree with Aspinall that it had been a mistake on Toftnes' part not to call him to the bridge sooner. One has the impression, in reading Toftnes' evidence, that, although he seemed to become flustered under cross-examination and even a little nonplussed at times (which may have been the language problem), he was quite a strong, outgoing character who may have resented the implication that he was not capable of dealing with any situation that arose. Andersen was in the witness box for a shorter time; his answers were generally brief and to the point. Reading the text at this remove can give only a tentative impression of the man but he seems to have been a rather more introvert character than his Chief Officer and one wonders who might have been the more dominant personality on the ship.

Toftnes' reaction to the indication from the *Empress* that she was stopping was to stop his own engines; he did not reverse them so the ship carried on, gradually losing speed. At this stage the *Empress's* crew all maintained that they could hear the *Storstad's* whistle blowing to their right, as expected. Likewise, the *Storstad's* crew testified that they could hear the *Empress's* whistle coming from their left as they expected. It is not necessary to suppose that any of the witnesses were lying to explain this anomaly. Determining the direction from which sound is coming in fog is dreadfully difficult and there is ample evidence that we tend to assume that it is coming from the direction that we expect.

At some stage, before the ships saw each other just prior to the collision, the order was given by Toftnes to turn the ship's wheel. In the witness box he said that he was worried that the current coming downstream in the St Lawrence would push the ship's head to the left and decrease the distance between her and the *Empress* so he wanted to counteract this effect. This was not the initial explanation for the manoeuvre that was given in the inquiry. In his opening remarks Haight argued on behalf of the *Storstad* that the order to turn the wheel had been with the intention not of keeping the ship steady on her course against the influence of the current, but of turning her to the right to keep farther away from the *Empress.* Either Haight had been incorrectly briefed or the story changed in the course of the inquiry. This was a point picked up by Mersey that appears to have had some influence with the tribunal.

Irrespective of the motive for the order, all of the crew on the bridge testi-fied that the ship had slowed so much that turning the wheel had no effect;

the *Storstad* had lost steerage way. What happened next is one of the most puzzling aspects of the whole tragedy. Seeing that the ship had lost steering way and was not responding to the rudder, Third Officer Jacob Saxe, who was on watch with Toftnes, pushed the helmsman away from the wheel and swung it hard over. He said that he did so because she was not responding and he was worried that the current might catch her and swing her round. Under cross-examination he agreed that he had not been given any order to put the wheel hard over, nor had he any indication from the compass that the current was having any such effect. It seems rather like someone reacting in something of a panic when, up to that time, there had been no indication of any danger according to the evidence that he and the others had given. In order to give the ship steering way, Toftnes then ordered the engines to 'slow ahead' and at last called the captain to the bridge.

Thomas Andersen was in his day cabin when the call came. His wife was accompanying him on the ship and told reporters afterwards that her husband had seemed worried, sensing something was wrong. Toftnes had not hinted as much, telling Andersen only that visibility had deteriorated and the light at Father Point, their destination to pick up the pilot, was no longer in sight. He did not mention the proximity of another vessel. Andersen had scarcely reached the bridge when the first indication of real danger appeared as the *Empress's* masthead light was seen above the fog quickly followed by her other lights and silhouette on the port bow of the *Storstad*. Andersen testified that he just had time to confirm that the *Storstad* was still pointing in the direction of her original course before ordering the engines full astern, knowing even then that a collision could not be avoided.

Whatever way the fog was lying or moving, it seems that the *Storstad* saw the *Empress* first, as those on her bridge estimated the distance between them at that point at about 200 metres. On *Empress* they thought that when the *Storstad* was first seen she was only 30 metres away, although this estimate seems remarkably low. This was not the only point of disagreement; those on *Storstad* thought that the *Empress*, far from being stopped, was moving through the water quite quickly, those on the *Empress* that the *Storstad* was close to her full speed of 10 knots. Again, it is not necessary to assume anyone was lying in order to arrive at such conflicting evidence. Witnesses were reporting momentary impressions of events in the dark in swirling fog and it is highly likely that those impressions were extremely unreliable. One must be a little suspicious at the degree of uniformity of the evidence within each ship, for there were opportunities for witnesses to chat amongst themselves and, if not to collude in falsehood, at least to reinforce in discussion a dominant impression that each then become convinced was his own. We know now more than was understood in the early part of the twentieth century about group dynamics and how suggestible we all are in arriving at agreed outcomes and convincing ourselves that these were our own beliefs from the beginning.

Whatever the speed of either ship, just a few seconds later the two collided. The bow of the *Storstad* travelled around 5 metres into the hull of the *Empress* almost in the middle of her right side and with dire consequences. It is important to reflect on how the tribunal judged the events up to this point. As we have seen, both Aspinall and Haight argued that only a change of course by one ship in the fog could have caused the collision. No evidence came from the *Empress* of any movement of the wheel or any indication of her changing the way that she was pointing, even after she came to a halt, assuming that she did so. Haight could offer no explanation as to why she might have altered course deliberately. He chose instead to produce evidence of problems with the *Empress's* steering gear that might have led to an involuntary change of course to which no-one on the ship was admitting. This was one of the areas in which he probably over-reached himself as he did not restrict his argument to one explanation of this steering problem but rather argued the case for three different explanations. Two years after being in service the *Empress* had had her rudder enlarged and a similar operation had been carried out on her sister ship the *Empress of Britain*. Haight argued, quite correctly, that this indicated a need to improve the steering qualities of the ships. Aspinall responded by saying that the rudder alterations had had the desired effect and that no further problem with the steering had been noted since. Haight then turned to the hydraulically operated telemotor steering system as a source of problems. One difficulty with presenting his evidence was the complete lack of understanding amongst the lawyers, the bench, or even some of the witnesses, as to how such a system worked. All get full marks for persistence; the transcript of this evidence runs to many pages and it is not easy reading. Haight tried to show that leaking fluid from a system, which, he claimed, with little evidence, might have been poorly maintained, could cause the ship to yaw about and not keep to a straight course. His called as witnesses representatives of the crew and the pilot of another Norwegian collier, the *Alden*, that the *Empress* had passed on the way down the St Lawrence that night. They maintained that the *Empress* had been swinging about erratically on her course but their evidence was contradicted by the pilot on board the *Empress*.

The now notorious Galway was called to give evidence that the *Empress's* steering gear was also prone to jamming. Galway said that when he had been on watch prior to midnight the steering had jammed briefly once and that when he went off watch he had warned both his successor at the wheel and the pilot. Both men flatly denied any such warning. If Haight appeared to be clutching at multiple straws in presenting his evidence on the steering, he tried in his summing up to hold tight to just one of them and magnify its significance. He presented a scenario in which, at the point just prior to the fog obscuring vision when the *Empress* had changed course, the steering had jammed, causing her to swing much too far to the right. Wrenching the wheel over eventually corrected the jam only to send the ship careering off to the left, right across the bows of the approaching *Storstad*. He went so far at this point as to suggest that Kendall was in a state of complete panic and had lost control of himself as well as his ship. These theatricals might have been the right approach for a New York jury but clearly did not have the desired effect on an elderly English judge and his learned Canadian colleagues. Kendall had come across as the sort who stayed calm in a crisis. We know from his earlier history (Chapter 6) that he had dealt with a number of dangerous situations in his life and the court's impression of him does not seem inconsistent with that history.

Aspinall argued his case in a more prosaic fashion, concentrating on a rather simpler argument that, despite protestations to the contrary from Andersen and the other members of the *Storstad* crew, the turning of the *Storstad's* wheel did alter her heading and that she was carrying sufficient forward motion, particularly once her engines resumed at slow ahead, to take her into the side of the *Empress*. This was the story that the tribunal accepted, although it still leaves some big questions unanswered. Perhaps the biggest was the fact that those on the *Storstad* were so emphatic that what they saw convinced them that the *Empress* would pass left side to left side and not, as those on the *Empress* maintained, right side to right side. At night, of course, observations depend on interpreting the lights that are seen. In this case Toftnes and Saxe both were adamant that, after the *Empress* made her change of course to head down river, they could see her red, left side, navigation light. Kendall and Jones were equally adamant that they were showing the *Storstad* their green, right side, light. Haight argued that 'his' crew were right; Aspinall tried to take the issue out of the equation by maintaining that, either way, the ships would have passed safely had not one of them changed course in the fog. What might the explanation be, given that it would seem that this might just be the crucial mistake that resulted in the tragedy? One explanation of course was Haight's supposed problem with the steering gear that caused the ship to weave. If, in making the change of course, the inadequacy of the rudder, or depletion of hydraulic fluid in the telemotor system, had caused the *Empress* to turn too far for a while showing her red light to the *Storstad*, the correction being obscured as the fog came down, then this would explain the discrepancy. However, Aspinall's defence of the steering gear on the *Empress* was quite robust and this explanation lacks credibility in the absence of better supporting evidence.

New helmsman on ships mostly make the error of oversteering. When ordered to alter course they swing the wheel over to start the turn, but fail to straighten up in time. The ship then swings past the desired course and a similar error of overcorrection leads to the sort of serpentine wake that gives officers of the watch nightmares. The author can testify to this, having been justly on the receiving end of abuse more than once from an officer of the watch on a sailing ship for exactly that offence. The quartermaster on the helm of the *Empress* was not a novice, but it is possible that he suffered a momentary lapse of concentration. It is a plausible explanation as an excess turn of only around 5° would have been sufficient to show the red light to the oncoming *Storstad* at least briefly. If that is indeed what happened and Toftnes and his colleagues had reason to believe that the ships would pass left side to left side, then making sure that the *Storstad* did not deviate at all towards her left made sense. Toftnes might have ordered the wheel turned, as Haight originally suggested, to increase the passing distance of the two ships although, if he did, he failed to indicate on his whistle that he was doing so. It seems a terrible thing to suggest that over a thousand people may have died as a result of a momentary lapse on the part of a helmsman, but it is a possibility that cannot entirely be ruled out.

Two aspects of events deserve particular attention at this stage. One is the decision by Kendall suddenly to throw his engines into reverse to stop the ship. The second is the suggestion of panic by Saxe on the bridge of *Storstad* before any real danger was apparent. The puzzling thing about Kendall's decision was not so much the fact that he made it but his reticence in explaining it in the witness box. Was there a reason other than his extreme caution that he did not want fully to share with the inquiry? Two possibilities present themselves. One is that he was aware of *Empress* having wavered on her turn and realised that this might have caused some confusion on the other ship. The other, probably more likely, is that he felt that the passing distance between the ships was safe enough in clear visibility but that there was not a sufficient margin of safety in foggy conditions. One can see why he might have been reluctant to share the former possibility with the court, but the second seems relatively innocuous. Perhaps he thought that it might not reflect too well on his seamanship in making his 30° turn when he did.

Saxe's behaviour in pushing the quartermaster away from the wheel and turning it to its maximum extent, without any order to do so, on the face of it seems even less explicable. Had he heard the *Empress's* whistle again and suddenly realised that it was not coming from the expected direction? Is it possible that he had even heard the sound of the other ship's machinery (her generators for example) which told him she was much closer than she should have been? Given the trauma that ensued soon afterwards, it is quite possible that he simply forgot the real reason for what he did and the story he gave the court of holding the ship against the current was the one that he then believed.

The issue that occupied more of the tribunal's time than any other was the speed with which the *Empress* sank immediately after the collision. There was lengthy evidence given concerning the ship's structure. When the ships came together, Kendall called through a megaphone to tell Andersen to keep his engines going ahead so as to hold the *Storstad* in the hole she had created, thereby reducing the inflow of water into the *Empress.* Andersen claimed that he had already given the order to go full ahead even before he heard Kendall shouting. No reply was heard on the *Empress*, possibly because Andersen had no megaphone, and within a few moments the ships separated as the *Storstad* twisted around and slid backwards down the right side of the *Empress.* Kendall maintained that the separation happened because Andersen had failed to respond. Andersen said that he had done his best but that the forward motion of the other ship had caused his to twist out of the hole. The argument between the lawyers on this point was protracted and probably pointless. It was important to Aspinall to establish that his ship was at rest when the collier had crashed into her. It was vital for Haight's case that the *Empress* was moving as it was her erratic movements that he blamed for the collision. Each lawyer produced an expert witness and each of the two experts proposed a different angle for the collision, Aspinall's that it had taken place almost at right angles, Haight's that the ships had been at an angle of only 40°. If Haight's expert was right about the angle (and he may well have been) then it actually would provide an explanation for the parting of the ships that did not require the *Empress* to be moving. If the collision took place at a narrower angle, the *Empress* would have absorbed the component of the *Storstad's* momentum that was driving her into the *Empress* but not the lateral component along the side of the *Empress.* With the *Storstad's* bows being stopped, her stern would then have swung on down the *Empress's* side until the two separated. The damage to the *Storstad's* bow was consistent with that scenario. Haight seems to have sensed that his own expert's evidence as to the angle of the collision was actually working against his desire to prove the *Empress* to be at fault, because in his summing up he referenced his argument to Aspinall's assumption of a collision angle of about 80°, at which angle there would be little lateral momentum to effect a separation; only movement on the part of the *Empress* could explain it.

After the separation, with fog still obscuring the scene, Andersen first ensured that his own ship was seaworthy and then brought her around in a circle to a position as close as he felt he could safely go to the sinking *Empress*. He launched the ship's lifeboats as quickly as possible and sent them away to pick people up from the water whose shouts they could already hear. From that point on his crew (including his wife) worked tirelessly to rescue and care for as many as possible, the *Storstad's* boats making a number of trips to fill up with survivors and bringing them back to such care as those on the *Storstad* were capable of giving them. The few of the *Empress's* boats that got away from her before she sank also brought some survivors to the *Storstad*, others went to the rescue ships once they arrived on the scene.

Only half a dozen boats got away from the *Empress*. Because of the rapid and severe list that she developed the boats on the port side were useless. Some even fell down across the deck of the ship injuring and possibly killing some people. On the starboard side the boats that were released were mostly dropped almost empty into the sea with few on board other than their allocated crew. This was done deliberately because of the rapidly deteriorating situation on the ship; their crews were instructed to pick survivors up from the water. Most of those who survived were picked up in this way either by the *Empress's* boats or those which rowed across from the *Storstad*. Most of the boats made several trips, their crews becoming exhausted in the process. Numbers rescued decreased rapidly with each trip, but initially were of the order of 50 or so. Contrast that scene with the situation when the *Titanic* sank and people were likewise being thrown into the sea. Third Officer Pitman was in boat No 5 and after leaving *Titanic* the half-filled boat sat off about 100 yards distant. This is what Pitman said about going back to pick up people struggling in the water:

As the *Titanic* sank and immediately after did you hear any screams?
— Immediately after she sank? Yes?
—Yes.
Were you able to go in the direction of the screams and render any assistance?
— I did not go.
But do you think you could have gone? I am not suggesting anything; I only want to get the facts from you. Do you think it would have been safe or reasonable to go?
— I do not.
What is your reason?
— Well, there was such a mass of people in the water we should have been swamped.
In your view you had a sufficient number of people on your boat. Is that so?
— No, but I had too many in the boat to go back to the wreck.

In Mersey's report on the loss of the *Titanic* he quite rightly expressed concern about the behaviour of those in the boats failing to pull people from the water, although his language was probably too measured to have the impact that it should have had. He was appropriately complementary about the work of the boats' crews in saving as many as possible from the wreck of the *Empress*.

Our last mention of Henry Kendall was when he was shouting across with the megaphone to the *Storstad*. Once the separation had occurred he considered the possibility of beaching, only to find himself in a similar position to Will Turner on *Lusitania* almost exactly a year later. The steam lines had been cut and there was no power for the engines. All that was left to do was to try to save as many lives as possible. He was, however, criticised at the inquiry on two counts. The first was that the order to close all watertight doors was not given until the collision had taken place. While this was not a breach of existing procedures, the view was expressed by Haight that a more prudent captain would have closed them when the fog appeared. This was the recommendation of the tribunal; in future all ships were advised to close watertight doors below bulkhead level in fog. It was suggested that they also be closed at night, along with all portholes below the same level. That was the second point of criticism of Kendall; the speed with which the ship sank was partly attributed to the fact that some of the portholes were open low down on the ship, something that was against the ship's own regulations. There was a suggestion that discipline was not sufficiently strict in enforcing that regulation, although the difficulty of doing so on a warm evening was recognised. Neither of these criticisms was included in the tribunal's report.

Captain Kendall, therefore, was almost given a clean sheet (bar slightly negative remarks about his changing course when he did and his caution in stopping his ship) and was exonerated from responsibility for the collision and for the loss of life that ensued. Neither did Andersen suffer any direct criticism, but his ship was found to have been at fault and there was an implication that he was not as fully in command as he should have been. Toftnes was found to have been negligent in turning the *Storstad's* wheel. Were these findings reasonable on the basis of the evidence presented? Like much of Mersey's work in this area there is an unjustifiable certainty about the way that the findings are expressed. It is as if no other explanation is now possible once he has arrived at his conclusions. However, expressed with more caution as a consequence of the conflicts in the evidence, what the tribunal concluded seems to be the most likely explanation for the disaster. It is necessary to set aside more evidence to arrive at any other explanation but Mersey and his colleagues too lightly dismissed the evidence of both Toftnes and Saxe regarding the sighting of the *Empress's* red sidelight. In the report they are simply described as mistaken, only because what they claimed does not fit in with the inquiry's preferred explanation. The tribunal should, at least, have allowed for the possibility that Toftnes and Saxe were correct in what they saw, even if it led to an erroneous assumption about the *Empress's* intention. Perhaps Newcombe was right at least in his suggestion that there was blame on both sides, a possibility that Aspinall and Haight had placed off limits in deciding how their personal jousting match was to be played.

Only one individual in all four disasters considered in this book was wise before the event, rather than after. It was reported that the ship's cat Emmy, who had never once missed a voyage, repeatedly tried to escape near the departure of the *Empress* on 28 May. The crew could not coax her aboard and the *Empress* departed without her. Apparently Emmy watched the ship sail away from Quebec City sitting on the roof of the shed at Pier 27, which would later temporarily house the dead pulled from the river after the *Empress* went down.

13

FREDERICK DAVIES AND WILL TURNER

The two inquiries into the wartime sinkings were both considerably shorter than those into the peacetime accidents. Those numbers do not provide a statistically significant sample, but even this very limited correlation may have had a reason. Much of the focus in the peacetime inquiries was on establishing the cause of the accidents and allocating blame. In the cases of the *Falaba* and *Lusitania* the causes of the sinkings were not in question and the allocation of the principal blame by a British inquiry under the circumstances could be taken for granted. However, there was still a question to be asked as to whether or not the actions of those on the two ships might have in some way contributed to their loss. Equally, it was necessary to ask if some additional actions might have been taken that would have improved the outcome.

The *Falaba* inquiry began on 20 May 1915 and had just four sittings. A total of 46 witnesses were heard. The four Assessors sitting with Mersey were the same four who were to sit with him through the *Lusitania* inquiry a few weeks later. It is the only inquiry in which neither of the two captains involved gave evidence. The inquiry took place at Caxton Hall in London and the report was published on 8 July, after the evidence of the *Lusitania* witnesses had been heard. The Solicitor-General, Sir Stanley Buckmaster, represented the Board of Trade for the first two days of the inquiry before being elevated to the post of Lord Chancellor, the role being continued in the other two sessions by the existing junior counsel. None of these inquiries would be complete without the presence of Butler Aspinall and, in this case, he represented the ship's owners, Elder Dempster, as well as the senior surviving member of the crew, Chief Officer Baxter and the company's Marine Superintendent, Fred Davies' brother-in-law Captain Thompson. The relatives of Captain Davies paid for their own barrister to be present on his behalf.

There was only one explicit reference to the *Lusitania* during the course of the inquiry. The witness who naively explained that he believed that the Germans only wanted to look at the ship's papers then incongruously pointed out that the *Lusitania* had been given no warning whatsoever. Mersey slapped him down by stating that he was not now 'trying the *Lusitania*'. It is apparent, however, in reading the transcript of the *Falaba* inquiry, that Mersey seems at times distracted. In the proceedings of all four inquiries there were examples of Mersey losing the thread of an argument by counsel or the examination of a witness, sometimes because of his deafness, sometimes because of his lack of nautical or technical knowledge, sometimes because what he was listening to did not actually make sense. In this inquiry there are a number of occasions when his interventions indicate that he has been missing quite significant stretches of input. It would hardly be surprising if the forthcoming *Lusitania* 'trial' were pressing on his mind.

Mersey and Buckmaster had an interesting exchange following the evidence given by one passenger who had asked to be allowed to give his evidence in his own words unprompted by questions. Mersey was unimpressed, but Buckmaster argued in support:

> *The Commissioner:* We had one gentleman here yesterday who asked to be allowed to tell his story in his own way. I said he might, and he did. He told us a very great deal of what we did not want to know and which was quite immaterial. Once you get a witness telling his story in his own way he will tell you the colour of his coat and how his hair had been brushed and all sorts of things.
>
> *The Solicitor-General:* I am as keenly alive to that as any one, but I can see something on the other side. These people have been in peril of their lives and they do not understand that matters which are of very real importance to them are matters which, for the purposes of this Inquiry, we do not want to know about.
>
> *The Commissioner:* You must as far as possible let them have their say.
>
> *The Solicitor-General:* I am obliged to your Lordship.
>
> The next witness, Mr. T. D. Woolley was sworn.
>
> *The Commissioner:* Now, Sir, will you tell us all you want to tell us?
>
> – I would rather have questions asked me.
>
> *The Commissioner:* I think you are quite right.

The *Lusitania* inquiry began on Tuesday 15 June 1915 in the Central Hall, Westminster. It lasted 5 days and there were just 36 witnesses. Part of the inquiry was heard in camera owing to the sensitive nature of the evidence. For obvious reasons, given the strategic political issues that the case raised, the cast of the *Lusitania* inquiry included some famous names. Leaving aside Mersey himself, who was quite well known as a result of the *Titanic* inquiry but probably not a name recognised in every household, there was the Attorney General, Sir Edward Carson representing the Board of Trade with the recently appointed Sir Frederick (F.E.) Smith, the Solicitor General. Smith was an extrovert, enormously self-confident and assured, with acknowledged courtroom charisma.

Carson's position as Attorney General was remarkable considering his recent political history. Less than a year before the *Lusitania* sinking he had been the political leader of what had threatened to become the most serious armed rebellion against the crown since Bonnie Prince Charlie in 1745. With large quantities of arms in the hands of the Ulster Loyalists and a threatened mutiny by sections of the British Army, Carson was set to create serious trouble for the government until the First World War intervened and the Irish problem was postponed for another day. His dramatic transition from rebel leader (even a 'loyal' one) to the senior law officer of the Crown was more reminiscent of events in the courts of the Tudor monarchs than in a twentieth century democracy. In Mersey's short parliamentary career, his party affiliation had been with the Liberal Unionists so we can assume that there was no frisson of political difference between him and the Attorney General.

Appearing for Cunard was the ubiquitous Butler Aspinall KC, by now regarded as a leading specialist in the field of maritime law. One of the questions it is fair to ask (although impossible to answer with any authority) is the extent to which a rapport had developed between Mersey and Butler Aspinall and the effect such an understanding might have had on the outcome. Aspinall had successfully represented the government interest in the *Titanic* inquiry in 1912 and Mersey had, in 1914, found that his defence of Henry Kendall's handling of the *Empress of Ireland* had been wholly convincing. As we shall see, his defence of the Elder Dempster interest in the case of the *Falaba* was likewise successful in persuading Mersey, in that case entirely in the face of the evidence. Aspinall had been given permission by Cunard to represent the interests of Will Turner in the *Lusitania* inquiry as well as the company interests. Was Mersey as swayed by the arguments that he heard from the same man yet again in defence of Turner?

The *Lusitania* inquiry might also have been relatively brief because the government wanted it so. Carson gave the distinct impression he was seeking brevity. In his opening statement he suggested that the 21 questions that made up Mersey's brief from the Board of Trade could effectively be reduced to just two. Did the navigation of the ship, in the light of Admiralty instructions, contribute to the disaster? Was everything done that could have been done to save life once the ship had been torpedoed? These are certainly the pertinent issues, particularly so far as Captain Turner is concerned; we are not addressing matters of strategic interest in relation to the war nor will we be adding to the debate on what level of conspiracy there may or may not have been in connection with the 'Lusitania incident'. We can therefore be content to accept Carson's narrowing of the focus, even if others see it as one element of an attempted cover-up.

Carson's two questions can also be used to assess the fundamentals of the Falaba inquiry. Was Davies' handling of his ship a contributory factor in its loss and was the evacuation of the ship as successful as it could have been in the circumstances? It makes sense to consider the first question for both Davies and Turner and then move on and do likewise for the second. In doing so the differences between the two incidents will be apparent and it will be of interest to consider whether or not Mersey's findings reflected those differences.

Prior to the sighting of the submarine, the Falaba was holding a steady course. Although in a known danger zone for submarines, Davies was not following Admiralty advice by zigzagging at irregular intervals because the advice had not yet been issued. Had von Forstner mounted an attack by torpedo without warning, as did Schwieger, the absence of zigzagging might have been important. However, as the Falaba was approached on the surface by U-28 in clear sight, it was immaterial. There is therefore no reference to zigzagging in the report. Once the submarine had been spotted, it was correctly assumed to be German and Davies did as his instructions told him to do. He turned away from the submarine and increased to maximum speed, sending a wireless message giving his position and the nature of the threat. The possibility of turning towards the submarine to ram it, the alternative Admiralty option, appears not to have been seriously considered, unsurprisingly given the fact that the ship was carrying passengers. Mersey made no comment about these actions in the report, simply referring to them in court as sound common sense. He also accepted without question the stopping of the ship once it was clear that escape was impossible.

Davies' attempt to run away from the submarine was fairly perfunctory. His call for full speed appears not to have had much effect as the ship was close to that anyway and he stopped when von Forstner threatened to open fire. To have continued was futile and would have put his passengers in immediate danger. Any shots would in all likelihood have caused casualties.

So far as the first question was concerned, Fred Davies was therefore entirely in the clear and it would be hard to dispute that finding. The one issue that might be raised was in relation to the wireless message. Sending the message was in accordance with Admiralty advice but was it really in the interests of the passengers on the *Falaba?* There was only one other ship in sight at the time. It was a small steam fishing drifter without either armament or means to summon help. Davies must have known that even if his wireless message succeeded in bringing a warship on the scene, his ship would have been long destroyed and the submarine departed. Knowing that the message had been sent, however, put pressure on those in the submarine to get the job done quickly and get as far from the scene as possible before help arrived. Visibility from the low height of a submarine conning tower is much more restricted than from the bridge of a substantial cargo liner. Von Forstner would have had little warning of the arrival of a destroyer. The Germans could have argued also that a wireless message aimed at bringing a warship to the scene put the *Falaba* outside the terms of the Cruiser Rules and made her eligible to be sunk without any further efforts to save those on board. However, it is vital to remember that this incident took place in the first few months of submarine warfare and of the first war in which wireless had been available on merchant ships. In the circumstances it is difficult to envisage Davies not sending that wireless message and impossible to guess how the result might have been altered, if at all, had he kept radio silence.

For Turner the issues that were raised about his handling of the *Lusitania* were much more complex and occupied a considerable amount of the inquiry's time. Questions had been asked in the press shortly after the sinking about the *Lusitania*'s course and speed, questions that were the result of some briefing of journalists by the Admiralty. Churchill himself, First Lord of the Admiralty at the time, was party to serious criticism of Turner in private and even gave hints of it in Parliament. The First Sea Lord, Admiral 'Jacky' Fisher was apoplectic and virtually demanded Turner's head on a plate, describing him as traitorous. This disgraceful outburst probably revealed more about Fisher's own mental instability at the time than the culpability of Will Turner. There were however significant and more rationally argued criticisms of Turner from lower levels within the Admiralty, particularly from within Naval Intelligence. Some of the criticism was obviously motivated by self-defence. Was it not the job of the most powerful navy in the world to protect the country's ships, especially those carrying large numbers of vulnerable passengers? How had such a failure of protection occurred – was poor intelligence to blame? Turner has frequently been described as the scapegoat, with some justification given the nature of the briefing against him. Nonetheless, given the evidence at the inquiry, there were real questions to be asked about the wisdom of Turner's decisions on the morning of the sinking.

The inquiry had a considerable amount of information before it concerning the events of 7 May 1915. There was evidence about the general advice to mariners given by the Admiralty in relation to the submarine menace as well as specific warnings issued about the situation at that time in the area the ship was passing through. Aspinall maintained that there was a tension between the two; Turner, he claimed, by obeying the general instructions would have increased his risk in relation to the specific warnings. F.E. Smith, who led the attack on Turner by the Board of Trade, argued that he had not used the options available to him and might have avoided the submarine if he had done so.

There was a second source of tension, one that Turner relied on in his defence, (which we identified back in Chapter 3) and which concerned the balance between the normal peacetime risks to a ship and the additional ones resulting from war. The need to navigate the ship safely as it completed the crossing of the Atlantic and approached land meant that an accurate determination of position was required. Turner argued that, on the morning of the 7 May he had to approach close enough to the Old Head of Kinsale to complete what is called a 'four-point bearing'. He pointed out that he remained at least ten miles farther out from the headland than he would in peacetime. Smith countered by suggesting that it was quite possible for Turner to have used other methods of fixing his position that did not require such a close approach to land.

The specific criticisms of Turner were that he ignored Admiralty advice by approaching land near a headland, that he did not zigzag and that he failed fully to exploit the speed of the ship as a means of protection. Aspinall's arguments in rebutting the first two of these criticisms were linked as the following passage demonstrated:

> *Butler Aspinall* ... Mr. Bestic [the Junior Third Officer], and those associated with him, were at the time in question doing what was perfectly legitimate, I submit, and perfectly proper, engaged in taking a 4-point bearing, and it was during that half an hour that the catastrophe happens. If they had been zigzagging, they could not have carried out the operation of taking the 4-point bearing.
> *The Commissioner:* Is that so?
> *Admiral Inglefield:* Yes. They must run steady on a direct course at a regular speed while the bearing is being taken.
> *The Commissioner:* So that the zigzagging would have defeated that object.
> *Mr. Butler Aspinall:* It would have defeated a legitimate operation in navigation.

Despite the apparent support given to Aspinall's argument by the Admiral, it was really quite specious on two counts. Firstly, it was not necessary, as the Solicitor-General pointed out, for Turner to have used that particular method of fixing his position. He could have achieved his objective without the necessity of keeping the ship on a steady course for an extended period. Turner was quite right in maintaining that he required assurance as to his position and it was normal practice in peacetime for him to approach the Old Head much closer. No doubt he then habitually used that headland to carry out a four-point fix. That procedure may well have been common to many of the Atlantic liner captains approaching the St George's Channel. Turner evidently felt that keeping an additional ten miles out to sea was sufficient to counter the submarine risk and then carried on as normal. On the previous wartime voyage in which he had been in command the ship had passed the Old Head at this same distance. As we have already seen with Captain Smith on *Titanic*, there was a powerful inclination to stick closely to standard practice irrespective of warnings received. In fact, had Turner taken the *Lusitania* a few miles farther out to sea, he might only have saved Schwieger the trouble of bringing U-20 closer inshore to get lined up for the shot.

Much was made at the inquiry and much has been made since of Turner's reaction to the warnings about submarine activity 20 miles south of Conninbeg lightship, warnings which resulted from Schwieger's activities the day before. Turner had not been told either that the reported activity was 24 hours previously or that it had resulted in the sinking of two ships. In one sense this is something of a red-herring because, although Turner had decided what he was going to do in response to the warnings, the attack by U-20 came before he took any action. There was still some 80 miles to go before he hit the supposed danger zone. It has been suggested that he came closer to the Old Head because he was intending to take an inshore course as he approached Conninbeg, to stay away from the supposed submarine lurking 20 miles out. However, as already noted, his distance off the Old Head was the same on this trip as it had been on the previous one when there had been no similar warnings. Furthermore, the 18-knot speed of the *Lusitania* had been set before the warning was received.

The second reason for Aspinall's argument being groundless was that Turner had not been zigzagging prior to taking the four-point fix and, it seemed, had no intention of doing so when it was completed. The fact that the ship was torpedoed during that procedure was entirely coincidental. The questioning of Turner in camera about his decision not to zigzag is one of the most crucial passages in the inquiry and so a lengthy extract (edited to omit some duplication) is given below to illustrate the nature of the questioning, Mersey's own part in the process and the character of Turner's responses. Carson, the Attorney General, has rightly been criticised for his overly forthright grilling of a man who was clearly very disturbed by what he had suffered and by the loss of so many of his close colleagues. At the same time, Haight's cross-examination of a similarly distressed Kendall had also been very direct and somewhat harassing. The general rule seems to have been to let the dead rest in peace but to lean heavily on the living.

The Attorney General: Now, tell me this. Did you zigzag the boat?
– No.
You were told to do that?
– I understood it was only when you saw a submarine that you should zigzag.
You had information that there were submarines about, and the instructions to you were to zigzag.
The Commissioner: And I think the reason is stated, too.
The Attorney General: Yes, my Lord. *(To the Witness):* You told me you read this: 'War experience has shown that fast steamers can considerably reduce the chance of a successful submarine attack by zigzagging – that is to say, altering course at short and irregular intervals, say ten minutes to half an hour. This course is invariably adopted by warships when cruising in an area known to be infested by submarines.' Did you zigzag?
– No
Why?
– Because I did not think it was necessary until I saw a submarine.
You were told zigzagging was a safeguard; you were told submarines were infesting the southern part of the Irish coast; you had plenty of time in hand, and you did not obey the orders?
– I did not.
You would have plenty of time. I understand zigzagging takes more time, but why did not you zigzag?
– Because I thought it was not necessary until I saw a submarine.
The Commissioner: But the whole point of that is that it is the submarine that is looking at you?
–Yes.
The Commissioner: And if you are zigzagging you confuse him and put him into difficulties?
The Attorney-General: How could you think that, because this is very clear: 'War experience has shown that fast steamers can considerably reduce the chance of a successful submarine attack by zigzagging' – nothing about when you see the submarine. You see, when you are torpedoed it is too late?
– Of course it is.
Do not you see now that you really disobeyed a very important instruction?
– (No answer.)

Turner later accepted that he had 'mis-read' the Admiralty advice. At a different point in the inquiry, Mersey himself picked up the logical flaw in Turner's
evidence. As he was at this time finalising the report of the *Falaba* inquiry, it
was perhaps natural that he would be the one to point out that Admiralty
advice to ships when a submarine was spotted was not to zigzag but to turn
away at maximum speed – exactly as the *Falaba* had done – or to turn towards
the submarine to ram it. Turner came across as someone who had not properly assimilated the thinking behind the Admiralty advice. It is worth pointing
out that in the case of the zigzagging instructions, he had had very little time
to consider them before his ship was torpedoed. They had only been issued
the day before the ship left Liverpool on the outward voyage and were not
drawn specifically to his attention at that time. It has been suggested that
Carson bullied him into agreeing that he had read a document that, in fact,
he had never seen, but Turner confirmed in the much friendlier questioning
by Aspinall that he had read it and never subsequently indicated otherwise. It
seems fair to assume that he had actually read the Admiralty advice to zigzag
but possibly had not given it the attention it deserved.

Although Mersey's was the only formal inquiry into the sinking of the
Lusitania there were other court proceedings at a later date in America resulting from claims for damages against Cunard. UK witnesses were not asked
to put themselves at risk by travelling across the Atlantic and depositions
were taken, including cross-examinations, in London in mid-1917. Naturally
Turner was one of the crucial witnesses and he was again questioned about
his decisions that morning, including the fact that he had not been zigzagging. His responses differed to those of two years earlier in that he no
longer claimed to have mis-read the instructions, interpreting them as only
applying after a submarine had been spotted. Instead, he maintained that he
thought them not to apply to a fast ship such as his, which is rather odd as
the Admiralty wording specifically indicated that zigzagging was particularly
effective in the case of faster ships. He also maintained that Admiralty advice
was little more than helpful suggestions to masters which they were under
no obligation to observe. Turner, probably with some degree of satisfaction,
pointed out that he had been torpedoed a second time when the *Ivernia* had
been sunk at the end of 1916 and he had been zigzagging at the time. There
were other captains who gave evidence to the American court in support
of Turner, indicating that few of their peers had paid any attention to the
advice on zigzagging when it had been issued. Indeed some had described it
as 'a joke'.

The zigzagging issue also connects through to the third element of the
criticism levelled at Turner, that of the 'slow' speed at which the ship was trav-

elling when it was hit. The ship, with its boiler capacity reduced deliberately by Cunard to save coal and so money, was capable of 21 knots but was only doing 18 knots when spotted by Schwieger. The Chairman of Cunard, Albert Booth, was first of all questioned about the reduction in boiler capacity and its effect on the ship's speed:

> *The Attorney General:* With that boiler power you have told us, and we have been told that they got an average maximum speed of about 21 knots?
> – That is right.
> Is that as fast or faster than most Atlantic-going steamers?
> – That is considerably faster than any Atlantic steamer which was running during last winter or is running now.

The inquiry seemed satisfied by Booth's point that 21 knots was faster than any other ship. Perhaps it should not have been. The level of safety depended on the absolute speed, not the speed relative to other ships. A ship travelling at 25 knots was safer than one travelling at 21 knots. There are echoes here of the 'maximum speed' issue as *Titanic* approached the ice. The real point was nothing to do with whether or not it was the fastest that the ship could go, it was the relationship of the absolute speed to the capacity of lookouts to spot things ahead that mattered. In the case of a submarine attack, the faster a target is moving the lower the chances of hitting it. Probability is all important here. Neither speed nor zigzagging offer any absolute defence against torpedoes. Each reduces the statistical probability of a strike somewhat and the combination of the two has even greater effect. Add an escort and the probability is reduced even further. Examples can still be found, nonetheless, of fast, zigzagging ships with escorts being torpedoed.

Booth was also questioned about Turner's decision not to use even the full speed he did have available and he defended his employee by arguing that, prior to the sinking of the *Lusitania,* no ship travelling at even 14 knots had been 'caught' by a submarine. Mersey immediately responded by (incorrectly) pointing out that the *Falaba* had been travelling at above that speed when caught by U-28. Booth had, however, provided an insight into thinking in Cunard, and probably other shipping lines as well. The primitive state of submarine technology and experience of it at work up to that point had created a sense, if not of invulnerability, at least of very limited risk. Despite the blustering of the German government in the adverts they had placed in the American press, the upper echelons of Cunard did not really believe that large, fast liners were seriously threatened by the new weapons. Hence Turner had given little more than perfunctory attention to Admiralty advice on the matter and had made only the minimum concession in his navigation to the supposed risk. One may wonder, in fact, how much he knew about the capabilities of submarines and how they operated. It is likely that a landlubber who has watched the film *Das Boot* has a better understanding of submarine operations than did Will Turner.

Turner's explanation of his decision to stick at 18 knots superficially seemed a good one because it did appear to be a response to one aspect of Admiralty advice. Captains had been told to try to arrive at their destination port at night and at a state of tide that allowed them to enter immediately. Turner had calculated that a steady 18 knots would bring him to the Mersey Bar just as the sun was about to rise and with water enough to allow him to cross it. F E Smith correctly pointed out that the time could just as well have been managed by zigzagging at greater speed. An erratic zigzag pattern at 21 knots would have taken much the same time to reach the Bar as 18 knots on a steady course. Aspinall defended Turner, rather lamely, by suggesting that zigzagging caused the ship to cover a slightly greater area and thus marginally increased the risk of being spotted by a submarine. As the extract given previously indicated, it is not the avoidance of being spotted that is the object of zigzagging.

In recording the events of 7 May in Chapter 8 we mentioned that, just before coming across the *Lusitania*, Schwieger had seen the cruiser HMS *Juno*. Although not a modern ship, sinking her would have made a fine ending to Schwieger's patrol. Despite being in range, Schwieger could not attack because the cruiser was travelling at speed and was zigzagging. This combination of speed and erratic changes of course had been recognised quickly as making an important contribution to defence against submarine attack and it remained so right through the Second World War. The two great Cunard liners of that period, the *Queen Mary* and the *Queen Elizabeth,* spent most of that war crossing the Atlantic, not in convoy, but travelling very fast and zigzagging, albeit with a heavy escort to reduce the probability of a successful attack even further. It was a successful ploy, the only loss of life coming from a collision between the *Queen Mary* and her escorting cruiser that may have resulted from confusion over the zigzag pattern. While recognising the benefit of hindsight, it does seem to be the case that, had Turner maintained the 21 knots his ship was capable of and steered an irregular zigzag pattern, it is less probable that Schwieger would have been able to mount a successful attack.

Given the criticisms of Turner that had been voiced even before the inquiry began, there was some surprise at the lack of criticism of him in the report. It was widely supposed (and still is by many) that Mersey himself was under pressure by the Admiralty to find Turner guilty of contributing to the loss of his ship. Admiral Inglefield was thought to be the assessor who was looking after the Admiralty's interest in the procedure, there being no counsel with that specific brief. In reading through the transcript, it does not seem that Inglefield showed any particular hostility to Turner and, as we have seen, he lent support to some of Aspinall's arguments in the captain's defence; but one cannot rule out pressure being exerted on Mersey through less official channels. The issue of the second torpedo does not concern us at this point, but the case is well made by Diana Preston in *Wilful Murder* that influence was brought to bear to persuade the inquiry that at least two torpedoes had been fired when in fact it was already known that there had only been one. There was also an incident in the inquiry when it was discovered that the Admiralty had prepared two versions of a communication sent to the *Lusitania*. The intention seemed to be to demonstrate that the instructions that Turner had received were less vague than in fact they had been. Mersey was extremely angry about the apparent deception and it may have made him more sceptical about the Admiralty position. There remains the possibility that Mersey, with agreement from the assessors, came to the conclusion without outside influence that Turner should not be blamed. A second possibility was that he resisted Admiralty pressure, possibly to demonstrate that, having been pushed around on the matter of the second torpedo, he was still his own man. A third possibility was that the government itself recognised that putting blame on Turner might detract from the anti-German propaganda value of the report, so that the influence on Mersey was in quite a different direction. Our focus must be to consider the merits of the outcome rather than to speculate without additional evidence about the murkiness of its origins.

The exoneration of Turner's handling of his ship on the morning of 7 May in the report is comprehensive – no blame was attached to him – but it was not unqualified. The section was obviously written with great care by a skilled wordsmith. It read:

> Captain Turner was fully advised as to the means which in the view of the Admiralty were best calculated to avert the perils he was likely to encounter, and in considering the question whether he is to blame for the catastrophe in which his voyage ended I have to bear this circumstance in mind. It is certain that in some respects Captain Turner did not follow the advice given to him. It may be (though I seriously doubt it) that had he done so his ship would have reached Liverpool in safety. But the question remains, was his conduct the conduct of a negligent or incompetent man. On this question I have sought the guidance of my assessors, who have rendered me invaluable assistance, and the conclusion at which I have arrived is that blame ought not to be imputed to the Captain. The advice given to him, although

meant for his most serious and careful consideration, was not intended to deprive him of the right to exercise his skilled judgment in the difficult questions that might arise from time to time in the navigation of his ship. His omission to follow the advice in all respects cannot fairly be attributed either to negligence or incompetence.

He exercised his judgment for the best. It was the judgment of a skilled and experienced man, and although others might have acted differently and perhaps more successfully, he ought not, in my opinion, to be blamed.

There are three points to note here. Firstly is the reference (unusual in Mersey's reports) to his having consulted with the assessors on a difficult judgment. Perhaps this was included deliberately in order explicitly to tie Admiral Inglefield into the exoneration of Turner. Second are the doubts expressed by Mersey that different decisions by Turner, more in line with Admiralty advice, might have saved the ship. He gives no reason for this view and there is nothing in the evidence given to the inquiry that would seem to justify it. Had Turner been travelling at any different speed on any different course in any different position around 2pm on that day the probability of a successful attack would have been altered. Like each of the other four ships whose sinking Mersey investigated, *Lusitania*'s fate depended on the coming together of a very particular set of circumstances on a specific occasion.

The third and most significant point to note is the last sentence, which implies that a different person might have made different, and more successful, decisions. Presumably such different decisions would have been more in line with Admiralty advice (they could hardly have been less so) and, if more successful, would, one assumes, have prevented the ship being lost – in contradiction of the opinion expressed in the first paragraph. If it was not negligence or incompetence that prevented Turner from making more successful decisions, what was it? Perhaps the answer lies in how Turner the man came to be viewed by Mersey during the course of the inquiry.

Butler Aspinall at times encouraged Turner to portray himself as the crusty old man of the sea, as in the following exchange:

Mr. Butler Aspinall: Is it your view that the modern ships, with their greasers and their stewards and their firemen, sometimes do not carry the old-fashioned sailor that you knew of in the days of your youth?
– That is the idea.
That is what you have in your mind?
– That is it.
You are an old-fashioned sailor man?

–That is right.
And you preferred the man of your youth?
–Yes, and I prefer him yet.

We will come back to the point concerning the seaman-like qualities of the crew later, but the passage also displays the brevity of Turner's answers, almost to the point of being curt. Reports at the time described him as ill at ease and clearly under stress from the dreadful experience of losing his ship and so many of the passengers for whose safety he was responsible. Mersey showed flashes of impatience with Turner on occasions in the earlier part of his evidence in particular, but then flashes of impatience from Mersey towards both witnesses and counsel were the norm rather than the exception. They do not appear to have carried any meaningful insight into Mersey's attitude to the person at whom they were aimed.

Towards the end of the inquiry there was a conversation between Mersey and Butler Aspinall about Turner as a witness, one that took place in camera in the absence of all of the witnesses. It was surprisingly frank and is worth quoting in full. It took place immediately prior to Aspinall beginning his defence of Turner's actions.

Mr. Butler Aspinall: At the outset of my remarks on behalf of the Captain what I want to emphasise, and I think it is a material matter, is this, that the Captain was undoubtedly a bad witness, although he may be a very excellent navigator.
The Commissioner: No, he was not a bad witness.
Mr. Butler Aspinall: Well, he was confused, my Lord.
The Commissioner: In my opinion at present he may have been a bad Master during that voyage, but I think he was telling the truth.
Mr. Butler Aspinall: Yes.
The Commissioner: And I think he is a truthful witness. I think he means to tell the truth.
Mr. Butler Aspinall: Yes.
The Commissioner: In that sense he did not make a bad witness.
Mr. Butler Aspinall: No.
The Commissioner: He made a bad witness for you.
Mr. Butler Aspinall: Well, what I was going to say about him was this, that it was very difficult to get a consecutive story from the man, but I was going to submit that he was an honest man.
The Commissioner: I think he is, and I do not think Sir Edward Carson or Sir Frederick Smith have suggested anything to the contrary.

The Solicitor-General: No, my Lord.

The Commissioner: The impression the man has made upon me is – I came here prepared to consider his evidence very carefully, but the impression he has made upon me is that he was quite straight and honest.

Mr. Butler Aspinall: Quite. He had gone through naturally the very greatest strain both physical and mental. He lost his ship; he lost his comrades, or many of them; there was very great loss of life, and he was in the water for a very long period of time.

It is interesting to see Mersey at this quite late stage (the penultimate session) saying that, in his opinion, Turner may have been a 'bad Master' during the voyage, but the main thrust of the passage is the recognition by all of the senior personnel taking part that Turner was honest and straight forward despite the brevity and lack of coherence of his answers. This is rather a different view to the hysterical picture painted by First Sea Lord Fisher of a captain traitorously presenting his ship to the enemy for destruction. The impression of Turner that comes across is akin to Jack Hawkin's portrayal of the Captain of the *Compass Rose* in the film of Nicholas Monsarrat's novel *The Cruel Sea* – taciturn, introverted, dogged and reliable, but not without charisma that inspired admiration and loyalty in others. A collection of photographs taken by him, many on board the *Lusitania*, were auctioned in the spring of 2011 and the catalogue described the 400 photographs as providing an intimate insight into the life of a captain who seemed fun-loving and happy.

The benefit of the doubt that Mersey gave to both Captains Smith and Turner in the handling of their ships may, in each case, have had a similar origin, despite the very different circumstances of the events they were associated with and the different characters of the men themselves. Butler Aspinall touched on it in his defence of Turner when he suggested to Mersey that 'He may have been a courageous sailor, but, after all, one has got to judge him by who he is and what experience he has had in the past.'

As we have seen, Mersey acquitted E J Smith of reckless speeding in the known proximity of ice because he was convinced, probably correctly, that other captains with similar experience to Smith would have done the same. There was evidence given in the *Titanic* inquiry to that effect. In the *Lusitania* inquiry there was, of course, no evidence given as to the practice of other master mariners so far as following Admiralty advice on the avoidance of submarines was concerned. In the sailing ship era there had been a resistance amongst merchant ship captains to being dictated to by their naval colleagues and convoy operations in the Second World War were often fraught with the same tension. Without hearing any evidence directly in court, Mersey may have been aware that Turner's non-compliance was very much in line with current practice amongst his peers on the larger, faster ships and he may, therefore, have been reluctant to single him out. The concern within the Admiralty at Mersey's failure to censure Turner probably arose not so much from a desire to punish that individual, but because they wanted their 'advice' to be regarded as instructions that were to be obeyed to the letter, except in the most unusual circumstances. Mersey appeared to endorse the notion that the captain's discretion was sacrosanct and should not be challenged. This is, perhaps, the critical issue so far as this inquiry is concerned. The Admiralty was collecting all of the data it could find about U-boat activity and was having considerable success in de-coding German signals. Using that intelligence it was providing the best advice it could in what were novel and difficult circumstances. That advice was the only source of expert help for merchant ship captains. While the requirements of safe navigation would always have to be taken into account, captains would have been well advised to stick as closely as possible to what the Admiralty believed to be the best way of avoiding attack. Our natural sympathy for Turner and understanding of Mersey's reluctance to censure him should not detract from the view that a strong exhortation in the report to captains to regard the Admiralty advice as instructions in all but name might well have been effective.

When Carson condensed the brief of the *Lusitania* into just two questions, his second one related to the steps taken to minimise the loss of life. Given the short time between the torpedo striking *Lusitania* and its sinking there was limited scope for a systematic evacuation. Mersey was satisfied that the lifeboats were in good order and that the collapsible boats designed to float free as the ship sank had been released to do so. One or two witnesses complained about lack of organisation, about lifeboats taking in water and about a degree of panic amongst the crew and some passengers. Mersey was not impressed by the complaints. Perhaps the fact that one of the complainants appeared to be motivated by the prospect of being paid to keep quiet prejudiced the Commissioner to some extent, but he was probably correct in suggesting that problems with lifeboats were a consequence of those on the port side crashing against the side of the listing ship as they were lowered. On the matter of panic, however, Mersey's wording left him open to an accusation of class bias. He suggested that any panic had only occurred when steerage passengers 'swarmed' onto the boat deck. It was an unfortunate choice of words. The class division in ships resulted in steerage passengers, who were aboard in larger numbers, having farther to go than passengers in the other classes to reach the lifeboats. When they began to get there, having climbed through a darkened, listing ship, they were suddenly faced with the appalling sight of the bow rapidly disappearing into the sea. It is not surprising that some became hysterical.

The loss of steam pressure from the boilers almost immediately after the *Lusitania* was hit prevented her engines being put into reverse in order to stop her. She carried on moving, gradually slowing down, right up until the time she sank. This created considerable difficulty in lowering the lifeboats as we noted in Chapter 8. Turner in his evidence mentioned that he had stopped the launching of lifeboats for some minutes in order to allow the ship to slow. As a consequence, some passengers reported that they had been ordered out of a lifeboat that they had already clambered into and this had obviously caused them distress. There was some confusion as to who told them to leave the lifeboat and how the instruction was explained to them. One witness said that the captain had shouted from the wing of the bridge to get out of the lifeboat as the ship was not going to sink. A second witness reporting the same incident said that it was Staff Captain Anderson who shouted to them. There may well have been some confusion as Anderson, who lost his life in the tragedy, carried the title of Captain and may have been better known to many than the passenger-shy Turner. Nonetheless, it is surprising that passengers were actually removed from lifeboats and even more surprising if they were assured that the ship would remain afloat at least until beached. It is an incident that has not been entirely explained but may indicate a communication glitch between captain and staff captain. Telling the passengers already in the lifeboats to get out because the ship was not going to sink may have been a white lie, to allow the ship time to slow.

Turner cast doubt on the competence of his own crew in manning the lifeboats. There are two sides to this. Like other captains he was very concerned about the number of good quality seamen who had been taken up by the navy as reservists and the difficulty in finding able replacements. At this stage of the war it was a major problem and, as we shall see in the next chapter, it was one of which the German submariners were well aware. However, in this criticism he was also exhibiting his old seadog nature, complaining that seamen in 1915 were not what they had been in his youth. He comes across as someone uncomfortable with the dramatic changes he has lived through and has found that for him they posed more threats than opportunities.

Turner's attitude to the passengers, from whom he made his living, was demonstrated when he claimed, without giving any specific instance, that their attempts to assist with the launching of the lifeboats had actually been a hindrance. While one or two other witnesses from the crew suggested that some of the efforts of passengers to help had been futile, there was not the same implication of interfering busybodies that emerged from Turner.

Surprisingly, Mersey reflected Turner's view, indeed seemed to amplify it in the inquiry report. It was an issue that had also surfaced in the *Falaba* inquiry; this from Henry Ashton, a steward on the ship giving evidence:

> You say the passengers meant to help, but were interfering with you?
> —Yes.
> At which boats?
> — At the two I was working at.
> You mean No. 2 and No. 4?
> —Yes.
> But they did not prevent your lowering No. 4?
> — No; but I mean most things would have been done much quicker and better and less lives lost if it had been left to members of the crew to do it.

One suspects that it may have been this evidence in the *Falaba* inquiry that influenced Mersey's comments in the *Lusitania* report as much as Turner's throwaway remark.

Fred Davies was not at that peak of the profession occupied by both Smith and Turner, but he was nonetheless on its higher reaches. He was not alive to give evidence on his own behalf, but his reputation did not suffer as a consequence. There is no hint of any criticism of him in Mersey's report. We have already observed that the two wartime inquiries were short by comparison with the peacetime ones but there was another significant difference. The inquiries into the *Titanic* and *Empress* disasters both finished with a set of recommendations intended to prevent similar disasters occurring or at least to ameliorate the consequences. Neither the *Lusitania* nor the *Falaba* reports contain any such recommendations. So, not only did Davies evade any criticism, there were no suggestions as to how things might be improved on future occasions. In the wartime context in 1915 it was almost certain that such occasions would arise with distressing frequency. The sinking of the *Falaba* was not a freak accident unlikely ever to happen again, as in the case of *Titanic*. Arguably the absence of recommendations in these two reports was one of Mersey's greatest failings. Not only did he not do what he should have done to support the Admiralty in their measures to help ships to avoid submarine attack, he missed entirely a crucial opportunity to highlight the failures in practice that led to so many casualties in the sinking of the *Falaba*.

In the evidence given to the *Falaba* inquiry Mersey was told that von Forstner's warning, shouted from the conning tower through a megaphone, had given Davies just five minutes to clear his ship. In fact only one witness, a passenger, claimed to have heard mention of five minutes in the hail from the submarine but admitted to being unsure of what he had heard. Another witness reported that, just before the torpedo hit, the captain remarked to him: 'They have only given us five minutes to clear the ship.' Other witnesses failed to decipher what had been shouted across the gap. The German side claimed that Davies had been given a ten-minute warning, but that 23 minutes actually elapsed before the torpedo was fired. In one sense the actual amount of time is immaterial. Davies knew that he had to evacuate the ship as quickly as it could be achieved. What followed was a shambles and although the last boat (a small one) was being launched when the torpedo struck, only two got away cleanly with the number of passengers they were expected to carry. Three were lost by accidents when being lowered, one broke up after launch and one was swamped. Why?

The inquiry report contains some answers to that question, but does so purely in the matter of fact manner that might be expected of an able journalist reporting events but making no comment or judgement. The difficulty of obtaining competent crew in wartime that we have already noted resulted in high turnover amongst crews from one voyage to the next. Over half of the crew that sailed on *Falaba* on her last voyage had not sailed on her previous one. Some of those may have been on the ship or her sister on another occasion but the majority were probably there for the first time. Some crew only arrived on board just before sailing time and this was the reason given for the fact that when she sailed crew members had not been allocated to lifeboats. The Purser was in the process of doing this when U-28 appeared.

It was the custom on Elder Dempster Line ships to conduct lifeboat drill on Saturdays or Sundays. The ship was attacked on Saturday morning and no drill had been attempted. Presumably, one would have been carried out sometime in those two days after the crew boat list had been completed. There were a series of vociferous complaints from the passengers who gave evidence about the equipment and the organisation on the ship. One, Cyril Bressey, summarised his five complaints and they mirrored the tone of the evidence given throughout the inquiry.

> The first thing is that there were no boat stations for the passengers – no list of boat stations and no passengers knew where they were to go to. Secondly, the submarine was apparently seen by a large number of passengers before any action was taken by the ship in altering the course to bring that boat directly astern. Thirdly, there were no instructions given to the passengers at the crisis, or to me anyhow. I say there were apparently no instructions given; in fact, I can say definitely that there were no instructions given me, as I heard none. Fourthly, the regulations also

provide for a crew, as far as I remember, from the ship's boats station list—it is somewhere about ten, with a competent officer in charge of each boat. The boat that I was dropped into the water in apparently had no officer. I heard none, because I had no directions given me there. The boat which ultimately picked me up was being steered and commanded by passengers, so that if there was a ship's officer on board he was not in charge and he gave no directions, he gave no orders. And the fifth is the apparently unsatisfactory condition of the boats.

The last complaint is one that was refuted with some degree of success by Aspinall and his team. Several of the passengers had described the timber in the boats as having been rotten. As some of the boats had been cast up on the Cornish coast they were examined and found to be sound. The boats on the *Falaba*'s sister ship were also examined on her next docking and were also found to be sound. While there may have been some doubts about the equipment in the boats and there was a possibility that one or two of the seams in the hulls had dried out and were leaking, the boats themselves do seem to have been generally fit for purpose.

Aspinall dealt with the complaints by passengers at length in his final statement. He began with a hand-wringing and patronising dismissal of the evidence from all of the passengers:

> A large number of them came forward, some seventeen or eighteen of them, in support of those charges, and I want those gentlemen to understand that in saying what I am going to say. I am speaking in no spirit of hostility to them. I am not attacking their veracity and I am not impugning their good faith. I have no doubt they perfectly honestly believed what they told the Court. They formed the impression at a time when their opportunities certainly for accurate observation were not good, but they undoubtedly have come to the conclusion that they have a grievance against the Elder Dempster Line, and against the sailors of the Elder Dempster Line who were managing the boats under the very trying circumstances of this lamentable tragedy.

Regarding organisation on the ship he was on particularly weak ground. This was his answer to the accusation about the lack of boat lists for crew members:

> Now with regard to the other points of attack, point No. 2 was that there were no boat lists for the crew or passengers. With regard to that, we have been told that the practice in this vessel, and I submit it is a reasonable

practice, is that the boat list is got out as soon as it can practically be got out. One cannot, of course, do impossibilities. I suppose perhaps it would be more desirable that one should have a boat list up as soon as ever the anchor is up and the vessel sails. But, in fact, that is impossible, if it could be done readily, of course, it would be done. The ship, no doubt, came out of dock at 6 o'clock in the morning, and did not sail until 6 p.m., 12 hours afterwards; but as Captain Thompson told us, it is very difficult to collect your men, and in this particular case four of the crew came on board as late as the passengers did, and that is, as common experience teaches one, what happens. Some of the sailors, unfortunately (not those of engine room staff as your Lordship elicited), came on board suffering from intoxication, and there always are out of a large crew unfortunately a certain number of men who do not act up to the higher standard of conduct, but when they get to sea they are not a whit worse as sailors. But we must deal with human nature as we find it, and I submit it is quite impossible under these circumstances for shipowners to do more than the Elder Dempster Line did in this case with regard to boat lists.

In a way it is rather sad to see a highly respected and intelligent lawyer being forced to come out with such claptrap in defence of his client. What on earth did the sobriety or lack of it amongst some members of the crew have to do with the purser putting a list of names and boats together unless the purser was himself amongst the intoxicated? This is perhaps the most transparent example across all four of the inquiries of a commercial interest pleading, and successfully pleading, innocence when the evidence so clearly pointed to guilt. At what point do crude financial considerations give way in the corporate mind to broader ethical concerns?

Aspinall's answer to the reports of the mishandling of the lowering of the boats that resulted in so many of the deaths was even less edifying. It consisted of a marriage of half-truth and innuendo in which he attempted to pass most of the blame onto the passengers concerned. The story of boat number 2 can serve to illustrate. This boat was one of the ones that had been lifted off its chocks and swung out ready for launching shortly after leaving Liverpool. When the emergency arose the first four people to go into the boat were four male passengers, including a father and son. Before any other people arrived the boat's stern suddenly fell and the ringbolt holding the bow broke. The boat fell heavily into the water still with the four men aboard and floated away, partially disintegrating in the process. It was held together with a rope that the passengers found and tied around what was left of the gunwale and it served to provide flotation for some of the other passengers who had been thrown into the water as a result of other boats being damaged. All four of the passengers who had climbed into the boat gave evidence. There was also evidence from one of the crew on the deck at the boat as the accident happened. He maintained that the ship's butcher had let go the fall at one end of the boat and the captain had told him to run out the other as quickly as possible. It had jammed and that was when the ringbolt had broken free. This was Aspinall's take on the story of boat 2, no doubt building on the evidence of the steward Ashton quoted earlier.

> That, my Lord, was the undoubted cause of this boat getting into trouble – the fact that the fall ran through the man's hand, and, possibly, the fact that the disaster was in some way contributed to by the efforts, and very zealous efforts, of these four passengers to get the boat into the water.

So, when von Forstner gave his warning, crew members did not know their duties and passengers did not know which boat to go to or what to do when they got there. Most of the casualties resulted from people being killed or injured in the accidents that occurred during the attempts to launch lifeboats or through being thrown into the sea when boats were upset. Mersey should have appreciated that a complete change in attitude to passenger safety was required if ships such as this were going to continue to sail with a major risk of submarine attack. The evidence he had heard had made it clear beyond any doubt that this ship had sailed into a submarine-infested zone totally unprepared to deal with the consequences of an attack. In all likelihood it was typical of many others. There should have been a clear recommendation that no ship should be permitted to sail unless all members of crew fully understood what was required of them in an emergency and all passengers had been well rehearsed in evacuation procedures. Habits that had become ingrained in peacetime, such as only holding lifeboat drill on a Saturday or Sunday, became quite absurd in wartime. Mersey might, yet again, have excused Davies personally as he was only following similar practice to others, but that did not detract from the need to ensure that obvious, life-threatening deficiencies in practice were addressed for the future. Instead Mersey, in his report, put all of the disorganisation of the crew and the catastrophes in the launching of the boats down to the haste engendered by von Forstner's inadequate warning.

The lack of recommendations in the two wartime reports may be associated with the desire to achieve maximum propaganda effect by heaping all responsibility for the loss of life onto the German submariners and their controllers. In the next chapter we will consider the nature of their culpability in relation to the terms in which Mersey chose to describe it.

14

GUNTHER VON FORSTNER AND WALTHER SCHWIEGER

When Mersey issued his report on the *Falaba* he summarised his findings as follows:

> The Court, having carefully enquired into the circumstances of the [sinking of the *Falaba*] finds … that the loss of the said ship and lives was due to damage caused to the said ship by a torpedo fired by a submarine of German nationality, whereby the ship sank. In the opinion of the Court the act was done not merely with the intention of sinking the ship but also with the intention of sacrificing life.

It is the final four words that we are concerned with, as all of the rest was already well established. While the first part of the statement is factual, those four words are an inference. Mersey did not question von Forstner and had no means of knowing what was in his mind during the attack. The inference seems to have been drawn from the brevity of the supposed five minute warning – Mersey was quite convinced that the torpedo had indeed been fired just five minutes after the ship was stopped. If von Forstner had no intention of killing people, why did he not allow adequate time for everyone to get clear? However, one might equally ask why he allowed any time at all. Had he fired immediately he could have sacrificed even more lives. Mersey presumably considered the five minutes a token behind which the Germans could hide their murderous intent.

In this case, we may be in a slightly better position to arrive at a judgement than was Mersey as we have access to more information about von Forstner and his pattern of behaviour as a submarine captain. Our view of Mersey's conclusions should not, however, be overly influenced by material of which he knew nothing. In Chapter 6 we referred to the journal that von Forstner published in 1917, following his transfer to a training role, and which included his descriptions of some of the actions in which he was involved. Before looking at what he says in his accounts of these actions, it is necessary to be absolutely clear that the journal must be regarded as a propaganda exercise. Those who lived through the Cold War will be attuned to a form of Soviet propaganda that was jargon laden. Words and phrases such as 'proletariat', 'workers' democracy' 'western imperialism' appeared so often as to become meaningless. Von Forstner's journal is not overt propaganda of that nature; parts of it seem almost to be extracts from training manuals, understandable considering his role at the time. He makes reference to British authorities in describing the nature of submarine warfare and uses the exploits of British boats in the Dardanelles as examples of what can be done. However, in his outline of submarine activity in the early part of the war, and in particular in his description of events in which he had been engaged, the journal is patriotic bluster, seeing the war as a glorious and often enjoyable exercise in the demonstration of German superiority over the hated enemy, 'our dear cousins across the Channel'. Needless to say the same sort of jingoistic material, replete with patronisingly contemptuous references to the 'Hun' was being produced in Britain; examples are not hard to find.

The journal was translated by Ana Crafts Codman and published in Boston in November 1917, America having entered the war that April. She added a foreword to the document which casts an interesting light on how the journal was regarded in the newly belligerent United States. This is her view of the Gunther von Forstner who emerges from the journal:

> Several chapters in this book are simple narratives of the commander's own adventures during the present naval warfare waged against commerce. His attempts at a lighter vein often provoke a smile at the quality of his wit, but he is not lacking in fine and manly virtues. He is a loyal comrade; a good officer concerned for the welfare of his crew. He is even kindly to his captives when he finds they are docile victims. He is also willing to credit his adversary with pluck and courage. He is never sparing of his own person, and shows admirable endurance under pressure of intense work and great responsibility. He is full of enthusiastic love for his profession, and in describing a storm at sea his rather monotonous style of writing suddenly rises to eloquence. But in his exalted devotion to the Almighty War Lord, and to the Fatherland, he openly reveals his fanatical joy in the nefarious work he has to perform.

In addition to personal recollections there are references to other aspects of the war in the journal, some surprisingly objective in tone. This is von

Forstner's take on the Battle of Jutland, which the German authorities at the time hailed as a great victory.

> If one should examine the course of this battle, which has been represented by lines graphically showing the paths of the British and German fleets, one could easily see how the British imposed their will upon the Germans in every turn that these lines make. It reminds one very much of the herding of sheep, for the German fleet was literally herded on May 31, 1916, from 5:36 in the afternoon until 9 o'clock that night. Admiral von Scheer, however, fought the only action which it was possible for him to fight. It was a losing action, and one which he knew, from a purely mathematical consideration, could not be successful.

There is also a brief passing reference to the *Lusitania* to the effect that 'destiny overtook her', surely one of the most euphemistic descriptions ever of such a terrible event. Our principal concern, however, is von Forstner's own actions during the spring and summer of 1915. There is a long description of his sinking of the *Leuwarden* in which great care is taken to ensure the safety of the crew and much made of their expressions of gratitude. The theme that runs through the journal is that captains who stopped their ships immediately and did precisely as ordered could thereby ensure the safety of their passengers and crew. Those who disobeyed, who attempted to escape or who tried to summon assistance could expect to suffer the consequences. Here is how he wrote of the sinking of the *Glitra* by another U-boat in October 1914.

> At the end of October, 1914, the first English steamer *Glitra* was sunk off the Norwegian coast. It carried a cargo of sewing machines, whisky, and steel from Leith. The captain was wise enough to stop at the first signal of the commander of the U-boat, and he thereby saved the lives of his crew, who escaped with their belongings after the steamer was peacefully sunk. If others later had likewise followed his example, innocent passengers and crew would not have been drowned; and after all, people are fond of their own lives; but these English captains were following the orders of their Government to save their ships through flight.

The problem that Britain was experiencing manning its merchant ships because of the massive expansion of the Navy was well known. Wages of merchant seamen had been increased in order to attract more and better people. In the journal, von Forstner claims that he had observed the effects of this problem and his observations were directly relevant to the sinking of the *Falaba*.

> I had made an interesting study of the manner in which the English crews
> of the present day were composed. Apart from the British officers there
> were but few experienced seamen on board. This was made evident by the
> awkward way the men usually handled the lifeboats. Even with the enor-
> mous increase of wages, sailors could not be found to risk their lives in the
> danger zone, and a lot of untrained fellows … revealed by their clumsy
> rowing that they had only recently been pressed into service.

To emphasise the point, he mentioned in his description of the sinking of the
Flamian the fact that the crew took to the boats with a perfect discipline 'we
were little accustomed to witness'.

The action in which we are particularly interested is one that took place
on the day prior to the sinking of the *Falaba*. As well as sinking the *Aguila*
that day, U-28 met the *Vosges* in heavy weather in the entrance to the Bristol
Channel. In this case the captain refused to stop and even, according to von
Forstner, turned and attempted to ram the submarine. The submarine's gun
was used to damage the ship and set it on fire and a running 'battle' went on
for four hours. The *Vosges* was damaged enough to sink when U-28 had to
leave because of fear of warships arriving. Von Forstner then reported what
happened after he returned to Germany.

> We had been truly impressed by the captain's brave endurance, notwith-
> standing his lack of wisdom, and we knew that the men-of-war were
> coming to his rescue. We read in the papers, on our return to a German port,
> that the *Vosges* had sunk soon after we had departed, and what remained of
> the passengers and crew were picked up by the English ships. The captain
> was rewarded for his temerity by being raised to the rank of Reserve officer,
> and the crew were given sums of money; but all the other officers had per-
> ished, as well as several sailors and a few passengers, who had been forced to
> help the stokers in order to increase the speed of the flying steamer.

The 'brave but stupid' theme was a recurring one in descriptions of British
master mariners. What is really odd about this passage is the acknowledgement at the end of the large number of people who had been killed, numbers
that he had obtained from a German newspaper. In fact there was only one
fatal casualty, the Chief Engineer, and four wounded, one of them a woman.
The suggestion that passengers were killed who had been forced to assist the
stokers was surely nonsensical.

Von Forstner makes no specific reference to the events of the following day. He simply says that in the next few days they stopped and searched many neutral steamers and sank many English ones. With regard to these actions he says:

> The captains were occasionally stubborn and refused to obey our signals, so a few accidents occurred; in one case, for instance, a stray shot struck some passengers in a lifeboat, which collapsed; but as a rule passengers and crews were picked up by the many sailboats and fishing boats which circulate in the Irish Sea and in St. George's Channel, and it was we who generally summoned these fishermen to go to the rescue of their shipwrecked countrymen.

We are left to wonder if the 104 deaths of passengers and crew from the *Falaba* was one of the accidents of which he speaks. There is no mention in the journal either of the sinking of the *Iberian* on 31 July that year, the event which later gave rise to the story of the sea monster. It is worth looking at as there was a report provided to the *New York Times* by the doctor on the ship, Dr Patrick S Burns, who happened to be American. As such the story in the paper was rather less partial than those syndicated across from London, as many of them were. Given that the incident happened two months after the sinking of the *Lusitania*, when sentiment in America was largely hostile to the actions of German submarines, the tone is surprisingly neutral. There are a couple of inaccuracies and inconsistencies in the report, which may be the result of mistakes by typesetters. The submarine is wrongly numbered as U-58 and the lifeboat that Dr Burns used to leave the ship is number 3 on one occasion and number 8 on another. The *Iberian* refused to stop when ordered to do so and attempted to outrun the submarine. Captain Jago had succeeded in escaping from a submarine on a previous occasion but this time von Forstner's gunfire proved conclusive. One shot killed six members of the crew and wounded a number of others while another blew away the aerial, although not before a message asking for assistance had been sent. Eventually Jago realised that escape was impossible and stopped the ship. The crew, including the wounded, were successfully evacuated before the torpedo was fired. Shortly afterwards there was a tremendous explosion inside the ship, probably as the result of a boiler coming into contact with cold water. Dr Burns made no reference to the sea monster which, twenty years later, von Forstner claimed to have seen.

Interestingly, the lifeboats came alongside the submarine and von Forstner lectured Jago on the foolishness of his refusal to stop. He also asked if a wireless message had been sent and Jago denied sending one. That seems odd, as one would have expected the submarine wireless operator to have detected the transmission himself. Von Forstner left the lifeboats to their fate around 75 miles from the Irish coast. Arguably that was his first departure from the Cruiser Rules in the attack as they were too far from land to be sure of getting there safely. Luckily the survivors kept the boats close together and they were picked up later that night.

So how does this additional information about the man commanding U-28 help us to second guess Mersey's assertion that his actions during the sinking of the *Falaba* were governed by a desire to kill? The term 'collateral damage' came to prominence in the first Gulf War as Western military leaders explained the regrettable deaths of civilians as a result of their operations. It was a phrase that came to have a callous ring from overuse and application to circumstances where its validity was, at best, dubious. Perhaps it does have value in the context that we are examining. Von Forstner, on the evidence we have available, suffered no moral anguish over the deaths of non-combatants as a result of the actions in which he was involved. He regarded them either as the inevitable consequence of a modern conflict at sea, or the result of the refusal of British authorities to be compliant in their part of the 'bargain'. He was quite prepared to shell a ship that he knew had passengers aboard and he left a group of filled lifeboats in deteriorating weather 75 miles from land. There is not, however, any evidence that he sought to magnify the number of casualties beyond what he regarded as the inevitable 'collateral damage' of submarine operations.

Mersey appears to have recognised this, despite his accusation of murderous intent. One of the questions that his inquiry was asked to consider was whether or not the submarine captain had made any attempt to save the lives of people struggling in the sea. The response was that he had not made any attempt as to do so would have risked the safety of the submarine. Mersey understood the pressure that von Forstner was under keeping his submarine on the surface for an extended period after a wireless call for assistance had been broadcast. The inclusion in the report of the phrase 'intention to sacrifice life' was pure propaganda – but it resonated with many people. Von Forstner had become a bête-noir with many newspaper readers around the world because of the stories of some of the survivors that were published. The *Falaba*, being the first passenger liner to be torpedoed, had been extensively covered in papers across the world before it was entirely overshadowed by the *Lusitania*. As mentioned earlier, amongst the stories reported by survivors was one that the crew of U-28 had lined the deck of the submarine and laughed and jeered at people struggling in the water. Several of the witnesses to the inquiry referred to this but, suspiciously, almost all used the same phrase, 'laughing and jeering', unprompted.

One witness however, a passenger called Primrose, one of the four involved in the accident to boat number 2, had a different slant:

> Did you notice the people on the submarine at all ?
> – Yes, I saw them quite plainly.
> Did you see them doing anything ?
> – I did not see them jeering at anybody in the water at that time, but when the *Falaba* heeled over I could see one or two men clinging on to the rail at the high side of the vessel, and it was then I heard the Germans shouting and pointing excitedly to these men as they fell off.

In the report, Mersey was judiciously non-committal:

> There was evidence before me of laughing and jeering on board the sub-marine while the men and women from the *Falaba* were struggling for their lives in the water; but I prefer to keep silence on this matter in the hope that the witness was mistaken.

In all likelihood the witnesses and the other survivors who gave the story to the press were mistaken. It is much more probable that some of the crew of the submarine were on deck (including those manning the gun) and were trying by shouting and with gestures to direct lifeboats to people that they could see in the water. What was the basis of an accusation of callous disregard for life may well have been the one attempt made at a humanitarian gesture.

As a final word on the time allowed for the evacuation of the *Falaba* it is worth noting that survivors' estimates in newspaper reports were varied but, in several instances, spoke of the torpedo being fired 'barely ten minutes' after the warning. Given the time taken to launch the boats, the five minutes assumed by Mersey seems much too short; on the other hand the 23 minutes claimed by the Germans seems rather long. Around ten minutes or a little more would be a reasonable guess and only a handful of people were on the ship when the torpedo struck. One passenger registering his anger at the bungled evacuation pointed out in his evidence that had the crew been well organised and the passengers well led, all of those on the ship could have been safely evacuated before the torpedo was fired. The sinking of the ship was down to von Forstner and U-28; responsibility for the loss of life, however lay with Elder, Dempster, their Marine Superintendent and his brother-in-law Fred Davies.

Before moving on to focus on von Forstner's colleague Walther Schwieger, we might just glance in passing at an example of what his translator described as the 'quality of [Gunther's] wit'. At one stage very early in the war, U-28 carried out an operation more akin to the privateering era than the First World War. A Dutch ship trading with the UK was captured in the Channel, a small prize crew of an officer and a seaman put on board and it was escorted as a prize, along with a second ship acquired similarly, to Zeebrugge. Von Forstner was initially concerned about the safety of the officer on the captive ship and wrote:

> So we proceeded towards the shores of Flanders; we, in the proud con-
> sciousness of a new achievement, and the Dutchman lamenting over the
> seizure of his valuable cargo. The passengers must have wondered what was
> in store for them. Many of the ladies were lightly clad, having been roused
> in fright from their morning slumbers, and their anxious eyes stared at us,
> while we merrily looked back at them.
>
> Our officer on board exchanged continual signals with us, and we were
> soon conscious, with a feeling of envy, as we gazed through our field glasses,
> that he was getting on very friendly terms with the fair sex on board our
> prize. We had feared at first that he might have some disagreeable experi-
> ences, but his first message spelled, 'There are a great many ladies on board,'
> and the second, 'We are having a delicious breakfast,' and the third, 'The
> captain speaks excellent German,' so after this we were quite reassured con-
> cerning him.

The women it turned out were members of a troupe going to perform in London. One suspects that the event did not seem quite so light-hearted from their perspective as it did for Gunther and his prize-captain officer.

Mersey's judgment on Wather Schwieger was, unsurprisingly, no less damn-ing than that on von Forstner. The language used to describe the German captain was uncompromising in its condemnation. In answer to the question, 'What was the cause of the loss of life?' Mersey wrote:

> The answer is plain. The effective cause of the loss of life was the attack
> made against the ship by those on board the submarine. It was a murderous
> attack because made with a deliberate and wholly unjustifiable intention of
> killing the people on board.

On the face of it the accusation of intent to kill is much more readily justi-fied than in the case of the *Falaba*. Schwieger gave no warning of the attack but launched a torpedo against a defenceless, unescorted passenger liner with dreadful consequences. For all the talk since of conspiracies, of Britain trail-ing the *Lusitania* like a bait across the Atlantic to tempt the Germans, of the German authorities secretly ordering Schwieger to lie in wait for the ship, few have attempted to justify the decision that Schwieger took that afternoon. The present author is not going to join their number. Schwieger's attack on the *Lusitania* was morally wrong, it should not have been made and there was nothing in the political or military context that justified it. That is not exactly the same as saying that he acted with the deliberate intention of killing the people on board.

Despite the evidence given to Mersey that the ship was hit by two torpedoes (and, indeed that there may have been a third that missed) we know that Schwieger only fired one. Later that day he fired another at a different ship, which missed. Why did he fire only one torpedo when he had the option to fire a second? He had used two torpedoes to sink the *Centurion* just the day before. Surely the *Lusitania,* the greatest 'prize' on the sea at the time, was worth two torpedoes if any ship was. German torpedoes early in the war were unreliable (something of which Schwieger himself had had recent experience) and sometimes failed to run true or to explode when they did hit a target. A second torpedo would have been an insurance against such a failure. What was Schwieger's real intention in firing just one torpedo? As well as keeping the formal ship's log, each U-boat captain was required to keep a war diary that was handed over to the German War Office on arrival back at base. Schwieger's war diary for that day cannot be relied upon to give any indication of his thinking, as there is clear evidence of it having been doctored, possibly even after his death.

What we can do is to look at the various possible outcomes and ask how they might have presented themselves to Schwieger in the circumstances of May 1915. His torpedo may have missed entirely and gone unseen by anyone on the *Lusitania*. It would probably have been too late at that stage to fire a second and the attack would have failed. Had the torpedo missed by a small margin and been seen by passengers and crew on the ship, that in itself would have been a propaganda coup for the Germans without the downside of a major loss of lives, particularly American lives. A similar outcome would have resulted if the ship had been hit but only damaged, stayed afloat and been taken in to Queenstown for safety. Any casualties would have been limited to those hurt by the explosion. A mortal blow which sank the ship, but which allowed sufficient time for a safe evacuation, might also have been a 'win-win' scenario for the Germans. The catastrophic destruction of the ship that actually occurred and the enormous number of deaths which resulted were what might be described as a 'win-lose' result for Germany. It was a win in the sense that the attack had succeeded, but a major loss in terms of the opprobrium that it generated and the consequent hostility towards Germany in the USA. When Schwieger fired just one torpedo at the *Lusitania,* then travelling at 18 knots and about 700 metres distant, he almost certainly considered this last possibility to be the least likely outcome and not the one he was hoping for. In that sense, and in that very limited sense only, he probably did not intend to cause the loss of life on the scale that took place.

Already by that point in the war a number of large ships had been sunk even by a single torpedo, some with big numbers of casualties. None had been as large as the *Lusitania* and most had been warships which lacked the life saving equipment of merchant ships. Nonetheless, there was ample evidence for Schwieger to be fully aware that a torpedo explosion in a vulnerable place could create sufficient damage to cause any ship to sink quite quickly. He must also have known that the rapid evacuation of the numbers of people on the *Lusitania* would have been a very dangerous process risking substantial loss of life. He had no right to take that risk with those on the ship. Mersey's condemnation in that respect was not harsh.

In examining the actions of the two submarine captains we have drawn a distinction between them, based on their modus operandi in a number of attacks on merchant ships. Von Forstner clearly made some attempt to follow the spirit of the Cruiser Rules and give passengers and crew an opportunity to escape before sinking their ship. Schwieger, on the other hand, rarely did and he fired torpedoes at a number of ships without ever coming to the surface. It was a pattern that continued after the *Lusitania*. On 4 September 1915 at 8.30pm he torpedoed without warning the Allan Line liner *Hesperian* approximately 70 miles off the Irish coast and about 130 miles west of Queenstown. The ship sank comparatively slowly and most of those on board were able to get into lifeboats and were picked up. The death toll still came to 32. The German authorities, still suffering embarrassment as a result of the *Lusitania,* tried to pretend that the ship had hit a mine. Schwieger was reined in and told to stick strictly to instructions which by then forbade no-warning attacks on passenger liners.

There is an intriguing question that probably should not be asked, a 'what if' kind of speculation that historians reject as invalid because it is not possible to change just one variable in history while keeping all of the others the same. The question is this. Had U-28 been the submarine that was in the track of the *Lusitania* on 7 May and not U-20, what action would von Forstner have taken? Would he have surfaced and ordered the ship to stop, firing his gun when she refused? Given how close the situation was to the naval base at Queenstown, that would have been a rather risky thing to do. Had he done so, however, the propaganda victory for Germany of the flagship of the British merchant fleet being fired at by a surfaced submarine a few miles from one of their own naval bases would have been tremendous.

Mersey was correct on the basis of the limited evidence in front of him in questioning whether von Forstner gave those on the *Falaba* sufficient time to make good their escape but wrong to blame the deaths that ensued solely on that time limitation. He was also correct in his outright condemnation of Schwieger in torpedoing a crowded passenger liner without warning. His failure was in not distinguishing between the two actions by ascribing the same murderous intent to both captains.

15

EIGHT CAPTAINS AND A JUDGE: THE LINKS

As an aid to drawing the threads of the four inquiries together, it might help just to summarise their findings so far as the eight captains are concerned. Even though it was acknowledged that *Titanic's* speed contributed to the loss of the ship, her captain was judged blameless as he had been following well attested custom and practice. E.J. Smith was not held personally responsible either for the disorganised evacuation that followed the accident nor was attention drawn to a lack of dynamic leadership during the time it took for the ship to sink. Neither government nor the White Star Line came in for serious criticism either. The principal focus of blame for the loss of life was someone who was many miles away when the ship sank. Mersey's castigation of Stanley Lord, the man who did nothing, was at least partially set aside by the MAIB inquiry over seventy years later. There still remains a question mark about the lack of response aboard the *Californian* to the rockets that were seen by Second Officer Stone and Apprentice Gibson. The MAIB inquiry regarded this as most likely a failure of communication, for which Lord must accept some responsibility, rather than a lack of will.

The *Empress of Ireland* inquiry turned into a pseudo-trial as a result of collusion between lawyers of the opposing parties. Mersey and his two fellow Commissioners came down firmly in favour of Kendall and against Andersen. Despite the strange and not fully explained action of Kendall in stopping his ship with dramatic suddenness when the fog obscured the *Storstad*, he was entirely exonerated. The Commissioners dismissed the *Storstad's* legal team's several attempts to cast doubt on the steering gear of the *Empress* and concluded that First Officer Toftnes on the bridge of *Storstad*, having failed to call his captain as instructed, had caused the ship to veer to the right into the side of the *Empress*. The appalling speed with which the *Empress* turned over and sank left little opportunity for a systematic evacuation and everyone involved on that ship, the *Storstad* and the rescue boats was judged to have done all that was possible to save life.

Although still called inquiries and still sponsored by the Board of Trade, the two wartime inquiries were quite different to the peacetime ones in many respects. Fred Davies and Will Turner were both held not to have contributed to the loss of their ships even though the latter disregarded Admiralty advice and the former followed it. Likewise, the two German submarine captains were dealt with similarly, each being accused of acting with intent to kill, despite von Forstner making some effort to preserve life while Schwieger made none. The manner of the rapid sinking of the *Lusitania* with a heavy list, like the *Empress*, left everyone on board struggling for survival and Mersey found no fault with Turner's leadership. Most of the casualties on the *Falaba* resulted from the crew being unbriefed and passengers not being properly informed, but still there was no censure of Davies personally and no attention drawn to the obvious deficiencies in practice in merchant ships at that stage of the war.

A constant theme running through all four inquiries was that of distinguishing lines of responsibility. Where did the responsibility of the government, either as regulator of the shipping industry in peacetime or as Admiralty in wartime, end and that of the shipping companies begin? For how much of what happened to their ships were the companies accountable and for how much the captains? Did the 'buck always stop' with the captain when it came to the mistakes of his subordinates? None of those questions was answered in any systematic way by the outcomes of the four inquiries and it is arguable that the failure to do so undermined their value.

As well as attributing blame, the purpose of holding an inquiry was to identify things that could be done to prevent a recurrence. The *Titanic* report is by far the best in this respect with a total of 24 formal recommendations. This compares with only three so-called 'suggestions' in the *Empress* report. Part of the discrepancy can be attributed to the fact that in the tragedy on the St Lawrence there was little to be learned from the post-collision phase. The recommendations in the *Titanic* report covered matters concerning the watertight subdivision of ships, provision of lifeboats and rafts, the manning of boats and boat drills, sight tests for look-outs, policing the passengers and, not surprisingly, the moderation of speed in the vicinity of ice. Then there was the pointed recommendation, already noted in the context of the *Californian* incident, that masters should be reminded of their obligation to go to the assistance of ships in distress. Finally, Mersey recommended the calling of an international conference to examine the issues raised by the *Titanic* disaster, particularly as regards mitigating the risk to ships of ice. We cannot tell to what extent Mersey was the author of this suggestion. He may well have been prompted by one or more of his assessors or by civil servants in the Board of Trade, but, if it can be said that his role between 1912 and 1915 as a Commissioner of Wrecks had any lasting legacy, this is it. The recommendation proved its worth not because the conference which was called in 1913 as a consequence dramatically improved safety at sea, but because it acted as the forerunner of a further series of such conferences which arguably have indeed had that effect.

Although the First World War prevented the ratification of the outcomes of the 1913 conference which Mersey chaired, some of its recommendations, for example in instigating an Ice Patrol to warn of serious ice hazards in the North Atlantic, were acted upon. Further Safety of Life at Sea or SOLAS conferences were held in 1929, 1948, 1960 and 1974, each incrementally adding measures to improve safety. Article VIII of SOLAS 1974 enabled further amendments to be put in place under the auspices of the International Maritime Organisation, without the need for further large international gatherings – provided a large number of nations did not dissent – and that process continues. In 2010 a number of the older cruise liners had to be withdrawn because the cost of bringing them into line with the latest SOLAS regulations was uneconomic. A number of people who, understandably, get great pleasure from seeing old, well-designed, attractive looking ships with character still at work were upset by their demise. It is perhaps ironic that there have been accusations that SOLAS has now become part of an overbearing 'health and safety' regime.

The suggestions at the end of the *Empress* inquiry were at a relatively low level, dealing with the closing of portholes and watertight doors at night or in fog, the provision of rafts on deck that would float off should the ship sink and the avoidance of ships crossing on the St Lawrence by staging the pick-up and drop-off points for pilots. The middle one of those is worth noting because it had a relevance to the *Lusitania*. Mersey clearly became quite engaged with his role as Commissioner of Wrecks. He mentioned in the *Empress* inquiry how, on his journey across the Atlantic on the *Mauretania,* he had noted the sort of lifebelts provided and their storage. In reading the transcripts one can see how he follows through on points from one to the other. One follow-through occurred in the *Lusitania* inquiry concerning the additional lifeboats that had been fitted as a consequence of his recommendation in the *Titanic* report. The *Lusitania* could not easily be adapted to take additional lifeboats on davits and instead a number of collapsible boats were placed, mostly underneath the existing boats on their davits. These were designed to be released easily so that, in the manner mentioned in the *Titanic* report, they would float free of the ship. Quite some time was spent in the *Lusitania* inquiry questioning Turner and other members of the crew so that Mersey could be satisfied that the collapsible boats were released and did float off as intended. Towards the end of the inquiry there was an odd exchange between Mersey and Turner about the value of the additional boats. When Turner was asked by Mersey if he thought that it had been worthwhile increasing the number of lifeboats as a response to the *Titanic* disaster, Turner responded that he did not think so. It was not clear whether Turner considered that they did not make any material difference in the particular circumstances of the rapid sinking of the *Lusitania* or whether he was of the view that cluttering up a ship's decks with extra boats was in general a bad thing.

The two wartime inquiries contained nothing even by way of 'suggestions', let alone recommendations. One cannot be sure if this was because the Commissioner and his Assessors found nothing of value to suggest, or because they were directed not to. The questions asked by the Board of Trade in those two instances were primarily retrospective and did not require forward looking responses. It is just possible that in either case (but probably more likely in the *Lusitania* one) Mersey provided some thoughts to the Board of Trade that were not included in the published report in case they might be of material or propaganda value to the Germans. If no recommendations were in fact made, one has to ask what purpose was served by holding the inquiries. Each report concluded that, as the whole world knew, the ship had been sunk by a German submarine and, as the Allies were in no doubt, the Germans were thereby failing to obey the accepted rules of warfare. It is hard to conceive that any propaganda gain from the reports was worth the trouble and expense of creating them. There is no evidence that either inquiry had any impact whatsoever on subsequent events. Their main benefit perhaps is to us a century later in providing additional windows through which we can observe some aspects of the first ever phase of submarine warfare, albeit at times as through a glass darkly.

There seems much to have been gained and little to have been lost if Mersey had stressed in the *Falaba* report the need for all merchant ships to be fully prepared before leaving port for an immediate evacuation and had pointed out in the *Lusitania* report the value of adhering as far as was possible to Admiralty instructions (the only source of expert advice for mariners) for the avoidance of attacks by submarines. In relation to both issues the inquiries had clearly shown that practice in the merchant service in the early stages of the war had failed to adapt with sufficient urgency to the new threat posed by the advent of submarines. As became clear from von Forstner's journal, this was at least as well understood by the German submariners themselves. They had nothing to learn from such recommendations in the report of a British inquiry.

In Chapter 4 we looked at the nature of inquiries of this type and wondered about the extent to which they were subject to external influence from government or from commercial interests. As the focus of this book has been on the men at sea and not those in Whitehall or in corporate boardrooms, we can only say that ship's captains, as has been noted, are company men and severe criticism of them may reflect badly on the company that employs them. That is exactly what happened with Stanley Lord. It was the Directors and not the Marine Superintendent of the Leyland Line that demanded his resignation for PR reasons following the criticism he received in the reports of both the American and British inquiries. The permission given to Butler Aspinall to represent Kendall, Baxter and Turner's interests, even though the shipowners were his clients, also seems to have been aimed at preventing any criticism of the captain making the company look bad. At the same time, given the public criticism of Turner, in particular, that had been aired prior to the inquiry, the fact that Cunard adopted this approach was a vote of confidence in Turner and in his ability to answer the criticisms that had been made. It might also be interpreted as an indication that Turner's decisions had indeed been in line with the company's view of Admiralty advice at the time.

The Canadian government may have had some concerns that Mersey would have found fault with the navigation system in the St Lawrence for which they were responsible and that may be why the junior Minister of Justice acted as their counsel in the *Empress* inquiry. In the event they had nothing to worry about. The final suggestion in the report that the pick-up and set-down points for the pilots might be staged was offered purely as a constructive idea without any hint of criticism. The British government had much more at stake, particularly the Board of Trade in the case of the *Titanic* and the Admiralty in the case of the *Lusitania*. Mersey has frequently been criticised for his lack of forthright condemnation of the Board of Trade for its anachronistic regulations governing lifeboats. At the same time, changing those was a matter for Parliament; responsibility lay with politicians rather than civil servants. With changing governments and changing faces in ministries it is rarely possible to pin blame on any particular politician (one of the attractions of the profession). The President of the Board of Trade had already initiated moves to have the regulations changed when the disaster occurred, albeit the pace of change would have made the movement of tectonic plates seem fast.

White Star Line also avoided censure for only fitting the minimum number of lifeboats to *Titanic*. The defence that 'we were only sticking to the inadequate regulations' obviously served its purpose. There is a debate to be had on corporate ethics in a situation of regulatory laxity but this is not the place for it. Arguably, the real criticism of White Star Line should have centred on the woefully inadequate corporate training provision for its officers in dealing with emergencies on its ships. No panic by the steerage passengers or by the 'black gang' from the stokeholds can justify the utter waste of valuable time between the collision and the sinking. Similar comments could be made about the disordered attempts at evacuating the *Falaba* even if wartime shortages of expertise exacerbated the crew's inadequacies.

Was this absence of negative comment on government and commercial interests the result of Mersey being leaned on or did it represent the outcome to be expected from inquiries headed up by an 'establishment man' who, in his previous role, had been close to the shipping companies? The only instance where there is circumstantial evidence of one of these inquiries being pushed is in the case of the *Lusitania*. We can now be reasonably certain that it was known in the Admiralty that only one torpedo had been fired but they did everything in their power to engineer a finding by Mersey of at least two torpedoes as a way of deflecting speculation on the cause of the second explosion. Mersey obliged, although there is no indication that he himself had any knowledge contrary to the evidence he heard in the inquiry. Turner has been criticised for being complicit in this deception and yet the matter was put to him in the manner of 'When did you stop beating your wife?'

> *The Attorney General:* Did you notice any other concussion that would lead you to believe there was a second torpedo?
> – One immediately after the first.

Turner acquiesced in response to a leading question to confirm, as he had to, that he had heard a second explosion, but he did not explicitly indicate that he believed that there had been a second torpedo. It was in character with his pattern of clipped answers that he did not try to provide any further explanation of his views. He seemed later in life to have come to the view that there was only one.

Butler Aspinall's maxim, already quoted in relation to Turner, that a man should be judged 'by who he is and by what experience he has had' is probably also a fair basis for us to come to a view on Mersey. Even before he had opened the first of his inquiries there were those voicing expectations of a 'whitewash' and few at the end of it came forward to say that their prediction had been wrong. One of the themes running through the book has been the inability of people in a variety of contexts to adapt practice to rapid changes in technology or to new risks suddenly emerging. If it was accepted as a valid excuse for Smith, Turner and Davies that they had simply done things the way that they had always been done, it surely was also a valid excuse for Mersey himself. Would it have been realistic to expect a judge in his seventies, a member of the House of Lords and with all of the connections that implied at the centre of the British establishment, to bring to his work as Commissioner of Wrecks a radical viewpoint, heavily critical of the status quo and the oversight of it by government legislation and corporate policy?

The view that in circumstances requiring a major public inquiry, confidence in the process can be assured by appointing a well-known legal brain to oversee it, is one that has had a long history continuing right up to the present day, despite the cynical expectations that often result. The appointment of Lord Hutton in 2004 to inquire into the circumstances surrounding the death of Dr David Kelly in the wake of the Iraq invasion is a case in point. From the time when the decision was announced until the publication of his report there were continual predictions that his findings would fail to point the finger at the 'guilty' parties. Few of those making the predictions were disappointed by the result. That is not to cast doubt on Hutton's findings; there is no basis here for such a comment. It is simply a matter of the historical record that the appointment of a Law Lord to undertake such an inquiry did not create confidence in the process; quite the opposite.

Perhaps the most positive judgment we can make of Lord Mersey is that, within the limitations of who he was and the experience he had had, he did quite an efficient job in the conduct of the four inquiries. He was diligent in ensuring that most of the issues that were raised during the inquiries were properly followed through. With the exception of the refusal to allow Stanley Lord representation, he was generally quite good in giving each of the parties involved in the tragedies full opportunity to put their cases. When the issue of the *Empress*'s steering was suddenly brought up after the inquiry was well underway he allowed considerable additional time to investigate it. His understanding of the maritime context within which he was working improved somewhat during the course of the four inquiries although it remained deficient and a source of misunderstanding and confusion to the end. As we have already hinted, the outcomes of the *Titanic* inquiry might just have been a little different had it been the fourth rather than the first of the series.

One of the unusual features of Lord Mersey's work as Commissioner of Wrecks was the number of very powerful men with whom he had to deal, both in government (Lord Chancellor, Home Secretary, Attorney-General, Solicitor-General, President of the Board of Trade) and in business (Chairmen of the two most prestigious shipping companies). Mersey did not appear to be daunted in having the likes of Isaacs, Carson and F E Smith appearing in front of him and there is nothing in the transcripts that speaks of subservience other than the rather overblown and at times apparently obsequious courtesies of legal protocol. The tasks that were given to him were challenging and he was subject to more intense public scrutiny than he had ever previ-

ously experienced. For all the inadequacies of the outcomes we must allow
Mersey credit for applying his legal experience and considerable intellect in
as effective a manner as could be expected of the man. Many people would be
content to rest on such laurels, as circumscribed as they are.

The sinking of *Titanic* was a freak accident; the *Falaba* and *Lusitania* were
both destroyed in a form of warfare that we hope will never return. The accident in the St Lawrence, however, was different in that it fitted a pattern, even
if it was unusual in its scale. Yachtsmen have a graphic description of this type
of collision. When racing yachts are tacking against the wind in close proximity, collisions frequently occur when a yacht with the wind on the port side
fails to see and give way as it ought to one with the wind on the starboard
side. Striking almost at right angles, the bow of one driving into the side of
the other, the collision is called 'T-boning'. That is exactly what happened to
the *Empress of Ireland;* she was T-boned by the *Storstad.* As we saw in Chapter 2,
other passenger liners that were also sunk by T-boning prior to 1914 included
Arctic, Ville du Havre, Oregon, Utopia and *Republic.* Just a month before the
Titanic disaster, an elderly liner, *Oceana,* also a product of Harland and Wolff
in Belfast, was setting out on what was intended to be her final trip to India.
Just off Beachy Head she was T-boned by a German sailing barque and sank
quickly, luckily with relatively small loss of life. There have been others since
including *Andrea Doria* (in 1956). Modern technology ought to ensure that
this type of accident should not happen, but the risk, however minuscule, is
always there and it continues to have the potential for dreadful consequences.
The effect of one of the new 200,000-ton super cruise liners with close to
5000 passengers and crew aboard being T-boned by a fully loaded modern
bulk carrier could be truly awful. Should such a terrible event happen, to
whom should a government turn to carry out the inevitable inquiry? The
second *Titanic* inquiry in 1992, limited to the role of the *Californian,* was conducted without the benefit of legal minds or legal trappings by the Marine
Accident Investigation Branch. This organisation professionally examines
each maritime incident with a UK involvement, however minor, and produces excellent reports designed to provide the maximum learning benefit
for all concerned. Following a major maritime disaster there might still be
media pressure for a 'public' inquiry headed by someone with establishment
status. Before acceding to any such pressure, a government might do well to
reflect on the record of such inquiries in the context of specialised technical
environments. It is the qualities of the findings that matter and not the standing of the inquirers. Mersey should not be blamed that, in the second decade
of the last century, governments failed to make that distinction.

POSTSCRIPT

There is a harmless joy in finding random historical connections. Just a few miles from Ballyferis, where the future Captain Turner was shipwrecked as a child, is my home town of Bangor in North Down. The author of *Shipwrecks of the Ulster Coast*, from which came the information that it was Turner senior's ship that was lost, is Ian Wilson, past Director of the North Down Museum. The Museum is housed in Bangor Castle, previously the home of Lord and Lady Clanmorris. One of the naval heroes of the First World War, Commander Barry Bingham, was a son of the family and grew up in the house. He was awarded the VC for leading his destroyer flotilla against the German High Seas Fleet during the battle of Jutland in an attack reminiscent of the Charge of the Light Brigade. Bingham's ship, *Nestor,* was sunk and he and the other survivors of the crew were captured.

At the end of the war, to commemorate the award of the VC, a gun removed from a surrendered U-boat was given to the town and installed on a concrete plinth in front of the War Memorial, where it remains. The submarine was U-19, the boat that torpedoed the *Calgarian* with Henry Kendall aboard and had also previously delivered the ill-fated Roger Casement on his mission to Ireland. At that time the boat's captain was Raimund Weisbach. Before taking over U-19, Weisbach was Torpedo Officer on U-20. It was his hand that, on Schwieger's order, pulled the lever that released the torpedo …

BIBLIOGRAPHY

Primary Sources

The proceedings and reports of the inquiries into the loss of the *Titanic* and the *Lusitania* are both available online via the *Titanic* Inquiry Project at www.titanicinquiry.org.

The proceedings and report of the American Senate Inquiry into the loss of the *Titanic* are also available through the same website.

The report of the second *Titanic* inquiry on the role played by the *Californian*:
Marine Accident Investigation Branch of the Department of Transport, *RMS Titanic- Reappraisal of Evidence Relating to SS Californian* (HMSO: London, 1992)

The proceedings and report of the *Empress of Ireland* inquiry:
Canadian Government Sessional Paper No 21B, *Commission of Inquiry into the loss of the British Steamship Empress of Ireland through collision with the Norwegian Steamship* Storstad (1915).

The proceedings and report of the *Falaba* inquiry:
Proceedings before the Rt. Hon. Lord Mersey, Wreck Commissioner of the United Kingdom ... on a formal investigation ordered by the Board of trade into the loss of the Steamship *Falaba*, (1915).

Gunther von Forstner's journal:
von Forstner, G-G, *The Journal of Submarine Commander von Forstner,* Trans: Ana Crafts Codman, Gutenberg Project, E-book #30114 (2009)

Lord Mersey's obituary appeared in *The Times* newspaper on 4 September 1929.

The report on the sinking of the *Iberian* appeared as 'Six of Iberian's Crew Slain With One Shell' in the *New York Times* newspaper on 31 July 1915.

Published Sources

Ballard, R.D., *Exploring the Lusitania* (Weidenfeld and Nicholson, London 1992)

Ballard, R.D., *The Discovery of the Titanic* (Madison Publishing Inc., Toronto 1987)

Bartlett, W.B., *Titanic, 9 Hours to Hell, The Survivors' Story,* (Amberley Publishing, Stroud, 2010)

Butler, D.A., *The Other Side of the Night* (Casemate, Newbury 2009)

Cameron, S., *Titanic Belfast's Own* (Colourpoint, Co. Down, 2011)

Eaton, J.P. and Haas, C.A., *Titanic Destination Disaster* (Haynes, Somerset 1987)

Eaton, J.P. and Haas, C.A., *Titanic Triumph and Tragedy* (Haynes, Somerset, 1988)

Flayhart, W.H., *Perils of the Atlantic* (Norton, New York, 2003)

Fox, S., *The Ocean Railway* (HarperCollins, London, 2003)

Gordon, A., *The Rules of the Game* (John Murray, London, 1996)

Harris, J., *Lost at Sea* (Guild, London, 1990)

Harris, J., *Without Trace* (Guild, London, 1988)

Keegan, J., *The Price of Admiralty* (Arrow, London, 1990)

Lee, P., The *Titanic and the Indifferent Stranger* (self published, 2008)

Lochner, R.K., *The Last Gentleman of War* (Arrow, London, 1990)

Lynch, D. and Marschall, K., *Titanic An Illustrated History* (Hodder and Stoughton, London, 1992)

Molony, S., *Titanic and the Mystery Ship* (Tempus, Gloucestershire, 2006)

Preston, D., *Wilful Murder* (Doubleday, London, 2002)

Ramsay, D., *Lusitania: Saga and Myth* (Chatham, Rochester, 2001)

Reade, L. and de Groot, E.P., *The Ship that Stood Still* (Haynes, Somerset, 1993)

Saward, J., *The Man Who Caught Crippen* (Moienval, France, 2010)

Stringer, C., 'Falaba's Sinking Begins March to War', *Voyage,* vol 53, pp.30-35

Thomas, L., *Raiders of the Deep* (Doubleday, Doran, New York, 1928)

Wilson, I., *Shipwrecks of the Ulster Coast* (Impact, Coleraine, 1997)

Zeni, D., *Forgotten Empress* (Avid, Merseyside, 2001)

INDEX

Admiral Gentaume, 32

Adriatic, 56, 57

Aguila, 65, 66, 169

Aleppo, 59

Alice Davies, 59

Allan Line, 61, 175

America, 70

Andersen, Captain Thomas, 55, 65, 74–75, 93, 94, 126–142, 177

Anderson, Staff Captain John C., 160

Andrea Doria, 74, 184

Andrews, Thomas, 111

Aquitania, 59

Arabic, 84

Arctic, 21, 23, 184

Arizona, 25

Ashton, Henry, 161, 165

Aspinall, Butler, KC, 96, 127–143, 146–163, 181

Asquith, H.H., 42

Asturia, 84

Athenia, 37

Baldaur, 21

Ballard, Dr Robert, 85, 104, 119

Baltic, 27

Baxter, Walter, 79, 144, 181

bearing, 41, 42, 121, 123, 134, 149

Bigham, John, 47

Binns, Jack, 26, 27

Board of Trade, 23, 38–42, 49–53, 59, 63, 68, 95–97, 107, 113, 116, 127, 133, 144, 146, 149, 178, 179, 180, 181, 183

boilers, 14, 15, 66, 71, 83, 86, 153, 160, 170

Booth, Albert, 153

Boxhall, Joseph, 71, 93, 104, 105, 106, 111, 119, 123

Boyle, Lieutenant Commander E.C. VC, 33

Bressey, Cyril, 162

Bride, Harold, 111, 123

Brittanic, 58

Browne, Father, 70

Brunel, Isambard Kingdom, 11

Buckmaster, Sir Stanley, 144, 145

bulkheads, 13, 23, 27

bunkers, 15, 86

Burns, Dr Patrick S., 66, 170

Buxton, Sydney, 38

Calgarian, 62, 185

Californian, 55, 62–63, 71, 72–73, 93, 97, 116–125, 133, 177, 178, 184

Canadian Pacific Railway, 61, 62, 96, 126, 127

Candidate, 84

Cannons, Captain Edwin G., 98–100

Carpathia, 72, 73, 101, 102, 103, 112, 116, 119, 124

Carson, Sir Edward, 42, 146, 150–153, 157, 159, 182, 183

Carson, Sir Edward, 42, 146, 150, 152, 157, 159, 183

Catalonia, 59

Celtic, 12, 55

Celtic, 12, 55

Centurion, 84, 174

Chamberlain, Joseph, 48

Cherbourg, 59

Churchill, Winston, 81, 148

City of Boston, 22

City of Glasgow, 21, 25, 28

City of Philadelphia, 21

Clermont, 11

coal, 12, 13, 15, 23, 33, 64, 83, 86, 103, 126, 153

Commissioner of Wrecks, 7, 38, 39, 40, 41, 46, 47, 54, 127, 179, 183

Conninbeg Lightship, 83, 84, 150

Crippen, Belle, 60

Crippen, Dr H.H., 55, 60, 61, 62, 74

Cruiser Rules, 30–36, 66, 76, 148, 171, 176

Cufic, 55

Cunard, 25, 51, 59, 60, 80, 96, 146, 152, 153, 154, 181

Davies, Captain Frederick, 55, 64–65, 79–81, 91, 92, 144–145, 147–148, 161–165, 172, 178, 182,

Derbyshire, 28

Dew, Chief Inspector Walter, 60, 61, 74

Dominion Coal Company, 126, 127

Donaldson Line, 37

E-14, 33

Earl of Latham, 84

Egypt, 73

Elder Dempster Line, 64, 78, 96, 144, 146, 162, 163, 164, 172

Emden, 31

Empress of Ireland, 7, 8, 24, 42, 44, 45, 55, 61, 62, 64, 70, 73–75, 91–96, 107, 119, 126–143, 146, 161, 177, 178, 179, 181, 184

Ethel Le Neve, 60, 61

Falaba, 7, 8, 36, 40, 51, 52, 55, 64, 65, 66, 68, 78–81, 91, 92, 94, 95, 96, 107, 144–145, 146, 147–148, 152, 153, 161–166, 169–172, 173, 176, 178, 180, 182, 184

Father Point (Point au Pere), 61, 74, 75, 133, 136

Feldkirchner, Kapitanleutnant, 32

Fisher, Admiral Jacky, 148, 158

Florida, 26, 27

Forstner, Kapitanleutnant Georg-Gunther Freiherr von, 55, 65–66, 67, 68, 78–81, 94, 95, 147, 148, 165, 166–173, 175, 176, 178

Fulton, Robert, 11, 13

Galway, James, 130, 132, 137

Gibson, James, 73, 93, 119–124, 177

Glitra, 32, 168

Graf Spee, 37

Grasmere, 58, 59

Great Eastern, 12, 14, 18, 23

Gul Djemal, 33

Hague Convention, 30, 31, 35

Haight, Charles, Sherman, 127–143

Halifax, 22

Harland and Wolff, 12, 33, 70, 184

Harrison Line, 84, 122

Hasselwood Rock, 26

heading 41, 42, 138

Hesperian, 175

HMS *Aboukir*, 76
HMS *Anson*, 24
HMS *Association*, 20
HMS *Cressy*, 76
HMS *Dreadnought*, 12, 32, 78
HMS *Eagle*, 20
HMS *Firebrand*, 20
HMS *Hawke*, 57
HMS *Hogue*, 76
HMS *Juno*, 85, 154
HMS *Pathfinder*, 76
HMS *Romney*, 20
Home Secretary, 40, 42, 183
Hutton, Lord, 183
Iberian, 66, 170
International Mercantile Marine (IMM), 45
Ireland, 70
Isaacs, Sir Rufus KC, 44, 49, 53, 96–101, 116, 183
Islander, 24
Ismay, Bruce, 43, 97, 103, 104
Ivernia, 60, 152
Jackson, Captain Henry, RN, 14
Jago, Captain, 170
Johannesen, W. Maithe, 45
Jones, Edward J., 134, 138
Jutland, Battle of, 168, 185
K-Class submarines, 14
Kelly, Dr David, 183
Kendall, Captain Henry, 55, 61–62, 74–75, 89, 91, 92, 94, 126–143, 151, 177, 181
Lady of the Lake, 25
Lake Superior, 61
Langsdorf, Captain, 37
Laurentic, 61
Lawther Latta Line, 63
Lemp, Oberleutnant Fritz-Julius, 37
Lightoller, Charles, 99–114

Lindsay, Captain, 127
Lloyd, George, 53
Loch Earn, 23
Lord, Captain Walter, 55, 62–64, 72–73, 89, 93, 97, 116–125, 133, 177, 181, 183
Lowe, Harold, 105, 109
Lusitania, 7, 8, 12, 26, 33, 36, 40, 42, 51, 52, 55, 58–60, 66, 68, 80, 81–87, 91, 92, 94–95, 96, 107, ,142, 144, 145–147, 148, 158–161, 168, 170, 171, 173–176, 179, 180, 181, 182, 184
Marconi Company 14, 26
Marconi Scandal, 53
Marconi, Guglielmo, 14, 53
Marine Accident Investigation Branch (MAIB), 118–124, 177, 184
Marquess of Dufferin and Ava, 49
Mauretania, 59, 179
McLeod, the Honourable Ezekiel, 126, 129
McQuitty, Bill, 62
Merchant Shipping Act, 38, 89, 98, 113
Mesaba, 71
Montreal, 62
Montrose, 61, 62, 74
Morgan J.P., 45
Muller, Captain Karl von, 31
Murdoch, William, 71, 109–111
Nelson, Horatio, 11
Newcombe, Edward, L., 127, 129, 143
Nomadic, 70
Norge, 24, 26
Norwegian Inquiry, 44, 45
Oceana, 184
Oceanic, 12
Old Head of Kinsale, 83, 149, 150
Olympic, 43, 56, 57, 58, 70
Oregon, 23, 184
Pacific, 22, 25, 28

Parsons, Dr Charles, 12
Persia, 25
Phillips, Jack, 105, 111, 123
Pitman, Herbert, 105, 106, 109, 141
Principessa Jolanda, 24
Q-Ships, 36
Queen of Nations, 59
reciprocating, 12, 13, 71
Republic, 14, 24–27, 92, 114, 184
Rostron, Captain Arthur, 101–103, 111
Routhier, Sir Adolphe, Basile, 126
Ryan, J.J., 80
Safety of Life at Sea (SOLAS), 179
Salvation Army, 74
Saxe, Jacob, 131, 136, 138, 139
Scheer, Admiral Reinhardt von, 168
Schmidt, Commander, 80
Schneider, Kapitanleutnant Rudolph, 33
Schwieger, Kapitanleutnant Walther, 55, 65, 66, 67, 68, 81, 84–86, 94, 95, 147, 150, 153, 154, 172, 173–176, 178
Sealby, Captain, 27, 92
Senator Weber, 55
Servia, 13
Shovell, Sir Cloudesly, 20
Smith, Captain E.J., 55–58, 60, 61, 62, 70, 71, 83, 89, 91, 92, 96–115, 123, 124, 150, 158, 161, 177, 182, 183
Smith, Senator William Alden, 44, 45, 97
Smith, Sir F.E., 146, 149, 154, 183
St Lawrence, 7, 61, 74, 75, 91, 131, 133, 134, 135, 137, 178, 179, 181, 184
Stockholm, 74
Stone, Herbert, 72, 93, 117, 119–124, 177
Storstad, 45, 55, 64–65, 74–75, 91, 93, 94, 119, 126–143, 177, 178, 184

Thompson, Captain, 144, 164, 172
Thrasher, Leon C., 78, 80
Thunderbolt, 59
Titanic, 7, 8, 9, 13, 21, 23, 25, 26, 38, 41–45, 47, 49–53, 55, 56, 62, 63, 69–73, 83, 86, 90–93, 96–115, 116–125, 127, 130, 133, 141, 142, 146, 150, 153, 158, 161, 178, 179–181, 183, 184
Toftnes, Alfred, 65, 74, 93, 131, 135–143, 177
turbine, 12, 13, 14
Turbinia, 12
Turner, Captain Charles, 58, 59
Turner, Captain William, 55, 58–60, 61, 62, 81, 82–87, 89, 91, 92, 142, 144–147, 148–162, 178, 179, 180, 181, 182, 185
U-17, 32
U-24, 33
U-30, 37
U-14, 67
U-21 76
U-29, 78
U-88, 67
U-9, 76
Ultonia, 60
US Senate Inquiry, 44, 45, 96–98
Utopia, 24, 184
Vagne, 59
Vesta, 21
Ville du Havre, 23, 184
Waratah, 24, 27–28
watertight doors, 13, 75, 83, 142, 179
Weddingen, Otto, 76
West Point, 60
White Star Line, 12, 14, 22, 26, 27, 33, 44, 45, 51, 55, 56, 57, 61, 66, 84, 97, 103, 104, 105, 114, 177, 181
Wilde, Henry, 105
Wright, Whitaker, 49, 53

Printed in Great Britain
by Amazon

29846220R00112